Using Technology with Elementary Music Approaches

Using Technology
with Elementary Music
Approaches

Amy M. Burns

Oxford University Press is a department of the University of Oxford. It furthers
the University's objective of excellence in research, scholarship, and education
by publishing worldwide. Oxford is a registered trade mark of Oxford University
Press in the UK and certain other countries.

Published in the United States of America by Oxford University Press
198 Madison Avenue, New York, NY 10016, United States of America.

© Oxford University Press 2020

All rights reserved. No part of this publication may be reproduced, stored in
a retrieval system, or transmitted, in any form or by any means, without the
prior permission in writing of Oxford University Press, or as expressly permitted
by law, by license, or under terms agreed with the appropriate reproduction
rights organization. Inquiries concerning reproduction outside the scope of the
above should be sent to the Rights Department, Oxford University Press, at the
address above.

You must not circulate this work in any other form
and you must impose this same condition on any acquirer.

Library of Congress Cataloging-in-Publication Data
Names: Burns, Amy M. author.
Title: Using technology with elementary music approaches / Amy Burns.
Description: New York : Oxford University Press, 2020. | Includes bibliographical
references and index.
Identifiers: LCCN 2019059944 (print) | LCCN 2019059945 (ebook) |
ISBN 9780190055653 (paperback) | ISBN 9780190055646 (hardback) |
ISBN 9780190055677 (epub)
Subjects: LCSH: School music—Instruction and study. | Educational technology—Planning.
Classification: LCC MT10 .B896 2020 (print) | LCC MT10 (ebook) | DDC 372.87/044—dc23
LC record available at https://lccn.loc.gov/2019059944
LC ebook record available at https://lccn.loc.gov/2019059945

9 8 7 6 5 4 3 2 1

Paperback printed by Sheridan Books, Inc., United States of America
Hardback printed by Bridgeport National Bindery, Inc., United States of America

CONTENTS

About the Companion Website

www.oup.com/us/utema

Oxford has created a website to accompany *Using Technology with Elementary Music Approaches*. Material that cannot be made available in a book is provided here. The reader is encouraged to consult this resource while reading the book.

1

What Is This Book About?

Amy M. Burns

Are you an elementary music educator who feels challenged and often frustrated by technology? Or are you one who likes your own personal technology, but needs ideas on how to use educational technology (edtech) in the classroom? Or are you one who was forced into technology when the pandemic closed your school and you now have a better handle on how technology works and wonders where it fits into the classroom? Technology can be a welcomed and valuable tool in the classroom. It also can be a challenging one.

Technology evokes numerous feelings in educators, from frustrations to joy, when we try to utilize it in the classroom. It is for this reason that I wrote this book. I wanted to assist teachers who may possess a variety of tech abilities, and who may have limited access to technology resources, to be able to use technology to enhance their current teaching methodology. I wanted to give them field-tested lessons, problem-solving solutions, and ideas that all involve technology as a tool that would enhance the approaches of Zoltán Kodály, Orff Schulwerk, and Dr. John Feierabend.

Why Technology?

"I just want to teach my students music." "Students get enough screen time at home. My music class is a time for them to take a break." These are valid concerns and statements from numerous elementary music educators with whom I have spoken over the past two decades. However, when elementary music educators attend professional development workshops, edtech buzzwords—from "21st-Century Learners/Skills" to "coding"—are ever present (Beckford, 2018; Cox, 2019; Gallo, 2019; Lane, 2011; Madda, 2017; Puentedura, 2015; Room 241 Team, 2019; Sanders, 2017). Many elementary music educators are evaluated by their administration on how their use of technology is integrated into the classroom (Fuller et al., 2012; Johnson & Mielke, 2013). In addition, teachers are evaluated on how they diversify their teaching to meet all learning styles. Educators are asked to demonstrate their use of learning styles, such as differentiated instruction or the current seven learning styles (visual, aural, verbal, physical, logical, social, and solitary), in their classrooms (Whiteley, 2020; Diaz et al., 2019). In addition, assessment and data are required to show student knowledge in the course subject (Alber, 2017; Konen, 2017). Technology plays a role in all of these types of instruction.

Schools are adopting more technology in their classrooms. In 2016, it was reported that public schools in the United States purchased at least one computer per every five students

Amy M. Burns, *What Is This Book About?* In: *Using Technology with Elementary Music Approaches*. Edited by: Amy M. Burns,
Oxford University Press (2020). © Oxford University Press.
DOI: 10.1093/oso/9780190055653.003.0001

(Herold, 2016). According to the national report conducted by Interactive Educational Systems Design (IESD) and STEM Market Impact, which is based on survey responses from 332 district leaders, 71% of the leaders stated that a quarter or more of their schools have adopted mobile technology. This is up from 60% in 2013. In addition, they quoted that only 12% had not adopted mobile technology, down from 21% in 2013 (Logan, 2015). With this survey, the leaders also stated that the major difficulties were teacher training and mobile device management. Finally, with the Every Student Succeeds Act (ESSA) that passed at the beginning of the 2017–2018 school year, Congress appropriated money to fund states in categories that include promoting the effective use of technology (Elements, 2019).

In 2013 and 2014, schools purchased more than 23 million devices for classroom use (Herold, 2016). In 2014, it was reported that Chromebooks overtook Apple's iPads, at 26%, as the bestselling device for that year, with more than 3 million devices being shipped. In 2015, it was projected that over 50% of K–12 classrooms would be 1:1 (defined as one device per student) in the next year (Molnar, 2015). In 2017, Futurescore reported that Chromebooks accounted for 58% of the mobile devices shipped to US primary and secondary schools. In addition, Apple's iPads dropped from 25% to 19% (Johnson, 2018; Singer, 2017).

The research found at code.org also supports the findings that technology is more prominent in schools. Currently, computing jobs are the leading source of new wages in the United States. There are more than 500,000 open jobs in computing. Projections show that these jobs will grow at twice the rate of all other jobs. Finally, research shows that 90% of parents want their children to study computer science, but only 40% of the schools offer computer programming (code.org).

What Does Technology Have to Do with Elementary Music Approaches?

The research is showing a trend in education in which technology will become a prominent tool. Whereas a decade ago, the elementary music classroom would be the last classroom to receive technology (think back to the introduction of the interactive whiteboards—i.e., SMART Board, Promethean Board, etc.—everyone was getting one except the music educator), in the current day, most elementary music classrooms have at least the basics: one device, a projector, and internet access. In addition, more schools are adopting 1:1 technology, and elementary students as young as kindergartners are walking into your music room with a device in hand. However, just because the students have access to technology, do we have to address that in elementary music class?

When I am asked this question in a workshop, I answer in this way: If technology can enhance and bring success to your students, then why would you not try to use it? I am not saying to use it every day, all day, or have it teach for you. I am saying that if it can be used to enhance your approach in your classroom, is it not worth it to try (Figure 1.1)?

Summary of This Book

My hope is that elementary music educators utilize this book to assist in using technology as a tool to enhance, and even engage and extend, one or more ways they teach

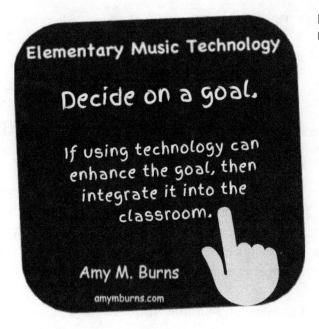

Figure 1.1.
Decide on a goal . . .

3

in their classrooms. In this book, each section begins with teachers who are prominent in the music education approaches of Dr. Feierabend (Dr. Missy Strong), Zoltán Kodály (Glennis Patterson), Orff Schulwerk (Ardith Collins), and Cross-Curricular and Project-Based Learning (PBL) (Amy M. Burns and Cherie Herring) describing each approach and how to apply it in the elementary music classrooms. Following those descriptions, there are ideas, lessons, and/or detailed activities that show the approaches enhanced with technological tools.

Materials and examples for the lessons are found on the book's accompanying website, http://www.oup.com/us/utema. This website icon⊚ will appear on the page when there are resources that can be downloaded from the accompanying website.

You can also type the URL, http://www.oup.com/us/utema, into a web browser to access the materials.

Readers of this book can vary from novice technology users to advanced techies. They can have access to one device in the classroom, multiple devices, bring your own 1:1 devices (BYOD), or a 1:1 music classroom. Most of the technology tools are multiplatform and can be used on web-based (any device that has internet access), Android, Google Play, and/or iOS devices. In addition, most of the activities described in the book do not require the students to have email addresses.

Important to Note

When using technology in the classroom, it is important to do the following:

- Check with your school administration about the proper use and protocol of using technology in the classroom.
- Check with your school's Information Technology (IT) Team so that you have support when you use technology in your classroom.
- Get to know and understand the proper policies set in place for the students, parents, and teachers when it comes to technology use.

- Have a Plan B, Plan C, etc. There are 26 letters in the alphabet. If Plan A does not work, there are 25 more letters. Or, as one of my favorite music technology trainers, Katie Wardrobe from https://midnightmusic.com.au/, states in her podcast, "Always have a contingency plan when things go wrong."

How the Educator Can Use This Book

Focusing on One Approach

Since there are four prominent approaches addressed in this book, educators can choose to focus on the one approach that they utilize in their classroom. They can read through the approach written by the expert teacher so that they can review it or learn more from the expert's point of view. Following the review of the approach are ideas, lessons, and activities that enhance that approach with technology.

Focusing on Multiple Approaches

Many elementary music educators choose to utilize multiple approaches in their classrooms for various reasons. Those reasons could range from what works best for them to what works best for their students. When using this book to focus on multiple approaches, you will find some of the ideas, lessons, and activities repeated throughout each approach.

Focusing on the Entire Book

This book is written for the educator to read and learn from its entirety. You will find that some of the ideas, lessons, and activities are repeated, when reading this book from front to back.

Introduction of Authors

Amy M. Burns (amymburns.com) (Figure 1.2) has been teaching elementary general music for over 25 years, with most of her career at Far Hills Country Day School, in Far Hills, New Jersey. She teaches general music to Grades pre-kindergarten through 4, directs the Far Hills Philharmonic for Grades 4–8, teaches a Mommy/Caregiver and Me music class for ages 0–3, and coordinates the Far Hills Conservatory. A widely known music educator, author, and clinician on how to effectively integrate technology into the elementary music classroom, she credits her colleagues, administration, and the members of the Technology for Music Education (TI:ME) organization and the New Jersey Music Educators Association (NJMEA) for her success in teaching music to elementary students.

During the summers, Ms. Burns teaches graduate courses on technology integration for Central Connecticut State University (CCSU), and she has taught courses for other Summer Music Institutes at Appalachian State University, Montclair State University, and William Paterson University.

Ms. Burns holds a bachelor's degree in music education/performance from Ithaca College and a master of science degree in music education from CCSU. She holds

Figure 1.2.
Amy Burns.

levels in Orff Schulwerk, Kodály, Technology for Music Education (TI:ME), Apple Teacher, Seesaw Ambassador, and Google Levels 1 and 2. She is also certified by the International Society for Technology in Education (ISTE). She was the president of TI:ME from 2010 to 2012 and is currently on the Board of TI:ME and of NJMEA as the Early Childhood Chair.

Ms. Burns has authored three books on how to integrate technology into the elementary music classroom. She has presented many sessions on the topic, including four keynote addresses in Texas, Indiana, Saint Maarten, and Australia. She is the recipient of the following awards: 2005 TI:ME Teacher of the Year, the 2016 NJ Master Music Teacher, the 2016 Governor's Leader in Arts Education, and the 2017 NJ Non-Public School Teacher. In 2019, she was featured on PBS's *Caucus NJ with Steve Adubato* discussing the benefits of exposing children from birth to age 7 to music to enhance their learning ability. Ms. Burns is also the proud mom of two daughters.

Dr. Strong (Figure 1.3) has joyfully served as an elementary general/vocal teacher since 1995. She is also the director of Children's Music Education at the Tenth Presbyterian Church in Philadelphia, overseeing Schola Cantorum, the weekly music school for Grades 1–6, as well as weekly preschool music classes. She frequently mentors young teachers and consults with churches and schools looking to implement music programs for children. Dr. Strong has presented several workshops and has addressed groups of parents and caregivers of young children regarding the importance of live music-making in the family and the community, a topic that serves as her primary research interest. In 2003, she earned the master of arts in music education from Rowan University. In May 2012,

Figure 1.3.
Dr. Missy Strong.

she earned a doctorate in music education, with an emphasis on early childhood development, from Rutgers University in New Brunswick.

After her first workshop with Dr. Feierabend 14 years ago, Dr. Strong immediately saw the excellence of the First Steps and Conversational Solfege programs and materials. Dr. Strong uses the First Steps in Music and the Conversational Solfege curriculum not only in her public school program, but also in her church music school program. She has also had her staff trained by Dr. Feierabend. She has since been dedicated to creating a more tuneful, beatful, and artful world, whether with her own students, or through student teachers, blog posts, workshops, conferences, or the Feierabend Fundamentals page she oversees on Facebook.

Dr. Strong, who is fully certified in the Feierabend method, is a founding member of the Feierabend Association for Music Education (FAME), served as vice president from 2012 to 2016, and is the current president. She is a Conversational Solfege Level 1 Teacher Trainer.

She and her husband, Jeremy (a composer, pianist, and church organist), enjoy making music together with their four children, Ethan, Owen, Lorelei, and Jackson, in southern New Jersey.

Glennis E. Patterson (Figure 1.4) teaches general music, band, and choir at Katharine D. Malone Elementary School in Rockaway, New Jersey. She earned her bachelor's degree in music education at Susquehanna University and Kodály certification at New York University. She is a clinician in the area of music and special learners and loves teaching children of all abilities. Glennis lives in New Jersey with her husband and three daughters, who are her constant support and source of inspiration.

Ardith Collins (Figure 1.5) teaches orchestra and general music at Columbia Grammar and Preparatory School in New York City and is adjunct faculty at Montclair State University Cali School of Music. Ardith has Orff Schulwerk and Kodály certifications, serves on the board of the New Jersey Orff Schulwerk Association, and is a member of the American Orff Schulwerk Association (AOSA).

She is an active writer, presenter, and Orff Levels teacher. Ms. Collins is on the AOSA *Reverberations* editorial board and the communications team for the American Center for Elemental Music and Movement. She performs with the Montclair State University Balkan Ensemble, and is a folk dancing and rounds singing enthusiast.

Figure 1.4.
Glennis Patterson.

Figure 1.5.
Ardith Collins.

Cherie P. Herring (Figure 1.6) has been teaching music for over three decades in a variety of positions. Presently, Ms. Herring is in her fifteenth year teaching general music to pre-kindergarten through Grade 4 students. The first faculty member at Hammond School to receive a SMART Board, Cherie has embraced interactive technology instruction and is now qualified as a SMART Certified Lesson Developer, SMART Certified Trainer, and SMART Notebook Education Instructor. In addition to SMART Technologies, Hammond is in its fifth year as a 1:1 Apple Distinguished School. An early adopter, Ms. Herring now uses the combination of 1:1 iPads and SMART interactive

Figure 1.6.
Cherie Herring.

technology to do what was previously inconceivable: augmented reality, green screen video techniques, a flipped classroom, and student-driven learning through Science, Technology, Engineering, Arts, and Mathematics (STEAM). In addition to sharing her passion to seamlessly integrate technology into her music classroom, Ms. Herring works to inspire, create, and support technology integration in the regular classrooms throughout Hammond School.

Ms. Herring has presented many workshops on integrating music technology into the elementary music classroom for district and state conferences in Florida, New Jersey, New York, North Carolina, South Carolina, Georgia, and Texas. Ms. Herring has also presented sessions at the regional conferences for TI:ME and the National Association for Music Education (NAfME). In 2015, she was the keynote speaker at the Music and Technology Conference in Houston, Texas.

Ms. Herring is also a Seesaw Ambassador and 2016 Apple Teacher for iPads and Mac computers. She has created over 45 interactive lessons for SMART Boards and/or iPads and shares them on the SMART Exchange and her blog: http://www.cphmusic.net. In 2018, she was named the TI:ME Teacher of the Year for her successful methods of integrating technology into the elementary general music classroom.

Resources

Alber, R. (2017, March 2). 3 Ways Student Data Can Inform Your Teaching. Retrieved July 19, 2019, from https://www.edutopia.org/blog/using-student-data-inform-teaching-rebecca-alber

Beckford, B. (2018, December 11). Education Buzzwords: A Rundown on Social & Emotional Learning. Retrieved July 19, 2019, from https://www.momsrising.org/blog/education-buzzwords-a-rundown-on-social-emotional-learning

Code.org (2017). Why Computer Science in K-12? [PowerPoint slides]. Retrieved from https://code.org/files/computer_science_advocacy.pptx

Cox, J. (2019, July 3). 7 Words You Need to Know If You're a Teacher. Retrieved from https://www.thoughtco.com/buzzwords-in-education-2081955

Diaz, C., Jon, Butcher, M., Fletcher, E., Walsch, N. D., Nichols, L., & Diamond, M. (2019, June 12). Understanding the 7 Types of Learning Styles. Retrieved July 19, 2019, from https://blog.mindvalley.com/types-of-learning-styles/

Elements, E. (2019). Technology in the Classroom: Insights for Optimization. Retrieved July 19, 2019, from https://www.edelements.com/technology-in-classroom

Fuller, W., George, C., George, L., Greene, P. J., Holmes, F., Kreul, M., . . . Wagner, J. (2012). Assessing Classroom Technology Integration. Retrieved July 19, 2019, from https://www.educationworld.com/a_tech/tech/tech243.shtml

Gallo, L. (2019, March). 2019 STEM Buzz Words: Definitions of Important Maker Education Buzz Words. Retrieved July 19, 2019, from https://www.whymaker.co/blog/post/2019-stem-buzz-words-definitions-of-important-maker-education-buzz-words

Herold, B. (2016, February 5). Technology in Education: An Overview. Retrieved July 19, 2019, from https://www.edweek.org/ew/issues/technology-in-education/index.html

Johnson, D., & Mielke, N. (2013, March). *Rubric for Effective Teacher Technology Use (Organized by the Four Domains of Danielson's Framework for Teaching1)* [PDF]. Alexandria, VA: Ascd.org.

Johnson, L. (2018, March 29). Apple's New iPads Still Can't Best Chromebooks in the Classroom. Retrieved July 19, 2019, from https://www.macworld.com/article/3267207/apples-new-ipads-still-cant-best-chromebooks-in-the-classroom.html

Koehler, M. (2012, September 24). TPACK.ORG. Retrieved July 19, 2019, from http://www.tpack.org/

Konen, J. (2017, December 23). Using Assessment in Instruction. Retrieved July 19, 2019, from https://www.teacher.org/daily/using-assessment-instruction/

Lane, C. (2011). Multiple Intelligences. Retrieved January 28, 2018, from http://www.tecweb.org/styles/gardner.html

from "The Distance Learning Technology Resource Guide"

Learning-styles-online.com. (n.d.). Retrieved January 28, 2018, from https://www.learning-styles-online.com/overview/

Logan, L. (2015). "Significant Growth in 1:1 Initiatives in Schools, National Survey Says." *Amplify*

Madda, M. J. (2017, July 11). Tired Edtech Trends That Teachers Wish Would Retire: From the Floor of ISTE 2017—EdSurge News. Retrieved January 28, 2018, from https://www.edsurge.com/news/2017-07-04-tired-edtech-trends-that-teachers-wish-would-retire-from-the-floor-of-iste-2017

Molnar, M. (2015, December 7). Half of K-12 Students to Have Access to 1-to-1 Computing by 2015-16. Retrieved January 15, 2018, from https://marketbrief.edweek.org/marketplace-k-12/half_of_k-12_students_to_have_access_to_1-to-1_computing_by_2015-16_1/

Puentedura, R. (2015, October 14). SAMR: A Brief Introduction. Retrieved July 19, 2019, from http://hippasus.com/blog/archives/227

The Room 241 Team. (2019, May 29). Education Terminology: Definitions of Common Buzzwords & Jargon. Retrieved July 19, 2019, from https://education.cu-portland.edu/blog/classroom-resources/education-terminology-jargon/

Sanders, J. (2017, January 4). 15 Educational Technology Definitions You Should Know. Retrieved January 28, 2018, from http://blog.whooosreading.org/edtech-buzzwords-defined/

Singer, N. (2017, March 2). Apple's Devices Lose Luster in American Classrooms. Retrieved July 19, 2019, from https://www.nytimes.com/2017/03/02/technology/apple-products-schools-education.html?_r=0

What's Wrong with This Picture? Retrieved December 31, 2017, from https://code.org/promote

Whiteley, S. (2020). Overview of learning styles. Retrieved February 26, 2020, from https://www.learning-styles-online.com/overview/index.php

2

Why Would We Use Technology in the Elementary Music Classroom?

Amy M. Burns

"My music room is for activities. There is already so much technology being used in the schools." These paraphrases come from numerous elementary music educators who experience the "balance question" when they teach. They feel that technology is consuming our youth, and there are many books and articles that support that thought. However, these music educators are also asked to address "21st-Century Skills," which include technology, whether it means that the students are using technology in the music classroom or the teacher is addressing technological skills such as digital citizenship and being a computational thinker (ISTE, 2018). With all of the pressures placed on educators, how do we find the balance? *Should* we find a balance? Should we deny technology in the elementary music classroom?

When I was performing research for a keynote address, titled, "How Technology Is Transforming the Way We Teach Elementary General Music Classes" (Burns, 2017), I directly addressed this question. When reading numerous music education professional learning network discussion boards, one observes a divide on this topic. Music educators will comment on how technology can enhance certain activities like composition and music-making for those who have limited abilities. Others will state that their music classroom is a "screen-free" zone because students need a break from screens. And there are others who are required to utilize technology because they must address 21st-Century Skills or their schools have become 1:1 (one device per student). Finally, there is the thought that technology is here to stay. If it can be used to hook a student or to connect a student to the subject, then it is a very useful tool for the music classroom.

When it comes to elementary music classroom approaches, such as Kodály, Orff Schulwerk, or Feierabend First Steps, technology can be utilized from the simplest ways, to assist with organization, to more complex ways as a significant teaching tool in the classroom. It can be used with one device in a classroom as well as in a 1:1 school. Technology can range from something as simple as Bluetooth speakers to students using an app to create and compose music.

Technology does not need to be the "end all, be all" in the elementary music classroom. It is an extremely useful tool for music educators that can enhance or transform their classrooms. Teachers could miss out on a way to connect to, relate to, assess, or even inspire their students when they deny integrating technology into the elementary music

Amy M. Burns, *Why Would We Use Technology in the Elementary Music Classroom?* In: *Using Technology with Elementary Music Approaches.*
Edited by: Amy M. Burns, Oxford University Press (2020). © Oxford University Press.
DOI: 10.1093/oso/9780190055653.003.0002

classroom. One way to determine and implement how to use technology in the elementary music classroom is to study Dr. Ruben Puentedura's SAMR model.

SAMR: Substitution, Augmentation, Modification, and Redefinition

SAMR is a model designed to assist teachers in integrating technology into their classrooms. Dr. Ruben Puentedura developed the model, which involves substitution, augmentation, modification, and redefinition, as a way for teachers to self-reflect on how they integrate technology into their classrooms. The model also gives the teachers a guide for how technology can be used as a tool from enhancing to redefining what is taught in the classroom. Though the SAMR model is usually shown as a ladder, beginning at S and moving up to R, it is more like a spectrum; at times, substitution is all that is needed.

Substitution

As defined through various resources, substitution is when technology is directly substituted for a more traditional tool. At this stage, elementary music educators would ask themselves if there was a benefit to substituting their current traditional tools with a technological tool (Gaudet, 2014; Puentedura, 2019; Shrock, 2013).

For example, when teaching my elementary music and movement classes, I like to use digital statue cards as opposed to paper ones (see Figure 2.1). When I print the cards, it is challenging for my young students to see them when performing the music and movement activity. However, if I project the cards onto a screen, the students can see and form the poses quite well. The technology used to project the statues is a form of substitution. An elementary music educator can use a variety of technologies to project the statue cards: (1) Download and print out the cards and use a document camera to project them onto a screen (see Figure 2.2). (2) Save the cards to your hard drive or to your Google Drive and click on the file so that they appear on the screen and you can project them from your

Figure 2.1.
Digital statue cards.

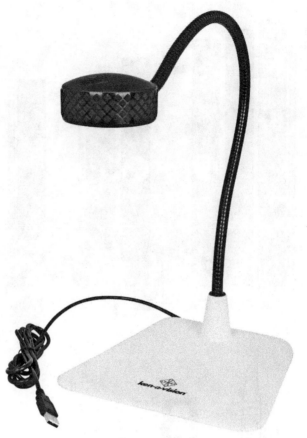

Figure 2.2.
Ken-a-vision is an example of a document camera.

computer with a projector connected to it. (3) When saved to your Google Drive, access your Google Drive from your mobile device, connect your mobile device to your projector through hardwiring it or through airplay, and project them onto the screen.

Augmentation

The augmentation stage also involves substituting a traditional tool with a technological tool. However, in this stage, there are great enhancements to the student's learning (Gaudet, 2014; Puentedura, 2019; Shrock, 2013). An example would be adding virtual instruments to your student's Orff ensemble. In my experience, not all elementary students can successfully play classroom instruments. Some have challenges that make it tough for them to hold mallets or to hold the instruments or to finger a note on a recorder. Virtual instruments can augment and enhance the students' experience with making music.

Tim Purdum's iOS Xylophone App (https://itunes.apple.com/us/app/xylophone-orff/id1092959126?mt=8) is a wonderful virtual Orff instrument that, when the iOS device is plugged into a decent pair of speakers, enables the student to play an Orff instrument without mallets and with just one or more fingers (see Figure 2.3). Or your student who might have difficulties performing rhythm patterns on a classroom instrument could use this virtual drumming website (http://www.virtualdrumming.com/drums/windows/joey-jordison-drums.html) on a laptop or Chromebook. In addition, coding a virtual instrument will work as well. An example is this virtual recorder I created with Scratch, found at https://scratch.mit.edu/projects/160843058/. This virtual recorder can

Figure 2.3.
Tim Purdum's iOS Xylophone App, found at accompanying website, www.oup. com/us/utema.

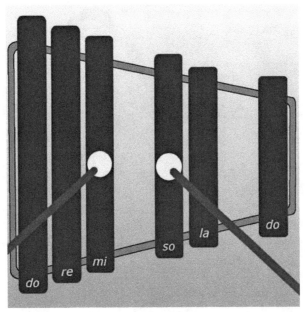

Figure 2.4.
Example of a virtual recorder coded with Scratch, found at accompanying website, www.oup.com/us/ utema.

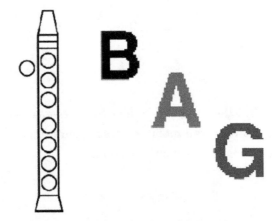

play the notes B, A, and G when the student clicks on the letters (see Figure 2.4). Virtual instruments are just one example of using technology as a way to augment your music classroom and your students' experiences.

Modification

The two previous examples showed how technology can enhance the elementary music classroom. When elementary teachers feel that a unit or lesson should be redesigned to form a more effective outcome, and they feel that technology is a tool that can achieve this, then a transformation of teaching occurs. This is when modification in the SAMR model comes into play (Gaudet, 2014; Puentedura, 2019; Shrock, 2013). An example from my elementary music classroom is when I want to assess what my students are learning on recorder. One way I do this is to have my students create beginning recorder books for next year's students. This can be done traditionally with paper, pencil, markers,

Figure 2.5.
An example of a
recorder ebook.

and a stapler. However, when my students use the iOS (https://itunes.apple.com/us/app/book-creator-one/id661166101?mt=8) or the web-based (https://bookcreator.com/) app Book Creator, they can add audio and video examples, as well as make the book interactive. They can also draw, take pictures, and add text. Finally, we can publish these ebooks online and share them with their parents as well as next year's recorder students (see Figure 2.5). The modification is apparent. If traditional methods of paper, pencil, and markers are used, the books lack the audio and video examples, and cannot be easily shared with an audience.

Redefinition

The redefinition stage comes when technology has made something possible that could not have been done with traditional methods (Gaudet, 2014; Puentedura, 2019; Shrock, 2013). In my classroom, one way that this occurs is when my students are sharing their music with other students from around the globe. With applications like Skype, FaceTime, Google Meets, Zoom, and Flipgrid, to name a few, classrooms can now connect virtually. In addition, students can also connect with the composer of their music. They can use thinking maps to outline questions to ask the composer.

Social networking also assists with this so that elementary music educators can find each other with a goal to connect and collaborate. Social networks like Twitter, Facebook Groups, National Association for Music Education (NAfME) Central Digest Network, and more, make it easier for elementary music educators to connect. In addition, Soundtrap (https://www.soundtrap.com) is a music-making digital audio workstation tool that my students have used to create music within a guided form and to share that music with other students to ask them to add to their songs. Soundtrap has a free version for anyone to use and collaborate; however, the educational (EDU) paid version has a better setup for a school setting.

The SAMR model helps elementary music educators re-examine why technology could be an effective tool to enhance or redefine their classrooms. It also reminds teachers that the tool might be for them to use and not their students, as with the example of projecting the statues onto the screen. Or they might want a tool that can be more effective for the students to use than a traditional tool, as with the Book Creator example.

Figure 2.6.
An example of a Seesaw Activity submission.

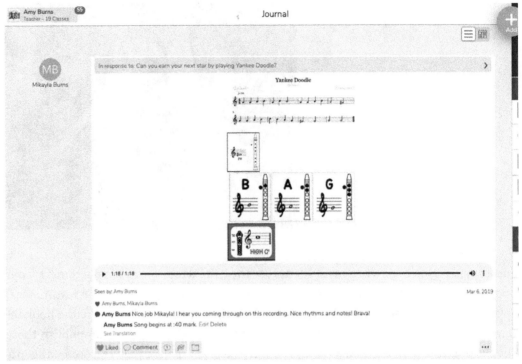

The Triple E Framework: Engage, Enhance, Extend

In 2017, Lisa Kolb authored the book *Learning First, Technology Second*, published by the International Society for Technology in Education (ISTE). She developed the Triple E Framework, which assists educators in measuring whether or not the technology tools being used are resulting in authentic student learning. It also helps educators in choosing the tools to integrate technology while keeping the subject's foundational concepts intact. It is based on the components of engagement in learning goals, enhancement of learning goals, and extension of learning goals. The Triple E Framework draws on research about what works and what does not work when teaching with technology. It emphasizes research from Dewey, Linnenbrink, and Pintrich, Mishra and Koehler, and others (Flaxman, 2019; Kolb, 2017, 2018; White, 2017).

I like the Triple E Framework as well as the SAMR model. The Triple E Framework helps the educator use the appropriate tech tools to achieve authentic learning outcomes that are meaningful to the students. It approaches technology as a tool to assist in teaching a step further. It encourages the use of technology in ways that extend learning outside the classroom.

An example of this in an elementary music classroom is using the student digital learning journal Seesaw (web.seesaw.me) (Figure 2.6). When used in the music classroom, the students have options to use various tools, from video to writing to audio recording themselves creating and performing music. They can also reflect on their performances and pose higher-order thinking skills. When they post to their personal digital journals, their parents receive a notification and can watch their children's progression and learning. When the students go home, they can continue their learning and progress. For example, they can log in to Seesaw from home and submit another recorder song to earn more recorder stars for their recorder belts. The teacher will receive their submissions and can comment on their performances.

In these examples, technology engages the students' learning outcomes. It also enhances learning opportunities by having students record and reflect on their performances. In addition, technology extends their learning by giving them the opportunity to perform and submit more music to the teacher from home.

However, with all of this, how could technology assist with the specific approaches of Dr. Feierabend, Zoltán Kodály, Orff Schulwerk, and Project-Based Learning (PBL)? Chapters 3, 4, 5, and 6 will address this question. Experts from each field will explain the approach. Each overview is followed by examples, ideas, and lessons that enhance and extend the approach with technology.

A Note About Technology and Distance Learning:

As this book was in its final phase of the editing process, many schools suddenly shut down due to a national pandemic crisis. This forced all educators to quickly convert their teaching to distance learning. For some, this meant creating resources that could be sent home. Others had to use creative technological ways to showcase their curriculum in an asynchronous way. And others had to teach live using tools such as Microsoft Teams, Zoom, and Google Meets. In whatever format that they were told to teach, they had to use some sort of technology, from xeroxing to a learning management system (LMS), to achieve some sort of teaching outcome.

The sudden closures of schools for a significant period of time, caused everyone to reevaluate their teaching methods, their performances, and more. From the technology integration point of view, it caused numerous teachers to become more familiar with the various technological tools that are offered in the educational world. Many music educators are now returning to their classrooms with a better foundation and comfort in educational technology. I hope that this book can give all music educators ideas, lessons, adaptations, and more, because they now have a better sense to how technology can enhance their approaches in teaching general music.

Resources

Burns, A. M. (2017, April 8). *How Technology Is Transforming the Way We Teach Elementary General Music Classes*. Lecture presented at Plugging In: Tech Symposium in Indiana State University, Bloomington.

Flaxman, J. (2019, February 5). The Triple E Framework. Retrieved August 1, 2019, from https://www.whatilearnedtodayinschool.com/the-triple-e-framework/

Gaudet, E. J. (2014). SAMR Model—Technology Is Learning. Retrieved February 29, 2020, from https://sites.google.com/a/msad60.org/technology-is-learning/samr-model

ISTE Standards FOR STUDENTS. (n.d.). Retrieved January 28, 2018, from https://www.iste.org/standards/for-students

Kolb, L. (2018). About. Retrieved August 1, 2019, from https://www.tripleeframework.com/about.html

Kolb, L. (2017). *Learning First, Technology Second: The Educator's Guide to Designing Authentic Lessons*. Portland, OR: International Society for Technology in Education.

Puentedura, R. R., Dr. (2019, February 26). Ruben R. Puentedura's Blog. Retrieved August 1, 2019, from http://hippasus.com/blog

Schrock, K. (2013, November). SAMR. Retrieved August 1, 2019, from https://www.schrockguide.net/samr.html

White, A. (2017, August 4). ILA's Blog. Retrieved August 1, 2019, from https://literacyworldwide.org/blog/literacy-daily/2017/08/04/the-triple-e-framework-learning-first-technology-second

3, PART A

The Feierabend Approach

Dr. Missy Strong

Dr. John Feierabend is the author of numerous music education resources as well as the *First Steps in Music for Preschool and Beyond* and *Conversational Solfege* curricula. Feierabend is Professor Emeritus of Music Education at the Hartt School of the University of Hartford and is a past president of the Organization of American Kodály Educators. According to the Feierabend Association for Music Education (FAME) website,

> Dr. Feierabend has been honored as a Lowell Mason Fellow by the National Association for Music Education (NAfME); named University Educator of the Year by the Connecticut Music Educators Association; received the outstanding alumni award from Wayne State University; received the Outstanding Educator Award from the Organization of American Kodály Educators, the James Bent Award for outstanding achievement in scholarship and creativity from the University of Hartford, and was the first U.S. recipient of the LEGO Prize, an international award given annually to "an individual who has made a distinctive contribution to the betterment of children." (https://www.feierabendmusic.org/john-feierabend/, para. 2)

Feierabend's curricula and other resources are utilized in classrooms throughout the United States and around the world, and the teacher certification courses FAME offers for both First Steps in Music and Conversational Solfege are highly sought after professional development opportunities. The success of Feierabend's ideas and programs can be attributed to the strength of a pedagogical approach based on high-quality literature, research, and best practices in music education in tandem with a vision of music education for all people. His ability to inspire teachers and students makes Feierabend's approach to music education provocative and appealing to educators the world over.

Influences

A close inspection of Feierabend's pedagogy quickly reveals that it is one predominantly steeped in the influence of Zoltán Kodály. His affinity for the Kodály approach is a result of years of his own study and careful analysis of Kodály principles, as well as the direct influence of some of Hungary's most esteemed Kodály practitioners, including Katalin Forrai, Katinka Daniel, Lenke Igó, János Horváth, László Vikár, and Arpad Darazs.

Dr. Missy Strong, *The Feierabend Approach* In: *Using Technology with Elementary Music Approaches*. Edited by: Amy M. Burns, Oxford University Press (2020). © Oxford University Press.
DOI: 10.1093/oso/9780190055653.003.0003

Feieraband holds strongly to the central tenets of the Kodály philosophy: progressing from a knowledge of folk song to great works of music, ensuring that singing is the primary mode for learning, and promoting the idea that quality musical experiences in early childhood should be the foundation for music literacy.

Added to these anchoring Kodály principles is the influence of Edwin Gordon's work as it pertains to the dynamic nature of musical aptitude, or the potential for achievement in music (Gordon, 1993). According to Gordon, musical aptitude is developmental and sensitive to instruction until around age nine (2003). During Feierabend's years as a doctoral student at Temple University he worked with Gordon, as well as with music and early childhood development expert Marilyn Zimmerman. Since Feierabend had already entered his doctoral work with a strong Kodály background, his further learning about the importance of music in early childhood, from Gordon and Zimmerman, led him to an increased focus on early childhood music in his own work.

Over time and supported by his own research, as well as that of his graduate students, Feierabend developed what he calls his "30-Year Plan" for all students (Feierabend, 2006). That is, with the right musical guidance in the elementary years, children will grow into adults who can sing "Happy Birthday" in tune, sway to the beat while singing in the seventh-inning stretch at a ball game, dance at their wedding, and feel the hushed wonder of singing a lullaby to their own children. They will, in essence, become musical people who are "tuneful, beatful, and artful" and ready for future learning (Feierabend, 2006).

First Steps in Music: Laying the Groundwork for Musicality

The best way to begin the journey toward a more musical adulthood is for infants and toddlers to experience music from and with parents and caregivers in the earliest years. The power of the parent/primary caregiver on music aptitude cannot be overstated (Illari, 2002; Hallam, 2006; McPherson, 2009). If parents are making music with their children on a consistent basis, they not only forge strong bonds between themselves and their child (Forrester, 2010; Custodero, Britto, & Brooks-Gunn, 2003), but also assist in "growing" their child's potential to make music in the future (Gruhn, 2002). Sadly, it seems that fewer children than ever are entering the elementary years having experienced a rich musical environment at home, and instead of tuneful, beatful, artful students, many teachers encounter young students who are not very musical at all (de Vries, 2007; Davidson, Faulkner, & McPherson, 2009).

Teachers faced with this situation can confidently utilize Feierabend's First Steps in Music in an effort to help their students become fundamentally musical. Feierabend created two programs for very young children: *First Steps for Infants and Toddlers* in 2001, and *First Steps in Music for Preschool and Beyond* in 2006. While both of these programs provide a wealth of engaging, developmentally appropriate musical experiences for students and help teachers remediate for any students who may come from a sparse home musical environment, this chapter will primarily discuss *First Steps in Music for Preschool and Beyond*.

First Steps in Music for Preschool and Beyond is a full curriculum that teachers can use on its own in the early childhood music class. As the title indicates, it is intended for students as young as three to four years of age. Activities for these students are arranged in what Feierabend calls an eight-part "workout" format. Students cycle through each of the eight parts every time they attend a music class. The intention is that throughout a First Steps lesson, students are challenged and their musical aptitudes developed via rigorous engagement in music-making activities. Since their musical aptitude is still in its dynamic phase, the impact of a program of this type in the early years is very powerful.

Activities in First Steps are centered on a rich repertoire of folk songs, rhymes, and classical masterworks. Students will sing, move, and play from start to finish in their music time. Doing this each time they meet for music ensures that they will make substantial progress on the road to becoming tuneful, beatful, and artful musicians. The end goal of these activities, according to Feierabend and Schall-Brazee (2018, pp. 81–82) is for students to:

- sing with the correct vocal placement;
- sing with accuracy in solo situations and with others;
- sing with expression;
- maintain beat motions in coordination with a rhyme, song, or recorded example;
- demonstrate a feeling of how beats are grouped in two and three, with beat motions;
- move expressively to reflect the expressive elements in recorded music;
- have emotional responses when listening to expressive music;
- create original musical thoughts.

Feierabend, like Kodály, believes that high-quality literature should be used to build a common musical language. In First Steps in Music (as well as in Conversational Solfege), Feierabend has provided repertoire from which teachers can make excellent choices. He also provides three years of sample lessons that utilize this repertoire if teachers desire to follow them. There are musical examples in Feierabend's programs from around the world. However, though the literature selected is high quality, it is not necessarily comprehensive. It is important that, in addition to building a common musical language, teachers are also choosing repertoire that is inclusive of all the students in their population. Therefore, teachers are the ultimate gatekeepers and should choose repertoire that best serves their demographic.

Getting Started with First Steps

At the beginning of First Steps lessons, many students will be awkward and faltering in their attempts. They will experience more challenges than successes. But the more students experience the eight-part workout, the more they will demonstrate increasing musical competence. Moreover, they will become comfortable and confident music makers who understand that music is simply an intrinsic component of everyday life. Students at the end of their First Steps years are more than prepared for formalized music instruction.

On page 2 of his Music and Movement in the Early Years handout (available at http://www.giamusic.com/pdf/Z153_2009.pdf), Feierabend outlines the eight parts (Figure 3.1).

Figure 3.1.
Dr. Feierabend's eight-part First Steps Approach (available at http://www.giamusic.com/pdf/Z153_2009.pdf).

First Steps in Music

AN 8-PART MUSIC READINESS CURRICULUM FOR 3-8 YEAR OLD CHILDREN

SINGING/TONAL ACTIVITY CATEGORIES

1. **Pitch Exploration/Vocal Warm-up** (Discovering the sensation of the singing voice)
   - Vocal glissandos
2. **Fragment Singing** (Developing independent singing)
   - Echo Songs
   - Call and Response Songs
3. **Simple Songs** (Developing independent singing and musical syntax)
   - 3-4 Note Songs
   - Expanded Range
4. **Arioso** (Developing original musical thinking)
   - Spontaneous created songs by the child
5. **SongTales** (Developing expressive sensitivity through listening)
   - Ballads for children

MOVEMENT ACTIVITIES CATEGORIES

6. **Movement Exploration/Warm-up**
   (Developing expressive sensitivity through movement)
   - Movement with and without classical music accompaniment
7. **Movement for Form and Expression**
   (Singing/speaking and moving with formal structure and expression)
   - Non-Locomotor (finger plays, action songs, circle games, with recorded music)
   - Locomotor (circle games, with recorded music)
8. **Beat Motion Activities**
   (Developing competencies in maintaining the beat in groups of 2 and 3)
   - Child-Initiated Beat Motions
     - Non-Locomotor
     - Locomotor
   - Teacher-Initiated Beat Motions
     - Non-Locomotor
     - Locomotor

© 1990 John M. Feierabend

The Eight-Part Workout Explained

As can be seen in Figure 3.1, the workout begins with Pitch Exploration, which gives students the opportunity to explore and warm up their voices. This is imperative, since they will often be doing a significant amount of singing during each class, especially as the semesters goes on. After this vocal "stretch," students will experience Simple Songs. These are pieces that are short and have a limited vocal range. Following this, students will engage in Fragment Songs, which means that they will either perform an echo or call-and-response song. Both of these will allow students to quickly engage vocally while also building their short-term aural memory for melody. Arioso is the portion of the lesson in which students are led by teachers to spontaneously create original tunes. Since the ability to do this is the pinnacle of musical thought, Arioso effectively closes out the tonal-focused portion of the First Steps Lesson.

Movement Exploration activities, both with and without music, come next in the workout. In these, children learn how to effectively move their bodies in order to express what they hear and feel in music. In the next section of the workout, Movement for Form and Expression, students experience movement as a vehicle to connect to the expressiveness of the music they hear. This is done through fingerplays, action songs, and circle games. Additionally, students engage in expressive movement to classical masterworks. To this end, Feierabend and Peggy Lyman (a former Martha Graham dancer) created two DVDs, entitled *Move It!* (2003) and *Move It! 2* (2008). Teachers may use these DVDs to learn the choreography so that they might model it for students along with the music, or they may choose to show the DVD to students. These resources, now beloved by teachers and students the world over, are greatly valued because of the many selections presented that guide students to demonstrate the form and expression of music through movement.

The penultimate part of the First Steps in Music workout is Beat Motion Activities. This is a time for students to move to classical music in order to develop a feeling for beat *and* meter. In other words, they are moving to demonstrate the steady beat in music, as well as learning to feel and show the beat groupings of two or three. Since Feierabend desires to include classical music in every First Steps in Music lesson, he created a CD of 36 recordings to use for this portion of the lesson. His *First Steps in Classical Music: Keeping the Beat* CD (GIA Publications, 2000) provides 2- to 3-minute recordings of classical masterworks that are at an upbeat tempo, perfect for this part of the workout.

The final part of the First Steps in Music eight-part workout is one that beautifully embodies "artfulness": SongTales. At the end of a rigorous and engaging workout students will, very simply, listen as their teacher sings them a story. They have no other task during this time but to sit (or recline) and experience a caring adult perform an expressive piece of music for them. Not only are they taking in the music they are hearing, not only are they learning the rare skill of sitting in rapt silence as someone performs, they are connecting with each other and with an adult who truly cares for them and is demonstrating that care through song. It is a beautiful way to end a class.

Students who have the benefit of consistently participating in music classes of this nature can hardly help but grow musically. In addition to being fun, these musical workouts are strengthening their neuronal networks for music and preparing students for future music learning. The music teacher who uses First Steps in Music has prepared them, and they are ready to start formal instruction in notational literacy. They can now fully embark on their journey to think musically and read and write notation.

Conversational Solfege: Building a Bridge to Musical Thinking

Who Should Use Conversational Solfege

After students have become tuneful, beatful, and artful, it seems reasonable to begin teaching more formal musical concepts and work on the reading and writing of notation. Because musical aptitude is still in flux until around 8–9 years of age, spending the early elementary years doing First Steps in Music lessons has truly "primed the pump" for students as they begin to embark on formalized instruction. If a teacher has been doing these immersive music-making activities with students since kindergarten, the students are most likely ready sometime around the end of 1st or the beginning of 2nd grade. But it is important to remember that Conversational Solfege is a developmental program. This means it is not strictly tied to a grade level or student age, but rather it is contingent on whether or not students are ready. Beginning to teach children musical concepts and terms and notation before they are truly musical is counterproductive, no matter what age. So, the deciding factor for starting Conversational Solfege is not age or grade, but student readiness.

In light of this, if a teacher begins at a new school and the 4th graders, for example, are unmusical, it is not helpful to begin Conversational Solfege. Rather, it is best to take a kind of "First Steps for Big Kids" approach. For ideas on how to create this type of program for older students, Feierabend has authored books that are on offer from GIA Publications, entitled *The Book of Song Dances*, *The Book of Canons*, *The Book of Playground Songs and Rhymes*, and *The Book of Song Tales for Upper Grades*. These resources provide rich and engaging repertoire that is appropriate for slightly older students in need of building a musical foundation before moving into Conversational Solfege.

Conversational Solfege will not be addressed in this book because of the focus on early to upper elementary and due to space limitations. I hope to address technology integration with Conversational Solfege in a future book. To learn more about Conversational Solfege, please read *Feierabend Fundamentals: History, Philosophy, and Practice* (GIA Publications, 2018).

Conclusion

In both First Steps in Music and Conversational Solfege, John Feierabend brings together the best of what research reveals about how children acquire musical knowledge in tandem with best practices in music education. First Steps in Music helps teachers foster musical readiness in young children and guides them toward being tuneful, beatful, artful musicians. Once they arrive at this point and can sing in tune with healthy voice production, can move to the big beat and beat divisions in music, and can connect to the expressive aspect of music, they are ready to blossom as musicians.

This is the point at which Conversational Solfege can be utilized as the notational literacy portion of the music lesson and to help students grow into independent musical thinkers/artists. Both of these programs, as well as Feierabend's numerous other resources, help teachers create an engaging and developmentally appropriate program that will help children become musicians. And teachers can feel confident that they are offering a high-quality, authentic musical experience as they seek to instill a true love for music in their students. In so doing, teachers are facilitating one of the most important end goals of an elementary teacher: students who leave school with a repertoire of songs, rhymes, games, and a lifelong love of music that they can take with them into adulthood. And regardless of whether they ever participate in any kind of musical group again after graduation, that they continue to truly enjoy participating in music at some level and seek musical experiences for a lifetime.

Resources

Custodero, L. A., Britto, P. R., & Brooks-Gunn, J. (2003). Musical Lives: A Collective Portrait of American Parents and Their Young Children. *Applied Developmental Psychology*, 24, 553–572.

Davidson, J., Faulkner, R., & McPherson, G. (2009). Motivating Musical Learning. *The Psychologist*, 22, 1026–1029.

de Vries, P. (2007). The Use of Music CDs and DVDs in the Home with the Under-Fives. *Australian Journal of Early Childhood*, 32(4), 18–21.

Feierabend Association for Music Education website (Paragraph 2). (n.d.) https://www. feierabendmusic.org/john-feierabend/

Feierabend, John, M. (2000). *First Steps in Music for Infants and Toddlers*. Chicago: GIA Publications.

Feierabend, J. M. (2006). *First Steps in Music for Preschool and Beyond*. Chicago: GIA Publications.

Feierabend, L., & Schall-Brazee, S. (2018). First Steps in Music in the Elementary Classroom. In J. Feierabend & M. Strong (Eds.), *Feierabend Fundamentals: History, Philosophy, and Practice*. Chicago: GIA Publications.

Forrester, M. A. (2010). Emerging Musicality during the Pre-school Years: A Case Study of One Child. *Psychology of Music*, 38, 131–158.

Gordon, E. E. (1993). *A Music Learning Theory for Newborn and Young Children*. Chicago: GIA Publications.

Gordon, E. E. (2003). *Learning Sequences in Music*. Chicago: GIA Publications.

Gruhn, W. (2002). Phases and Stages in Early Music Learning: A Longitudinal Study on the Development of Young Children's Musical Potential. *Music Education Research*, 4(1), 51–71.

Hallam, S. (2006a). Musicality. In G. E. McPherson (Ed.), *The Child as Musician: A Handbook of Musical Development* (pp. 93–110). New York: Oxford University Press.

Ilari, B. (2002). Music Perception and Cognition in the First Year of Life. *Early Child Development and Care*, 172, 311–322.

McPherson, G. E. (2009). The Role of Parents in Children's Musical Development. *Psychology of Music*, 37, 91–110.

3, PART B
Technology Integration with First Steps

Amy M. Burns

Important Note: Before you use any tool with your students, please check with your school's administration regarding the technology policies of your school to make sure you can use students' information, including images, and that you have their support.

Tech Resources

There are numerous resources for elementary music educators using the Feierabend approach in their classrooms, so one can easily obtain folk songs, manipulatives, connect with others using the approach, and more. Here is a list that I have found helpful:

Accompanying Website for This Book

- Type in any web browser, www.oup.com/us/utema, or click on the icon.⊙

Organization Websites

- **Feierabend Association for Music Education (FAME)** (https://www.feierabendmusic. org/): This organization was founded in 2012. Its purpose it to assist music educators in using Dr. Feierabend's materials, as well as create a network for members to share ideas, videos, materials, and more.
- **Feierabend Fundamentals Facebook Group** (https://www.facebook.com/groups/ feierabendfundamentals/): This group is for anyone who is interested in Dr. Feierabend's approach. It also is a great place for those who have questions, which will be answered by experts in the field.
- **FAME Podcast** (https://www.feierabendmusic.org/the-tuneful-beatful-artful-music-teacher-podcast/): This will lead you the official homepage of the podcast so that you can easily subscribe to it on the music service of your choice. The podcasts feature experts in the field of First Steps and Conversational Solfege.
- **Perform a Google Search to find FAME organizations in your country and your local chapter.**
- **Website to Assist with the Rule of Thumb**: *Sing for the children, not with the children.* Utilize https://classroomscreen.com/ and click on the traffic light. You now have a great interactive and visual took for them to know when they are to listen to you sing and when they are to sing.

Amy M. Burns, *Technology Integration with First Steps* In: *Using Technology with Elementary Music Approaches*. Edited by: Amy M. Burns, Oxford University Press (2020). © Oxford University Press.
DOI: 10.1093/oso/9780190055653.003.0004

Pitch Exploration

Creating Pitch Explorations to Assess and Share in a Classroom with One Device

Curriculum Note: *Pitch explorations give the students the time to warm up and explore their voices. This is the first step of the eight-step workout and can take a relatively short amount of time from your daily classroom routine to accomplish. However, there are times when I want to extend this portion so that the students' parents, caregivers, or possibly another music classroom can share in their pitch explorations. Or, there are times when a class is distracted by an upcoming break or they will have a class party right after music class, so I want to creatively extend the pitch explorations with technology. In this lesson, the goals are assessment, creativity, and sharing.*

Objective: To create and record pitch explorations to assess or share with parents/caregivers or other music classes.

Grade Levels: PreK–2

Materials: This lesson can be done with one device in the classroom. For this lesson, you can use traditional paper with marker/pencil and a mobile device, or an iOS device/or a web-based device such as a Chromebook with the Seesaw app (web.seesaw.me). *First Steps in Music for Preschool and Beyond* (GIA Publications, 2006), *The Book of Pitch Explorations* (GIA Publications, 2003), and/or *Pitch Exploration Pathways—Flashcards* (GIA Publications, 2004) by Dr. John Feierabend.

Standards: Creating: MU:Cr2.1.PreKa, MU:Cr2.1.PreKb, MU:Cr1.1.Ka, MU:Cr1.1.Kb, MU:Cr2.1.Ka, MU:Cr2.1.Kb, MU:Cr1.1.1a, MU:Cr1.1b, MU:Cr2.1.1b, MU:Cr1.1.2a, MU:Cr1.1.2b, MU:Cr2.1.2a, MU:Cr2.1.2

Essential Understanding: The singing voice can produce high and low sounds. By exploring our voices with pitch explorations, the students will find their head voices.

Procedures:

Traditional Paper with Marker/Pencil and a Recording Device:

- Review pitch explorations using *First Steps in Music for Preschool and Beyond* (GIA Publications, 2006), *The Book of Pitch Explorations* (GIA Publications, 2003), and/or *Pitch Exploration Pathways—Flashcards* (GIA Publications, 2004) by Dr. John Feierabend.

- Pass out a marker or pencil and some paper and have the students draw a line. The line can curve, loop, or whatever they choose, but use examples like the flashcards so that they do not make them too complex.

- Have each student sing their drawing, with the class echoing the drawing.

- Using a device that can record video or audio (this can be a school device or a personal device, if allowed in the classroom, such as a mobile phone, tablet, iPad, etc.) and record the student singing the pitch exploration with the class echoing it. Video is optimal so that those who view it can see how the student drew the pitch exploration.

- **Assessing the pitch exploration**
  - Assess the pitch exploration later using Dr. Feierabend's method of 3: consistently competent in singing in the head voice; 2: competent in singing in head voice; 1: emerging in singing in the head voice. This can be done with paper and pencil or using technology such as Google Sheets or Microsoft Excel, a digital portfolio such as Seesaw, or an iOS app like iDoceo.

- More examples of these tools will be used throughout the book. Also check the Feierabend Facebook group in the file section for those who have shared their online spreadsheets and iDoceo files with the assessment charts already made for you.
- **Sharing the pitch exploration**
  - Sharing the pitch exploration has many benefits. If you share with parents, the parents can experience what their children are experiencing in music class. You can also use the video/audio as an assessment tool to share with parents if you are required to write progress reports. If you share with other teachers who are using the First Steps approach, your class can sing the other class's pitch explorations. Find some classes to share by asking on the Feierabend Fundamentals Facebook group.
  - To share the pitch exploration with parents or other classes, you can email the video, post it on a digital portfolio (see an explanation of the Seesaw app in Appendix of this volume, "Links Listed Throughout the Book and Descriptions of Programs"), or post it on a class website.
  - A class website can be made on such platforms as Google Classroom (https://classroom.google.com), Google Sites (https://sites.google.com/), Weebly (https://education.weebly.com/), Adobe Pages (https://spark.adobe.com/make/website-builder), Wordpress (https://wordpress.com/), and other sites.

One Device in the Classroom with Seesaw Student-Learning Digital Portfolio and Engagement Platform App:

- Review pitch explorations using *First Steps in Music for Preschool and Beyond* (GIA Publications, 2006), *The Book of Pitch Explorations* (GIA Publications, 2003), and/or *Pitch Exploration Pathways—Flashcards* (GIA Publications, 2004) by Dr. John Feierabend.
- Launch Seesaw (web.seesaw.me) and create an account. Create a journal for this class and add the names of the students. Connect the parents to their child's journal by sending the printed QR code or generated email found within Seesaw. To see how to do this, please visit the accompanying website found at www.oup.com/us/utema.⊚. Have the journal set up before class begins.
  - Click on the + sign > Post to Student Journal > Drawing (Figure 3.2).
  - Have the students draw a line. The line can curve, loop, or whatever they choose, but use the pitch exploration flashcards as an example so that they do not make them too complex. There are a variety of fun drawing tools for them to choose.
  - Click the record/microphone button and have each student sing the pitch exploration that he or she created.
  - Once finished, click the check button and click the student's name to assign it to his or her journal. Since you are running this through the teacher account, once you assign it to the student, it is automatically approved.
  - With Seesaw, you can set it up to have the parents connected to their child's journal. Therefore, when you post a pitch exploration for the student, parents can receive a notification on their mobile device that will bring them to their child's digital portfolio so that they can listen to the pitch exploration.

Figure 3.2.
Tools used in Seesaw.

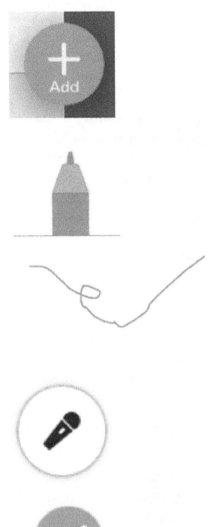

- **Tech tip**: This is if the teacher is directing the activity with one device. You can also do this with the students logging in on their 1:1 devices, drawing a pitch exploration, click the record button, and submitting it to their journals with your approval (see next lesson).
- **Tech tip**: This takes longer than the video of the students singing their own drawings with one mobile device. You would use Seesaw for the purposes of recording, assessing, organizing, and sharing their work with their parents/caregivers.
- **Website example**: Visit the website that corresponds with this book at www.oup.com/us/utema to see an example of this activity.⊛
- **Alternative student-learning digital portfolio and engagement apps**: Seesaw is just one of many platforms that showcase students' works. Others are ClassDojo (classdojo.com), Flipgrid (flipgrid.com), FreshGrade (freshgrade.com), ClassTag (classtag.com), and Bloomz (bloomz.net), to name a few.

Higher Order Thinking Questions to Ask the Students:

- When the pitch exploration began at the bottom of the screen, was your voice high or low?

- When the pitch exploration began at the top of the screen, was your voice high or low?
- *These questions will be challenging for younger students to answer. However, it helps them to begin to experience the concept of high and low pitches.*

Extensions: Utilize a cross-curricular connection with writing by having the students write the first letter of their name and record themselves singing the letter.

Creating Pitch Explorations to Assess and Share in a 1:1 Classroom

This is similar to the preceding lesson. The difference is that your students in Grades K–2 have 1:1 devices. Here is how you can do this lesson with 1:1 devices.
Using 1:1 Devices in the Classroom (example uses Seesaw):

- This can be done with one device per student by using Seesaw (web.seesaw.me). The device can be an iOS device, a Chromebook, a computer, an Android, or a Kindle. To read a detailed description of Seesaw, please visit Appendix, "Links Listed Throughout the Book and Descriptions of Programs."
- **Website example**: To see how to set up a class in Seesaw, please visit the website that corresponds with this book at www.oup.com/us/utema.⊚
- The students log into their journals by using a QR code login or an email/text code login. Since they are in grades K–2, the QR code login would be the most intuitive for this age group.
- Once they are logged in, have them tap the plus tool and then the drawing tool.
- Have them draw a pitch exploration. There are a variety of fun tools for them to choose.
- Have them spread out so that the recording will focus in on their voices and not so much on the background sound.
- Have them press the microphone, introduce themselves, and then sing their newly drawn pitch exploration into the device.
- When finished, click the check button so that they approve their recordings, and then press the check button again to approve it. They will need to select their name to post the pitch exploration.
- In the teacher account, you will receive their posts, where you can listen and assess their pitch explorations.
- **Assessing the pitch exploration**
  - Assess the pitch exploration later using Dr. Feierabend's method of 3: consistently competent in singing in the head voice; 2: competent in singing in head voice; 1: emerging in singing in the head voice.
  - You can approve or delete the post (Figure 3.3). When you click the check button (approve), it will be posted on their journals and their parents/caregivers can now listen to the pitch explorations as well. When you click on the trashcan (delete), it will be deleted and will never post to their journal.
- **Activity tip**: I have the students introduce themselves before they record so that if they accidentally post it to another student's journal, you can still assess them accurately.
- **Website example**: Visit the website that corresponds with this book at www.oup.com/us/utema to see an example of this activity.⊚

Figure 3.3.
Seesaw's approve or discard tool for teachers only.

- **Alternative student-learning digital portfolio and engagement apps**: Seesaw is just one of many platforms that showcase students' works. Others are ClassDojo (classdojo. com), Flipgrid (flipgrid.com), FreshGrade (freshgrade.com), ClassTag (classtag.com), and Bloomz (bloomz.net), to name a few.

Making Pitch Exploration Stations

Curriculum Note: *In this lesson, we are using the interactive whiteboard or a device, such as an iOS device, or a website, to draw the pitch exploration at one of the stations.*

Objective: To create and record pitch explorations to assess or share with parents or other music classes.

Grade Levels: PreK–3

Materials: This lesson can be done with one device in the classroom or in a classroom with 1:1 devices. For this lesson, you can use an interactive whiteboard or a projector with a screen, an iOS device, or a laptop/desktop with internet access/or web-based device such as a Chromebook that can access https://drawisland.com/. *First Steps in Music for Preschool and Beyond* (GIA Publications, 2006), *The Book of Pitch Explorations* (GIA Publications, 2003), and/or *Pitch Exploration Pathways—Flashcards* (GIA Publications, 2004) by Dr. John Feierabend. For the stations besides the one with technology, purple yarn and traditional paper with markers/crayons.

Standards: Creating: MU:Cr2.1.PreKa, MU:Cr2.1.PreKb, MU:Cr1.1.Ka, MU:Cr1.1.Kb, MU:Cr2.1.Ka, MU:Cr2.1.Kb, MU:Cr1.1.1a, MU:Cr1.1b, MU:Cr2.1.1b, MU:Cr1.1.2a, MU:Cr1.1.2b, MU:Cr2.1.2a, MU:Cr2.1.2

Essential Understanding: The singing voice can produce high and low sounds. By exploring our voices with pitch explorations, the students will find their head voices.

Procedures:

Using an Interactive Whiteboard as a Station:

- Review pitch explorations using *First Steps in Music for Preschool and Beyond* (GIA Publications, 2006), *The Book of Pitch Explorations* (GIA Publications, 2003), and/

or *Pitch Exploration Pathways—Flashcards* (GIA Publications, 2004) by Dr. John Feierabend.

- Assign stations for students to create pitch explorations.
- **Station One**: Using a string of yarn, each child in the group creates a pitch exploration for the other students in the group to sing.
  - The line that they create can curve, loop, or whatever they choose.
  - From Dr. Strong's First Steps Certification Class, reference the book *Harold and the Purple Crayon* by Crockett Johnson and use a purple string for the students to create their pitch exploration.
- **Station Two**: Use the traditional paper and pencil/marker for each student to create his or her pitch explorations for the rest of the students to sing.
- **Station Three**: Use a device with Seesaw or another type of student-learning digital portfolio and engagement app and have the students add a pitch exploration to their journals (see previous pitch exploration lesson in this chapter).
- **Station Four**: Have the students use an interactive whiteboard to draw a pitch exploration for the other students in the group to sing. Use the eraser to erase the pitch exploration for the next group to use. If you do not want to erase the pitch explorations, then have them add a new page to the file and create more pitch explorations.
  - Turn on the interactive whiteboard.
  - Launch the software that comes with the interactive whiteboard.
  - Once launched, use the markers, pens, stylus, or writing utensils that come with the board to draw (Figure 3.4). Use the eraser to erase. Add a new page to the file to create more pitch explorations.
  - **Website example**: To see how to do this, please visit the website that corresponds with this book at www.oup.com/us/utema.⊚

If you do not have an interactive whiteboard, the following are alternatives.

Figure 3.4.

A pitch exploration written on an interactive whiteboard using a creative pen.

Using Laptop/Desktop with Internet Access/or Web-Based Device Such as a Chromebook That Can Access https://drawisland.com/:

- Open https://drawisland.com/
  - Instruct the children (Grades 1–3) to use the pencil and delete tool. Before they enter the class, make sure the pencil tool is set to a different color than black and that the size of the tool is 15+.
  - The children use the pencil tool to draw the pitch exploration.
  - The students sing it.
  - The student clicks the delete button and the next child draws the pitch exploration.
- **Website example**: To see how to do this, please visit the website that corresponds with this book at www.oup.com/us/utema.⊛
- **Tech tip**: Lay a mobile device near this station to video record their pitch explorations to assess later.

Using an iOS/Google Play/Chromebook App:

- Visit https://www.showme.com/create to download the free version of the app to the appropriate device. The free version will suffice for this activity.
  - Lay the device at the station and have the students use their fingers or a mouse (depending on the device) to create their pitch exploration.
  - The other students sing the exploration.
  - The student uses the "undo" tool or the eraser tool to erase the pitch exploration and have the students take their turns.
- **Tech tip**: Lay a device nearby this station to video record their pitch explorations to assess later.
- **Tech tip**: ShowMe can record and draw at the same time. With the free app, there are a lot of steps and it can be complex for young students to master.

Higher Order Thinking Questions to Ask the Students:

- When the pitch exploration began at the bottom of the screen, was your voice high or low?
- When the pitch exploration began at the top of the screen, was your voice high or low?
- *These questions will be challenging for younger students to answer. However, it helps them to begin to experience the concept of high and low pitches.*

Extensions: Utilize scarves to create pitch explorations. Take a photo of their creation and then have them use the drawing tool to draw, sing, and record the pitch exploration on an interactive whiteboard, in a student digital portfolio engagement app like Seesaw (web.seesaw.me), or in an interactive whiteboard app like ShowMe or Explain Everything (explaineverything.com).

Visualizing a Pitch Exploration

Curriculum Note: *This lesson can be used to show mastery of high and low or to help children who are challenged by the concept of high and low sounds.*

Objective: The students will create pitch explorations with the website, https://creatability. withgoogle.com/seeing-music/. This website visualizes their pitch explorations. This could be used to show assessment with high and low sounds, as well as helping students who are challenged with high and low sounds to visualize the concept.

Grade Levels: PreK–3

Materials: The website https://creatability.withgoogle.com/seeing-music/ can be used in a classroom with one device that has a microphone, internet access, and can be projected onto a screen, as well as in a 1:1 classroom. *First Steps in Music for Preschool and Beyond* (GIA Publications, 2006), *The Book of Pitch Explorations* (GIA Publications, 2003), and/or *Pitch Exploration Pathways—Flashcards* (GIA Publications, 2004) by Dr. John Feierabend.

Standards: Creating: MU:Cr1.1.PreKa, MU:Cr2.1.PreKa, MU:Cr2.1.PreKb, MU:Cr1.1.Ka, MU:Cr1.1.Kb, MU:Cr2.1.Ka, MU:Cr2.1.Kb, MU:Cr1.1.1a, MU:Cr1.1b, MU:Cr2.1.1b, MU:Cr1.1.2a, MU:Cr1.1.2b, MU:Cr2.1.2a, MU:Cr2.1.2b, MU:Cr1.1.3a, MU:Cr1.1.3b, MU:Cr2.1.3a, MU:Cr2.1.3b

Essential Questions:

- What happens when I sing from low to high?
- What happens when I sing from high to low?
- How does music and art work together?

Procedures:

- Before class, make sure that the device you are using has internet access, a microphone (internal or external), and can access the website https://creatability.withgoogle.com/seeing-music/. Click the "Start Playing" button. You might need to approve the microphone to be used with this site on your browser.
- Greet the class and begin with the pitch exploration using *First Steps in Music for Preschool and Beyond* (GIA Publications, 2006), *The Book of Pitch Explorations* (GIA Publications, 2003), and/or *Pitch Exploration Pathways—Flashcards* (GIA Publications, 2004) by Dr. John Feierabend.
- Use a slide whistle for students to echo with their singing voices.
- Launch https://creatability.withgoogle.com/seeing-music/
- Ask the students to watch as you sing or play an instrument like a slide whistle (Figure 3.5).
- Ask the students to tell you what they saw. Answers will vary from lines moving across the screen to a variety of colors appearing on the screen.
- Play again and encourage the students to tell you what is happening musically.

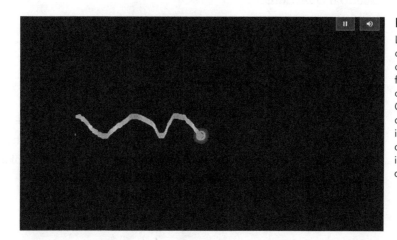

Figure 3.5.
Link to https://creatability.withgoogle.com/seeing-music/ found at www.oup.com/us/utema. Creatability is a set of experiments made in collaboration with creators and allies in the accessibility community.

- Ask a student to sing a pitch exploration and have the other students echo. As this happens, remind the students to watch the screen.
  - **Activity tip**: If a student uses a silly voice when you want them to use a singing voice, encourage them to use them singing voice. If it continues, ask them to sit and watch another student who will demonstrate.
- As students sing solos, ask the other students to musically describe the line. You can pause the microphone when you ask questions.
- **Website example**: To see how to do this, please visit the website that corresponds with this book at www.oup.com/us/utema.⊛

Higher Order Thinking Questions to Ask the Students:

- When your voice moves from high to low to high, what is happening on the screen and why?
- How does this website show music, art, and science all working together?

Extensions: This site has some more features. You can change the visualization to Hilbert, Spectrograph, Spectrogram, Waveform, and Oscilloscope. You can also show the examples of voice, saxophone, violin, guitar, and tabla. These examples can encourage wonderful discussions about volume, attack of sound, and more. You can add an mp3 file and it will interpret visually. Finally, you can turn on the note grid and see where the children are singing in relation to note names.

Creating a Pitch Exploration ebook to Share

Curriculum Note: *This lesson works well right before a break because it brings together something that you have been doing at the beginning of each class. This is also a great way for First Steps classes to share with each other across the country and the globe.*
Objective: To create a pitch exploration ebook to share with another class for them to sing.
Grade Levels: PreK–2
Materials: *First Steps in Music for Preschool and Beyond* (GIA Publications, 2006), *The Book of Pitch Explorations* (GIA Publications, 2003), and/or *Pitch Exploration Pathways—Flashcards* (GIA Publications, 2004) by Dr. John Feierabend. Book Creator app (bookcreator.com) for iOS or the web-based app that can be used on Chromebooks. For this lesson, we will use one device in the classroom projected to a screen with speakers.
Standards: All Creating and Performing Standards
Essential Questions:

- When is a creative idea ready to share?
- When is a performance ready to share?

Procedures:

- Before class, launch the Book Creator app.
  - For the iOS app, it will allow you to create one book in the free version. If you purchase the app, you can currently create an unlimited amount of ebooks.
  - For the web-based app that you would use on Chromebooks, you can create a free account that allows 40 free ebooks to be made.
  - This may change, so check bookcreator.com for their most current free and subscription options.

- Review pitch explorations using *First Steps in Music for Preschool and Beyond* (GIA Publications, 2006), *The Book of Pitch Explorations* (GIA Publications, 2003), and/or *Pitch Exploration Pathways—Flashcards* (GIA Publications, 2004) by Dr. John Feierabend.
- Launch Book Creator (bookcreator.com) on your device.
- Click a new ebook (square mode, not in comic book mode, will work fine), click the + button, and click the drawing tool.
- Ask a student to come and draw using her finger (iOS app) or the mouse.
- Press the plus button and then the microphone so that the students can record themselves singing their pitch explorations. You can solo if you want to assess or have the group sing the pitch exploration together.
- Once finished, press stop and approve the recording (Figure 3.6).
- Press the + button on the side to add a new page. Continue until every child has had a turn. If attention is waning, go for as long as you feel will work best with your class.
- The ebooks save automatically.
- Once finished, you have an ebook of pitch explorations. *How can these be shared?*
  - *Exporting ebooks from Book Creator:*
  - On a web-based device using the bookcreator.com site, these can be shared to be published online at their website, downloaded as an ebook, or printed, all by clicking the share icon. The easiest is the link-sharing so that it can be accessed from multiple devices.
  - On an iOS device using the Book Creator app, epub (for reading in an ebook app), pdf (for printing), video (for posting to the web, Seesaw, Google Drive, Dropbox, Google Classroom, etc.), and online (for posting on book creator's website). The easiest is video, as most devices can play it and the audio files will be included.
  - Go to the Feierabend Fundamentals Facebook page to find another First Steps class to share the ebook.
  - Export it as a video and send it to them via email, google drive, dropbox, etc.
  - Have the teacher in the other class video record his or her students singing your students' ebook.
  - Have the teacher send you the video of them singing and have your children respond. The response can be a thankful one or a response that has them using their design thinking skills of, "I like the way you sang my pitch exploration. I wonder why you started low when mine started high. What if you started with a high sound and then went low?"

Figure 3.6.

An example of a page from the kindergarten pitch exploration ebook.

- **Website example**: To see an end product, please visit the website that corresponds with this book at www.oup.com/us/utema.⊛

Higher Order Thinking Questions to Ask the Students:

- We finished our ebook. Do you feel that it is ready to share with a class at another school? Why or why not?
- Do you perform differently when you know that someone else besides the teacher and your classmates will listen to it?

Extensions: Try using Skype, especially the website Skype in the Classroom (https:// education.microsoft.com/skype-in-the-classroom/overview), to find another music classroom to skype into your classroom when you are ready to share the ebook.

Fragment Singing (Song Fragments)

Curriculum Note: *This goes with the song fragment/fragment singing portion of the eight-part music workout. This lesson will enhance this portion and encourage independent singing. This lesson works well when being used before a school break or when finding more ways to comfortably encourage solo singing along with creativity. It is also a good way to connect across the curriculum through reading, writing, and creating rhyming words.*

Creating an ebook with New Verses to the Song "Down by the Bay"

Objective: To create and record rhyming words to the song *Down by the Bay*, and place them in an ebook to share with parents and other music classes.

Grade Levels: PreK–2

Materials: This lesson can be done with one device in the classroom or in a classroom with 1:1 devices. For this lesson, you can use traditional paper with marker/pencil, an interactive whiteboard or a projector with a screen, an iOS device, or a web-based device such as a Chromebook or a laptop. For this lesson, we will use Book Creator (www. bookcreator.com), a web-based program or an iOS app that can create ebooks. The web-based version can currently create 40 ebooks for free. The iOS version can create one ebook for free or numerous ebooks with the paid app. *First Steps in Music for Preschool and Beyond* (GIA Publications, 2006) and/or *The Book of Echo Songs* and/or *The Book of Call and Response* by Dr. John Feierabend.

Standards: Creating: MU:Cr2.1.PreKa, MU:Cr2.1.PreKb, MU:Cr3.1.PreKa, MU:Cr3.2.PreKa, MU:Pr6.1.PreKa, MU:Cn11.0.PreKa, MU:Cr1.1.Kb, MU:Cr2.1.Ka, MU:Cr3.1.Ka, MU:Cr3.2.Ka, **Performing**: MU:Pr5.1.Ka, U:Pr6.1.Kb, MU:Cn11.0.Ka, MU:Cr1.1.1a, MU:Cr1.1b, MU:Cr2.1.1a, MU:Cr3.1.1a, MU:Cr3.2.1a, MU:Cn11.0.1, MU:Cr1.1.2a, MU:Cr1.1.2b, MU:Cr2.1.2a, MU:Cr2.1.2b, MU:Cr3.1.2a, MU:Cr3.2.2a, MU:Cn11.0.2a

Essential Question:

- When you improvise new lyrics, does it change the mood of the song?
- Does it change the rhythm of the song?

Procedures:

One Device in the Classroom Projected onto the Screen:

- Review the song *Down by the Bay* from *First Steps in Music Preschool and Beyond*.

- Ask the students what is special about the pairs of words like "bear and hair," "llamas and pajamas," "whale and tail," "bee and knee," "goose and moose"? (They are rhyming words.)
- Ask the students, "Can you think of more rhyming words?" Ask for a couple of examples.
- **For PreK–1:**
  - Pass out paper and markers/pencils.
  - Ask the students to draw two pictures that rhyme.
  - For younger students, this could be challenging, so ask them to draw a picture and you will find the rhyming word for it. In addition, have the students work in groups if you feel that this would work well for your class.
- **For Grade 2:**
  - Pass out paper and markers/pencils.
  - Ask the students to draw two pictures that rhyme and to write the words below the pictures. If your school wants students' works that are published to have the correct spelling, make sure to assist the students with accurate spelling.
  - If you are pressed for time, assign partners to work together.
- Ask the students to show their pictures.
- Everyone sing the song again with their new rhymes.
- Launch Book Creator (www.bookcreator.com) from the device that is projecting onto the screen. This can be an iOS device or a device, like a Chromebook or a computer, that has internet access.
  - Create a new book. You can choose portrait, square, or landscape depending on the device that will view it. Default to square if you are not sure what to choose.
  - The cover is the first square that appears; your students can create that during another class, or you can create one after class.
  - Click the + button on the side.
  - You are now on page 2. Click the + button, and scroll down to the camera.
  - Take a picture of the students' rhyming pictures. To save time, take one picture of the two rhyming pictures.
  - Click "Use Photo" to use the photo or "Retake" to retake the photo.
  - Do the steps again until the ebook includes all pictures.
  - Now it is time to record. For younger students, you might want them to sing the entire song together. Only help them when you need to, but try to have them sing by themselves. For older students, have them sing the song independently.
  - Go to page 2.
  - Click the + button and scroll down to the microphone.
  - Click the red record button and have either the entire class sing that verse with the new rhyming words that match the pictures, or just the student artists who drew the pictures. Accept the recording and go to page 3, unless you need to redo the recording (Figure 3.7).
  - Repeat the steps again until all students have sung. You will have separate recordings for each page. If a student is too shy to sing independently, encourage other students to sing with him or her.
- **Share the ebook.**
  - Once you or your students have created the cover, your ebook is complete.
  - To export the ebook:

Figure 3.7.
An example of Song Fragment ebook created by kindergartners.

- Click the share icon under the book and you will see the following choices for the iOS app: epub (for reading in an ebook app), pdf (for printing), video (for posting to the web, Seesaw, Google Drive, Dropbox, Google Classroom, etc.), and online (for posting on book creator's website). The easiest is video as most devices can play it and the audio files will be included.

- On a web-based device using the bookcreator.com site, these can be shared to be published online at their website, downloaded as an ebook, or printed, by clicking the share icon. I find it best to share it as a link so that it can be viewed on multiple devices.

- Share the book as a video or link and you can now post it to their digital learning portfolios, post it on a music classroom website, post it on the school's website, or email it to parents. From there, students can tell their parents about the ebook and how they made it, or music classrooms can share their ebooks with each other. To find a music classroom to connect with, search through the Feierabend Fundamentals Facebook group or at one of their get-togethers to find other music educators to discuss the possibility.

- **Website example**: To see an end product of this, please visit the website that corresponds with this book at www.oup.com/us/utema.⊚

1:1 Devices: This is similar to the procedure in the preceding, but your students would need to be able to access your free account and there would be a limit to 40 books (web-based), or one book (iOS device with the free app). The biggest difference is that when the students create their ebooks, it would just have a cover and their two pictures. They will most likely record their verse as a solo. You can either share numerous small ebooks or combine them into one large ebook, as long as they are all the same shape (i.e., they are all square or portrait or landscape). If you have the paid web-based versions, students can collaborate in real time. The paid app would be ideal for a 1:1 classroom.

Higher Order Thinking Questions to Ask the Students:

- What happened to the rhythm when we added new words?
- What happened to the mood of the song when we added new words?

Extensions: Have the older students review each other's ebooks. Use a design thinking process of "I like . . . I wish . . . I wonder . . . What if . . ." to assist with commenting on the ebooks. For example, "I like your picture. I wish it had more of the color blue for the bird. I wonder what it would look like with more of the color blue. What if you add more of the color blue to your picture?" For older students, this promotes the process of digital citizenship in a respectful way, even if they are commenting on it without writing it.

For younger students, show a cross-curricular connection by writing the letter that their picture begins with on the picture. For example, if they drew a bear, ask them what letter the word bear begins with, and then guide them to write the letter on the picture.

Simple Songs

Curriculum Note: *When assessing a solo singer, many music educators like to use pencil and paper for a checklist so that they can check off items on a rubric that they are using to assess the solo singing. This is a wonderful tool and if it works for you, then continue to use it. However, what if there were a way that technology could "level up" the organization of the assessment? What if technology could help share the solo singing with the parents or caregivers so that they could hear the performance? What if technology could be used to show why a grade was given on a progress report based on this solo singing?*

Recording Simple Songs for Sharing with Caregivers and to Show Students' Progress in a Classroom with One Device

Objective: After phases 1 (teacher has sung the simple song to the class for two or more meetings), and 2 (the whole group has sung the song a few times without the teacher's assistance), the students will voluntarily sing the simple song as a solo. Technology is used as a tool to keep track of the students' solos and to be able to share the achievement with their parents.

Grade Levels: PreK–2 (but can be used for older students with more mature songs)

Materials: The assessment for the solo singing can be done with the following tech devices: (1) One device in a classroom, which can be a laptop, mobile device, tablet, iOS device, or Chromebook; (2)1:1 devices in the classrooms, which could be laptops, Android devices, Kindles, iOS devices such as iPads, generic tablets with internet access, or Chromebooks. You will also need *First Steps in Music for Preschool and Beyond* (GIA Publications, 2006) and/or *Simple Songs & Circles* by Dr. John Feierabend. The tech devices offered in this lesson are iDoceo (idoceo.net—iOS only), online-voice-recorder.com (a free online voice recorder that saves audio to your Google Drive or hard drive), Vocaroo (another free online voice recorder tool that requires Adobe Flash, which will be discontinued in late 2020), GarageBand (iOS or Mac app), or Soundtrap (soundtrap.com—a free online digital audio workstation).

Standards: Performing: MU:Pr6.1.Pk, MU:Pr6.1.K, MU:Pr6.1.1, MU:Pr6.1.2

Essential Questions:

- When is a performance ready to present?
- How do the context and the manner in which the musical work is presented influence the audience's response?

Procedures:

- This is phase three of Simple Songs, which is step three in the eight-part workout. It is understood that the students know the song and have been able to sing it without the teacher's assistance.
- Review the song of choice found in *First Steps in Music for Preschool and Beyond* (GIA Publications, 2006) and/or *Simple Songs & Circles* by Dr. John Feierabend.
- **Solo Singing Attempts: One Device in the Classroom**
  - iDoceo (www.idoceo.net—iOS only)
- iDoceo is an iOS paid app that acts as a teacher's assistant. It serves as a gradebook, planner, diary, timetable, seating chart, resource manager to keep track of PDFs, audio, video, links, images, and more, that can export as PDFs, Excel files, and more. iDoceo is stored locally on your iPad. Therefore, no internet is needed. You can back it up to a google drive, dropbox, etc.
- Launch iDoceo. To add a class, you can ask for an Excel file that contains class lists. Have them emailed to you. Make sure the first name on the class list begins in the second cell. On your iPad with iDoceo, click open your email app and tap and hold the attachment file. The iPad will ask you for the app to open the file. Click on iDoceo, and iDoceo will launch. iDoceo will then ask you if you want to create a class from the attachment. Once you approve this, the class list is ready in iDoceo. I find that making separate excel files for each class works best. However, you can always type in the names of the students into iDoceo.
- I create a tab in iDoceo called assessments. I create a column next to the children's names by tapping at the top of the screen. Once the column is titled and dated, I tap the cell next to the child's name. I tap the microphone symbol and click the red record button. Once the student is finished singing, I click the green check button and now have the recorded assessment to grade later.
- **Grading**: In that same cell with the recording, I will add a symbol for grading. I might use a number system from 1 to 4: 4 is that the child sang the simple song in tune and on pitch; 3 is the child sang the song in tune with teacher assistance of the starting pitch; 2 is the student could only sing the song when starting on a lower pitch; and 1 is the child is still emerging as a solo singer. Or I might use smiley faces or some type of icon included in iDoceo.
  - The assessments are now recorded and organized so that they can be used for future planning or grading purposes.
  - **Bonuses**: On the Feierabend Fundamentals Facebook Group, there are teachers who share their lesson plan templates and unit templates created in iDoceo.
  - **Website example**: To see how to do this, please visit the website that corresponds with this book at www.oup.com/us/utema.⊛
  - **Similar app**: Teacherkit: http://teacherkit.net/
- **Online Voice Recorder** (https://online-voice-recorder.com/beta/)—a free online voice recorder that saves audio files as mp3 files and downloads them to the computer's hard drive or to a Chromebook's Google Drive. Use the beta version as it currently saves files much faster and is not based in Adobe Flash (which will be discontinued in late 2020).
  - Launch the website, (https://online-voice-recorder.com/beta/).

- Press record.
- Ask the student to sing.
- **Activity tip**: Mention the student's name in the recording to make it easier to assess later.
- When finished, end the recording and download it to the computer's hard drive or to Google Drive (if you are using a Chromebook). Since you named the student at the beginning of the recording, you have a reference of who is singing on each recording.
- Grading: See preceding example.
- **Vocaroo** (https://vocaroo.com/)—This is a free online recorder that saves audio files that can be shared via social media, or downloaded onto the computer's hard drive or Google Drive (if you are using a Chromebook).
  - This is similar to using online voice recorder.
  - When it loads, you would do essentially the same thing as online voice recorder. You can share vocaroo recordings via social media, but you can also download them onto the computer's hard drive or Google Drive (if you are using a Chromebook), embed them on a website, or create a QR code for them.
  - Grading: See previous example.
- **GarageBand** (MAC—https://www.apple.com/mac/garageband/?cid=oas-us-domains-garageband.com, or iOS app https://itunes.apple.com/us/app/garageband/id408709785?mt=8)
  - Launch GarageBand on your iPad or MAC laptop.
  - If it asks you to choose an instrument, choose the microphone (audio).
  - Click record (enable microphone) and record the child singing a simple song. You can change the instrument track's name to the name of the child, or when you record, speak the child's name or ask the child to introduce him- or herself.
  - Once finished, listen to the recordings and assess accordingly.
  - Grading: See previous example.
- **Soundtrap** (https://www.soundtrap.com)—This is a web-based digital audio workstation that is online and involves music creation, collaboration, and recording tools. There is a free version that can be set up for the teacher to use to record students.
  - Launch soundtrap.com and create a free account.
  - Tap the red record button and record the child singing a simple song.
  - You can change the instrument track's name to the name of the child, or when you record, speak the child's name or ask the child to introduce him- or herself.
  - Once finished, listen to the recordings and assess accordingly.
  - Grading: See previous example.

Higher Order Thinking Questions to Ask the Students:

- How would you describe your singing?
- How would an audience describe your singing?
- *Give guidance to the younger children's answers by always encouraging a positive reflection on their solo singing. Examples could be, "I like my singing because . . ." "The highlight of my singing is . . ." "The audience would like . . . about my singing." If a child is not singing at this time, you can encourage a reflection by using examples such as, "When I sing, I will sound like . . ." "I did not want to sing today because . . ."*

Extension: If the child sang a solo, give the child a type of "badge" that reads, "I sang a solo in music class today!" or "Ask me about my solo in music class today!" If you are using a student digital portfolio like Seesaw, ClassDojo, ClassTag, Flipgrid, FreshGrade, Bloomz, etc., then share the post with the student's parents or caregivers, with a comment on how proud you are that the student sang a solo in music class.

Recording Simple Songs for Sharing with Caregivers and to Show Students' Progress in a 1:1 Classroom

Curriculum Note: *This is the same lesson as the one previous, with the one exception that the students will use their own devices to perform the activity instead of as an entire class with one device. The change would occur here:*

Solo Singing Attempts: A Few Devices in the Classroom or a 1:1 Classroom

- **Seesaw (web.seesaw.me)**—a student engagement platform for digital portfolios.
  - An in-depth description of Seesaw is listed Appendix, "Links Listed Throughout the Book and Descriptions of Programs."
  - **Website example**: Visit the supplemental website at www.oup.com/us/utema to see how to create an activity in Seesaw.⊙
- **Flipgrid (flipgrid.com)**—A free app and web-based tool that empowers students' voices. Engage and empower every voice in your classroom by recording and sharing short videos. I would suggest for kindergarten and above.
  - Create a free account at flipgrid.com.
  - Create a grid titled "My Music Classroom [insert grade level and or identification of that class, such as KP]. A grid is your classroom. Add topics to your grid to encourage performance and reflection.
  - There are options for sharing grids.
  - You can have students log into your grid with their email addresses.
  - For students with no email addresses, you can create student logins so that they will have a QR code to scan to join the grid.
  - Or you can make the grid public with a password to enter the grid.
  - *If you use Flipgrid, check with your school's administration for approval and the proper protocol.*
  - Add a new topic within that grid titled, "Simple Songs."
    - The recording time for each video submitted will default to one minute and thirty seconds.
    - In the section marked "Prompt," type the instructions.
    - In the section marked "Focus (Optional)," you can video yourself giving the instructions or an example of a Simple Song.
    - Have the students access your grid (via email addresses or QR code) and click the green + button.
    - Have them video record themselves singing a simple song.
      - If they are shy, have them click the whiteboard button, where they can add emoji stickers and record their singing without having to appear in the video (Figure 3.8).
      - Once they finish their video, they can add a selfie as their thumbnail (you can turn this off in the settings if needed).

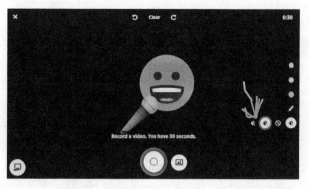

Figure 3.8.
Example of the whiteboard tool in Flipgrid.

- In the settings, you can turn on the item that allows you to approve each video that is submitted.
- **Website example**: Visit the supplemental website at www.oup.com/us/utema to see how to create an activity in Seesaw.⊚
- **Similar programs**: Others are ClassDojo (classdojo.com), FreshGrade (freshgrade. com), ClassTag (classtag.com), and Bloomz (bloomz.net), to name a few.

Higher Order Thinking Questions to Ask the Students: see previous example.

Arioso

Curriculum Note: *Many music educators have commented that this is the step they tend to hesitate on when utilizing the eight-step workout in the classroom. However, there are also music educators who will state that this is the most intuitive one to implement because students naturally perform Ariosos. Here are some creative ways of using technology to help an elementary music educator feel more comfortable when assisting a student in creating an Arioso.*

Taking a Trip to Arioso Land

Objective: Encouraged by the teacher, the student will spontaneously create an original tune with more than two pitches.

Grade Levels: PreK–2

Materials: This Arioso lesson can be done in a classroom with one device that can access one of the following tech tools with the following tech devices: a laptop, mobile device, tablet, iOS Device, or Chromebook that has access to Google Slides (web-based), PowerPoint (PC or Mac), Notebook (for SMART Boards), or can display a pdf file. You will also need *First Steps in Music for Preschool and Beyond* (GIA Publications, 2006) by Dr. John Feierabend and the file "Arioso Lands" by Amy M. Burns found on the supplemental website at www.oup.com/us/utema. In addition, the websites or apps listed in the procedures could also be used.

Standards: Creating: MU:Cr2.1.PreKa, MU:Cr1.1.Kb, MU:Cr1.1b, MU:Cr1.1.2b
Performing: MU:Pr4.1.PreKa, MU:Pr4.1.Ka, MU:Pr4.1.1a, MU:Pr4.1.2a,
Responding: MU:Re8.1.PreKa, MU:Re8.1.Ka, MU:Re8.1.1a, MU:Re8.1.2a
Connecting: MU:Cn10.0.PreKa, MU:Cn10.0.Ka, MU:Cn10.0.1a, MU:Cn10.0.2a
Essential Question:

- How can we tell a musical story through Arioso?

Procedures:

- Arioso is step four of the eight-part musical workout. Before this step, the students would have warmed up their voices with pitch explorations and have performed echo and simple songs to develop independent singing.
- **"Going to Arioso Land" using technology**:
- There are many fabulous music educators who have created Arioso Lands for their students. These lands consist of a part of the classroom that is transformed into a magical land where students will create Ariosos. However, what do you do if you are on a cart or teach in multiple classrooms? This is where technology can be a very useful tool.
- **Website example**: Go to www.oup.com/us/utema and download the file "Arioso Lands." It is a zip file that will open with a folder carrying Arioso Lands as a pdf file, a PowerPoint file, a Notebook file, and a link to a Google Slides file.◉
- **Arioso Land pdf** (found on website: www.oup.com/us/utema):
  - Open this file and project it onto a screen. This can be done digitally, or you can print it out and project it using a document camera like an ELMO.
  - Choose a background for your Arioso Land (this file comes with 15 backgrounds).
  - Choose four students to sing an Arioso for today using the background of cupcakes.
  - Have them make up a song about cupcakes and sing it to the class.
- **Arioso Land PowerPoint** (found on website: www.oup.com/us/utema): If you are using a PC or Mac with PowerPoint installed on it, you can use this file for your Arioso Land. Follow the preceding directions.
- **Arioso Land Notebook** (found on website: www.oup.com/us/utema): If you are using a SMART Board with the Notebook software installed on it, you can use this file for your Arioso Land. Follow the preceding directions.
- **Arioso Land Link** (The Google Slides Version; found on website: www.oup.com/us/utema): (https://docs.google.com/presentation/d/1_Yz3IDaV1N6S8a6BnZGhY4CGg1ypl6Fo0BCidA9O61k/copy) is the same as the other version and allows you to access the file through a web browser. Therefore, if you are on another teacher's device, you just need to open the web browser, input the link, and Arioso Lands will appear using Google Slides.
  - The link will ask you to copy the file. This is so that you can edit it. If you want the original file, you just use the link noted in the preceding bullet and it will bring you back to the original file. The links can be found at www.oup.com/us/utema.

Higher Order Thinking Questions to Ask the Students:

- Did your Arioso turn out the way you thought?
- Did you Arioso change as you were singing? Why?

Extensions: This lesson can be extended by sharing the movies or ebooks created with the student's parents or caregivers.

Using the iOS GarageBand App to Assist with Creating an Arioso

Curriculum Note: This idea comes from Dr. Feierabend's Live Facebook Interview with Dr. Missy Strong in 2018.

Objective: Encouraged by the teacher, the student will spontaneously create an original tune with more than two pitches while the teacher gives a background accompaniment in the key of F or G and records the Arioso.

Grade Levels: PreK–2

Materials: GarageBand's Virtual Acoustic Guitar (iOS only- https://itunes.apple.com/us/app/garageband/id408709785?mt=8). You will also need *First Steps in Music for Preschool and Beyond* (GIA Publications, 2006) by Dr. John Feierabend.

Standards: Creating: MU:Cr2.1.PreKa, MU:Cr1.1.Kb, MU:Cr1.1b, MU:Cr1.1.2b
Performing: MU:Pr4.1.PreKa, MU:Pr4.1.Ka, MU:Pr4.1.1a, MU:Pr4.1.2a,
Responding: MU:Re8.1.PreKa, MU:Re8.1.Ka, MU:Re8.1.1a, MU:Re8.1.2a
Connecting: MU:Cn10.0.PreKa, MU:Cn10.0.Ka, MU:Cn10.0.1a, MU:Cn10.0.2a

Essential Question:

- How can we tell a musical story through Arioso?

Procedures:

- Arioso is step four of the eight-part musical workout. Before this step, the students would have warmed up their voices with pitch explorations and have performed echo and simple songs to develop independent singing.
- Launch the GarageBand app on your iOS Device. Since one child at a time will be singing the Arioso, you do not need to plug it into speakers.
- Click the + and scroll to find the guitar virtual instrument.
- Turn the "Autoplay" dial to 1, 2, 3, or 4.
- Click the F tab and it will play a loop of an acoustic guitar playing an arpeggio of an F chord.
- Have the students create Level 1 Ariosos, where they are creating tunes on neutral syllables. With GarageBand playing the looping F arpeggio on an acoustic virtual guitar, the student can create tunes staying within the key.
- **Tech tip**: Need to change the tempo? Click the wrench tool>click Tempo>change the tempo. It currently defaults to 110 beats per minute.
- **Tech tip**: Want the G tab? Click the wrench tool>Key Signature>G Major, then click out of the menu.
- **Tech tip**: Would you like to video record and assess them? The simplest way is to use a separate device's camera app and video the Arioso.
- **Assessment**: 4: Sings competently with numerous pitches; 3: Sings competently with three pitches: 2: Sings competently with two pitches; 1: Still emerging as a solo singer.

Higher Order Thinking Questions to Ask the Students:

- Did you like singing with the guitar? Why or why not?
- Did the guitar change the way you sing? If so, how?

Extensions: You can use GarageBand to audio record the students singing their Ariosos. To do this:

- Change the number of measures by clicking the + button located under the wrench tool. Click "8 bars" and then turn on "Automatic." This will give you unlimited measures.
- Turn the blue metronome off by clicking on it.
- Click the red record button, turn the dial to 1, 2, 3, or 4.

- After two minutes, click the stop button.
- Tap the track view button Add a new track by clicking the + at the bottom left-hand side of the screen.
- Scroll to the microphone (Audio Recorder) and click "Voice."
- You can click record and you will hear your two-minute guitar track. The students can sing and the audio track is recording them.
- When finished, click the stop button.
- You now have a recorded Arioso to assess later. See the preceding assessment.
- **Website example**: Visit the supplemental website at www.oup.com/us/utema to see how to perform this activity using the iOS GarageBand app.⏺

Students Creating Their Own Arioso Lands

Objective: Encouraged by the teacher, the student will spontaneously create an original tune and Arioso Land.

Grade Levels: PreK–2

Materials: This Arioso lesson can be done with the following tech devices: (1) one device in a classroom, which can be a laptop, mobile device, tablet, iOS Device, or Chromebook that has access to Google Slides (web-based), PowerPoint (PC or Mac), Notebook (for SMART Boards), or can display a pdf file; (2) 1:1 devices in the classrooms that could be laptops, Android devices, Kindles, iOS devices such as iPads, generic tablets with internet access, or Chromebooks. You will also need *First Steps in Music for Preschool and Beyond* (GIA Publications, 2006) by Dr. John Feierabend. In addition, the websites or apps listed in the procedures could also be used.

Standards: Creating: MU:Cr2.1.PreKa, MU:Cr1.1.Kb, MU:Cr1.1b, MU:Cr1.1.2b **Performing**: MU:Pr4.1.PreKa, MU:Pr4.1.Ka, MU:Pr4.1.1a, MU:Pr4.1.2a, **Responding**: MU:Re8.1.PreKa, MU:Re8.1.Ka, MU:Re8.1.1a, MU:Re8.1.2a **Connecting**: MU:Cn10.0.PreKa, MU:Cn10.0.Ka, MU:Cn10.0.1a, MU:Cn10.0.2a

Essential Question:

- How can we tell a musical story through Arioso?

Procedures:
   One Device in the Classroom:

- **Use https://byrdseed.com/emoji2/ to assist with creating Ariosos**

  - This website is an emoji creator. Tap the "and then" button four times (Figure 3.9).
  - Have the student look at the four emojis and have the student create an Arioso using those emojis.
  - Use your own mobile device or tablet's video recorder and record the students creating the story and Arioso.
  - **Assessment**: 4: Sings competently with numerous pitches; 3: Sings competently with three pitches; 2: Sings competently with two pitches; 1: Still emerging as a solo singer.
- **Using the free app Story Dice to assist with creating Ariosos**
  - Download the app for iOS (https://itunes.apple.com/us/app/story-dice-story-telling/id1105668334?mt=8) or Android/Google Play/Chromebook app (https://

Figure 3.9.
Link to Creating Ariosos with emoji prompts, found at http://byrdseed.com/emoji found at www.oup.com/us/utema.

play.google.com/store/apps/details?id=com.zuidsoft.storystones&hl=en_US&pageId=none).

- Launch the app. You can use the settings to select how many dice you would like to use (currently, you can have up to 10) and which backgrounds should appear on the dice (currently, they include General, Kids, Mystery, and Star Wars). I suggest one of each.
- You can also click on the settings further to change the background of the app and to turn the sounds on and off.
- Once you have the settings completed, click the button (or shake the iOS device) to roll the dice.
- Have the student look at the four die and sing an Arioso to match the pictures.
- Use a mobile device or tablet's video recorder to record the student's Arioso.
- **Alternative app: Rory's Story Cubes (https://www.storycubes.com/app)**
- **Using a book to create an Arioso**
  - Many teachers will use a book to assist with creating Ariosos. Some books that have been mentioned on the Feierabend Fundamentals Facebook group are *CHALK* by Bill Thomson, *Journey* by Aaron Becker, *Andy Warhol's Colors* by Susan Goldman, *La La La: A Story of Hope* by Kate DiCamillo, and *Yellow Umbrella* by Doug Il Sheen and Jae-Soo Liu.
  - Before class, using the iOS app Book Creator (the free version allows you to create one ebook) or the web-based Book Creator app (the free web-based version allows you to create 40 ebooks), launch the app.
  - With the app, tap the + button and using the camera button, take a screenshot of the cover of *La La La: A Story of Hope* by Kate DiCamillo.
  - On a blank page, tap the + button and using the camera button, take a picture of the first illustrated page of *La La La*.
  - Continue this until all of the pages have been taken. Depending on the class size, you can take a picture of two pages together so that this activity will not take too much time.
  - When the students enter, launch Book Creator on your device. If your device can project to the screen, it will be beneficial as the younger students can see the pages.
  - On the first page with "La," ask a student to create an Arioso using the word, "la" for that page. Press the + button and then the record button. Click "Start Recording" and it will give you three seconds. Record the student and click "Stop Recording" when finished. You can then accept or delete the recording. When you accept it, it will now appear on the screen.
    - **Activity tip**: In this particular book, the "La" varies across the book's pages. I make a reference of this to the students so that they can see and create their Ariosos a little differently for each "La."
    - The device's internal microphone will work for this activity.
  - Continue with each page until all students have had a turn.
    - **Activity tip**: If a student will not sing, encourage him if you feel that a little encouragement will help him sing. If you feel that it will not, move on and continue with the other students.

- **Activity tip**: If there are not enough pages, pair two students up or just have half the class sing a solo. Make another ebook during the next class to accommodate the other half of the class.
  - **Activity tip**: If there are too many pages, have the students perform the extra pages as a group.
- When finished (and with permission since this is a copyrighted book), you can publish the ebook online and share it with administration, parents, etc., or if you are using the iOS version, you can export it as a video, and share it through their student learning journals like Seesaw, ClassDojo, Flipgrid, or in their Google Classrooms, Google Drives, etc.

Multiple Devices in the Classroom or a 1:1 Classroom:

- **Using a book to create an Arioso (ideal for Grade 2 and above)**
  - You can do the preceding activity, but share the book to their devices and have them sing one page. In Book Creator, you can merge the books or combine the books together to make one book of Ariosos.
- **iMovie (iOS)—In a 1:1 classroom, do this with Grade 2 or higher**: On an iOS device, take a photo of a page in the book. Then launch the app, click +, click movie, click the photos you took of the book, and click create movie. To record singing, click the microphone on the left side of the screen, click record, click stop, and click accept. If the recording was longer than the picture, click on the picture and drag it to match the recording's length.
  - **Website example**: See www.oup.com/us/utema to see a video on how to do this.⊛
- **iMovie (MAC)—If 1:1 classroom, do this with Grade 2 or higher**: On a MAC, launch iMovie, click +, click movie, find the photo you took of the book, and drag it to the iMovie timeline. To record singing, click the microphone on the screen, click record, and click stop. If the recording was longer than the picture, click on the picture and drag it to match the recording's length.
  - **Website example**: See www.oup.com/us/utema to see a video on how to do this.⊛
- **Seesaw (web.seesaw.me)—This can be done with K–2**: Seesaw is a student-learning digital portfolio and engagement app that allows you to sign up for free and set up to 10 classes. You can have the parents connect to their child's journal and see only their child's work when their child posts something from the music classroom. You must approve the post before it can be seen. In Seesaw, you can set up an activity with the picture from the book and have them press the microphone to record themselves singing the Arioso.
  - **Website example**: See www.oup.com/us/utema to see a video on how to do this and see Appendix, "Links Listed Throughout the Book and Descriptions of Programs," for a more detailed description of the programs.⊛
  - **Similar apps**: ClassDojo (classdojo.com), Flipgrid (flipgrid.com), FreshGrade (freshgrade.com), ClassTag (classtag.com), and Bloomz (bloomz.net), to name a few.
- **WeVideo (https://www.wevideo.com)—If it is a 1:1 classroom, do this with Grade 2 or higher**: WeVideo is very similar to iMovie, but it is web-based and therefore can be used on most devices with internet access and a web browser. There is also an iOS version that has limited features. Currently, a free account on WeVideo allows you to create 5 minutes of video per month with 1GB of cloud storage. Login to WeVideo and click +

to begin a video project. Click media and you can take any media that is stored in your Google Drive or upload it from your hard drive. Once uploaded, drag the picture to the timeline. To add a recording, click the microphone button toward the top of the screen, then click the red microphone that appears, click stop when you are finished recording, and click the check to approve the recording.

- **Website example**: See www.oup.com/us/utema to see a video on how to do this.⊕
- Once completed, have the student save the recording and you now have the Arioso that has a picture with a recorded song. You could share this with the parent via email, Google Classroom, a student-learning digital portfolio, or on your music classroom website.

Higher Order Thinking Questions to Ask the Students:

- Did your Arioso turn out the way you thought?
- Did you Arioso change as you were singing? Why?

Extensions: This lesson can be extended by sharing the movies or ebooks created with the student's parents or caregivers (again, with permission if you are using a copyrighted book). In addition, older students can create a soundtrack by adding the movie to the MAC version of GarageBand.

Using Book Creator iOS App or a Web-Based Program to Create Comic ebook Ariosos

Curriculum Note: *My second graders adored making these Arioso comic ebooks because they connected to it. They love comic books. Even my shiest, emerging singers were able to shine with this lesson.*

Objective: To create an Arioso comic ebook.

Grade Levels: 1+

Materials: Book Creator iOS or web-based app (bookcreator.com). This can be done with one device connected to a screen and each student coming up to record a comic book page. However, I did this in small groups. Book Creator allows you to collaborate on the same book with separate devices if you have the paid version. If not, take a few devices, create the ebook with the free or paid versions by following the steps listed here, and have the students work on shared devices. You will also need *First Steps in Music for Preschool and Beyond* (GIA Publications, 2006) by Dr. John Feierabend.

Standards: MU:Cr2.1.PreKa, MU:Cr1.1.Kb, MU:Cr1.1b, MU:Cr1.1.2b **Performing**: MU:Pr4.1.PreKa, MU:Pr4.1.Ka, MU:Pr4.1.1a, MU:Pr4.1.2a, **Responding**: MU:Re8.1.PreKa, MU:Re8.1.Ka, MU:Re8.1.1a, MU:Re8.1.2a **Connecting**: MU:Cn10.0.PreKa, MU:Cn10.0.Ka, MU:Cn10.0.1a, MU:Cn10.0.2a

Essential Question:

- How can we tell a musical story through Arioso?
- How do the pictures influence the song?

Procedures:

- Book Creator (bookcreator.com) is an iOS app (currently $4.99) or a subscription web-based program (free and up) that allows your students to create and publish ebooks. This can be done with Grades 1 and up.

- *If you use the iOS app, your school would purchase it through Apple's Volume Purchase Plan to install on the students' iPads.*
- *If you use the web-based app, you can create one class with up to 40 ebooks for free. If you pay for the subscription, you can create more classes and more books, along with students collaborating on books.*
- With this lesson, I set up the book for them by utilizing images of comic-style musicians through a labeled for reuse Google image search of cartoon musicians that I downloaded.
- I launched Book Creator, clicked +, clicked New Book, scrolled down, and clicked on 1:1 comic. I clicked the + button to add panels, speech bubbles, thought bubbles, text, and stickers. I added the cartoon musician images and text for the directions.
- The students looked at the images, thought about the story, and clicked the + button and then media to add sound.
- Once finished, they had an Arioso comic ebook.
- Share their Arioso ebooks with each other.
- **Website example**: See www.oup.com/us/utema to learn how to do this and to hear an example.⊚
- **Activity tip**: I use a thinking map to help the students to create ideas about the topic. In this example, they are creating a comic Arioso book using musician comics and a thinking circle map to create their ideas.

Higher Order Thinking Questions to Ask the Students:

- How did the pictures influence your Arioso?
- If it had not been a comic ebook, do you think that you would have created a different type of Arioso?

Extensions: Book Creator, app or web-based, has the ability to share to their website or app-smash into other apps such as Seesaw, Google Classroom, etc. Share their Ariosos with their parents/caregivers or other classes that use First Steps. When sharing an ebook with sound, exporting it as a video is the most intuitive way. The second most intuitive is publishing it on their website and sharing the private link.

SongTales

Curriculum Note: *As Missy stated earlier in this book, SongTales is listed as the fifth portion of the musical workout, but also can be the final part of the musical workout. When SongTales are introduced, the teacher sings and the students simply listen. After the SongTale has been sung for two or three classes, then add the book. In this lesson, technology is integrated to assist the teacher.*

How to Project a SongTale for All to See

Objective: Ways to utilize SongTales in the classroom when your students cannot see the book.

Grade Levels: PreK–2

Materials: *First Steps in Music for Preschool and Beyond* (GIA Publications, 2006) by Dr. John Feierabend, a projector, a device with internet access, the SongTale books

54

found at www.giamusic.com (like *The Crabfish; The Frog and the Mouse; There Was a Man and He Was Mad; My Aunt Came Back; Father Grumble; The Derby Ram; Risseldy, Rosseldy; The Tailor and the Mouse; There's a Hole in the Bucket; The Other Day I Met a Bear; Jennie Jenkins; Over in the Meadow;* and *Momma, Buy Me a China Doll*), and the YouTube channel https://www.youtube.com/user/GIAPublications (the GIA publications YouTube channel) or the Kindle app (which can be installed on most mobile devices and laptops).

Standards: Responding: MU:Re8.1.PreKa, MU:Re8.1.Ka, MU:Re8.1.1a, MU:Re8.1.2a, **Connecting**: MU:Cn10.0.PreKa, MU:Cn10.0.Ka, MU:Cn10.0.1a, MU:Cn10.0.2a

Essential Understanding:

- Students will experience an expressive song performed for them by a caring adult.

Procedures:

- **Utilizing the Kindle app**
  - You can purchase a SongTale ebook via Amazon (https://www.amazon.com).
  - To project it onto the screen, you will need the free Kindle app on your device found at amazon.com (https://www.amazon.com/kindle-dbs/fd/kcp). Ask your IT to install it if you do not have permission to install it yourself.
  - Once purchased, you can open the Kindle app and find the book in your Kindle Library.
  - Open the book in the Kindle app and the book will project onto your screen.
  - Sing the SongTale to the children.
  - Remember that if you are using the app, hold off at least two lessons before showing the ebook. This helps students build their imagination.
  - Having the ebook projected onto the screen helps the students see the book, especially if you have a large class.
- **Projecting the SongTale book using a document camera**
  - There are various document cameras available at schools, such as an ELMO, that teachers can use to project books, or other items, onto a screen.
  - If you can find one, hook the document camera into the projector.
  - Place the book under the document camera and it will appear on screen.
- **Creating an ebook using a mobile device**
  - If you own the book for your classroom, you can take pictures of each page on your mobile device.
  - From your mobile phone's photo app, you can connect your mobile phone to your projector and display the book onto the screen.
  - These photos can only be used in the classroom in which the book was purchased to be used. The book cannot be shared or used in another classroom.

Higher Order Thinking Questions to Ask the Students:

- Did the images in the book match the images in your head about this SongTale?
- If so, how?
- If not, what were the images in your head when you first heard the book?

Extensions: Level up by creating an ebook or video with the pictures and audio of you singing to display during class (see next lesson).

How to Project and *Listen* to a SongTale for All to See

Objective: Ways to utilize the SongTales in the classroom when your students cannot see the book and you do not have the voice to sing it.

Grade Levels: PreK–2

Materials: *First Steps in Music for Preschool and Beyond* (GIA Publications, 2006) by Dr. John Feierabend, a projector, a device with internet access, the SongTale books found at www.giamusic.com (like *The Crabfish; The Frog and the Mouse; There Was a Man and He Was Mad; My Aunt Came Back; Father Grumble; The Derby Ram; Risseldy, Rosseldy; The Tailor and the Mouse; There's a Hole in the Bucket; The Other Day I Met a Bear; Jennie Jenkins; Over in the Meadow;* and *Momma, Buy Me a China Doll*), and the YouTube channel https://www.youtube.com/user/GIAPublications (the GIA publications YouTube channel) or the Kindle app (which can be installed on most mobile devices and laptops).

Standards: Responding: MU:Re8.1.PreKa, MU:Re8.1.Ka, MU:Re8.1.1a, MU:Re8.1.2a, **Connecting:** MU:Cn10.0.PreKa, MU:Cn10.0.Ka, MU:Cn10.0.1a, MU:Cn10.0.2a

Essential Understanding:

- Students will experience an expressive song performed for them by a caring adult.

Procedures:

- **What if you have no voice? Is there a way to prepare a SongTale in advance, so when you have a day with no voice, you have a pre-recorded SongTale ready to go with your voice?**
  - **Creating an ebook using Book Creator (bookcreator.com)**
    - Book Creator (bookcreator.com) is an iOS app ($4.99) or a subscription web-based program (free and up) that allows your students to create and publish ebooks.
    - If you use the iOS app, your school would purchase it through Apple's Volume Purchase Plan to install on the students' iPads.
    - If you use the web-based app, you can create one class with up to 40 ebooks for free. If you pay for the subscription, you can create more classes and more books, along with students collaborating on books.
    - Launch Book Creator, click +, click New Book, and click on square.
    - Click the + button at the top (media tools) and scroll down to camera.
    - Take a picture of the cover.
    - Click the + button on the side to add a page.
    - Click the + button at the top and scroll down to camera.
    - Take a picture of the first page.
    - Continue to do this for the remainder of the book.
    - Once finished, go back to the first page and click the + button at the top.
    - Scroll down to audio or the mic icon to record yourself singing the words on the page.
    - Continue to do this for the remaining pages so that each page has a separate recording.
    - When finished, you have an ebook with a recording of you singing the song that you can project onto the screen from the app on the device where you created it. Since there is a recording per page, it will not have the same fluency as if you were singing the song as a solo.

- If you need to export it, in the iOS app, export it as a video and then share it to wherever you would need to access it, i.e., store it in your Google Drive for later. In the web-based app, publish it online and use the private link to access it from any device that has internet access.
  - **Tech tip**: Book Creator gives you the option to add a soundtrack to the entire book when in the iOS app. You can record yourself singing the song, place it in your iOS Music App (formerly iTunes) app, and add it as a soundtrack in Book Creator. It will only play in books that are exported as an epub into iBooks.
- **YouTube**:
  - Go to https://www.youtube.com/user/GIAPublications.
  - Find items by Dr. John Feierabend. They are sometimes listed under a header or listed as a playlist.
  - In this list, you can find some SongTales, such as *The Crabfish*. It is a sample of the book with Jill Trinka singing the song.
- **Creating your own video of a SongTale:**
  - Simply use a screen recording tool like Screencastify (www.screencastify.com) or Loom (www.loom.com) to record yourself singing the kindle version of the SongTale.
  - Using the hard copy of the book or the ebook that you have purchased, take pictures or screenshots of each page of the book. These pictures of screenshots are only to be used in the classroom that you purchased the book for and only for educational purposes. They are not to be shared outside your classroom.
  - Place each picture in a media app like iMovie for Mac or iOS device (https://www.apple.com/imovie/) or WeVideo (https://www.wevideo.com/), a cloud-based online video editor. If you are using iMovie, place the pictures on the hard drive or Photos. If you are using WeVideo, place the pictures in your Google Drive (https://www.google.com/drive/).
- **iMovie**: On a MAC, launch iMovie, click +, click movie, find the photos you took of the book, and drag it to the iMovie timeline. To record singing, click the microphone on the screen, click record, and click stop. If the recording was longer than the picture, click on the picture and drag it to match the recording's length. Once finished, save to the computer's hard drive and play on days when you have no voice.
  - **Website example**: See www.oup.com/us/utema to see a video on how to do this.⊛
- **WeVideo**: Currently, a free account on WeVideo allows you to create 5 minutes of video per month with 1GB of cloud storage. Login to WeVideo and click + to begin a video project. Click media and you can take any media that is stored in your Google Drive or upload it from your hard drive. Once uploaded, drag the picture to the timeline. To add a recording, click the microphone button toward the top of the screen, then click the red microphone that appears, click stop when you are finished recording, and click the check to approve the recording. Once finished, export the video to play on days when you have no voice to sing.
- **Website example**: See www.oup.com/us/utema to see a video on how to do this.⊛

Higher Order Thinking Questions to Ask the Students:

- Did the images in the book match the images in your head about this SongTale?
- If so, how?
- If not, what were the images in your head when you first heard the book?

Extensions: Using the recording you made of your voice with the pictures of the book, create another audio track (in iMovie, just press the record button again to create a second audio track and WeVideo, tap the + button and add an additional audio track), and have the students use classroom percussion instruments to enhance the SongTale. For example, in the SongTale *Momma Buy Me a China Doll*, the students could add bells pitched in an F pentatonic scale (F G A C and D) every time the teacher sings the word "sleep."

Movement Exploration (Movement Warm-ups)

Displaying Movement Shapes on the Screen for Students to See

Curriculum Note: *As shown in Dr. Feierabend's* First Steps in Music for Preschool and Beyond *(GIA Publications, 2006) the movement exploration portion of the eight-step workout is for movement warm-ups. They include movement themes of Rudolf von Laban adapted by Dr. Feierabend. Technology is used to enhance the movement exploration portfolios and presentations.*

Objective: The students will become aware of movement shapes and how to create these shapes individually and with partners and groups.

Grade Levels: PreK–2

Materials: *First Steps in Music for Preschool and Beyond* (GIA Publications, 2006) by Dr. John Feierabend, a projector, a device with internet access, your choice of music for students to move to (suggested: *First Steps in Classical Music: Keeping the Beat* CD by Dr. Feierabend, GIA Publications, 2000), and the projectable downloadable movement cards found at the corresponding website to this book, www.oup.com/us/utema. These movement cards are basic stick figures for students to freeze in various shapes when you pause the music. They are found in the following formats: PowerPoint (for any device with this app or software), Keynote (for MAC or iOS with this software or app), Google Slides (for any device with internet access), Notebook (for SMART Boards), and pdf (to print out or project with a document camera like an ELMO.

Standards: **Creating**: MU:Cr1.1.PKa, MU:Cr1.1.Ka, MU:Cr1.1.Kb, **Performing**: MU:Pr4.2.PKa, MU:Pr4.2.Ka, MU:Pr4.2.1a, MU:Pr4.2.2a, **Connecting**: MU:Cn10.0.PKa, MU:Cn10.0.Ka, MU:Cn10.0.1a, MU:Cn10.0.2a

Essential Understanding:

- The movement warm-ups will assist the students in broadening their movement possibilities, especially focusing on the awareness of shapes, the awareness of levels, and the awareness of others.

Procedures:

- Project the Movement Exploration file onto a screen.
  - **Laptop/Desktop:** If the laptop/desktop connected to the projector has PowerPoint, keynote (MAC only), Notebook software (for SMART Boards), or an internet connection, then you can choose which format of the file to project.
    - **Website example**: The file is found at www.oup.com/us/utema◉
  - **Activity tip**: If you travel to the classroom and have to use a teacher's device that has an internet connection, then use the Google Slides link, as then you will not have to worry if the teacher's device has any software applications needed for PowerPoint, Keynote, or Notebook.

- **Document camera**: Print out the pdf version of Movement Explorations and place them under the document camera to project onto the screen. The document camera must be hooked up to the projector in order to do this.
- **iOS device**: If the iOS device has the PowerPoint app, the Keynote app, or the Google Slides app, you can use those formats for this lesson. If not, and the iOS device has internet access, then use the Google Slides link.
- **Chromebook**: If you are using a Chromebook, use the Google Slides link.
- **Android or Kindle**: The simplest solution is the Google Slides link, unless you have the PowerPoint, Keynote, or Google Slides app.
- Most devices listed in the preceding should also be able to project the pdf file.
- **Why project the cards when I can just print them and hold them up?** You can always choose this option. However, the students can have a challenging time seeing the cards that you are holding up in the air. When they are projected, the students have an easier time seeing the card and creating the movement shape.
- Choose a piece of music for this movement warm-up. Suggested: *First Steps in Classical Music: Keeping the Beat* CD by Dr. Feierabend (GIA Publications, 2000).
  - If your school district will accommodate the cost, I suggest having a subscription to Spotify, Google Play, or Apple Music so you have access to music when you have an internet access.
- Have the students spread out in the room (if they cannot spread out because they are seated at desks, then feel free to adapt the movements).
- Tell the students that when the music pauses, they must create the movement shape that is displayed on screen. Remind the students that when the music pauses and they are performing the movement shape, they can always breathe, blink, and swallow.
- Begin playing the music and have the students move independently to the music.
- Pause the music with one of the shapes projected onto the screen. The students are to pause and create the shape with their bodies.
- Ask the students if their movement shape is high, middle, or low (to reinforce the awareness of levels)?
- Resume playing the music and showcase another shape onto the screen.
- Pause the music again and have the students create the shape that is projected onto the screen.
- Continue until you present all 22 shapes. Feel free to arrange them in a different order than presented. Encourage groupings by showing the slides that have 2+ stick figures in them.
- For the final shape, have the students create their own shape with their bodies and walk around the room to compliment the students on their shapes and statues.

Higher Order Thinking Questions to Ask the Students:

- What movement shape did you create?
- What level is your movement shape (high, middle, or low)?

Extensions: Guide the students to use stick figure drawings to create their own shapes. Take pictures of the drawings and add them to a PowerPoint, Google Slides, Keynote, or Notebook file, or project them directly from your device to the projector by using Airplay, Reflector App, Apple TV (MAC/iOS), Miracast (PC/Android), Chromecast, etc., (for wireless results), or attaching the adapter from the device to the projector (for hard-wire results). Play another piece of music and have the students become these new shapes when the music pauses.

Saving Your Voice or Freeing You Up to Assist Students during a Movement Exploration

Curriculum Note: *Sometimes, you will have classes that need you to narrate and demonstrate the movement exploration while the music is being played. In addition, there are times when you need to do this as you position yourself near children who need more assistance. This can be overwhelming at times. Here is a way to simplify this.*

Objective: The teacher will create a vocal track to direct the movement explorations so that the teacher can be moving around the room to assist students who need more guidance to perform the movements.

Grade Levels: PreK–2

Materials: For this lesson, you can use recorded music of your choice for the movement exploration. In addition, you will create a vocal track to use with the recorded music using Audacity (https://www.audacityteam.org/) or Soundtrap (https://www.soundtrap.com).

Standards: **Creating**: MU:Cr1.1.PKa, MU:Cr1.1.Ka, MU:Cr1.1.Kb, **Performing**: MU:Pr4.2.PKa, MU:Pr4.2.Ka, MU:Pr4.2.1a, MU:Pr4.2.2a, **Connecting**: MU:Cn10.0.PKa, MU:Cn10.0.Ka, MU:Cn10.0.1a, MU:Cn10.0.2a

Essential Understanding:

• The movement warm-ups will assist the students in broadening their movement possibilities, especially focusing on the awareness of shapes, the awareness of levels, and the awareness of others.

Procedures:

• Before class, launch either Audacity or Soundtrap to create a vocal track over the music you selected for the movement exploration. For this example, let's use Pachelbel's Canon in D.

• **Audacity** (https://www.audacityteam.org/)

  • Developed by Dominic Mazzoni and Roger Dannenberg at Carnegie Mellon University in 1999, Audacity is a free digital audio editor and recording application software, available for Windows, MacOS/OS X, and Unix-like operating systems. You will need to download it onto your computer. It is not currently a cloud-based software, so it cannot be used on a mobile device, tablet, or Chromebook.

  • Once downloaded, launch Audacity.

  • Find the music file on your computer and drag it to Audacity's project window.

    • **Tech tip**: Audacity can import a number of music file formats. WAV, AIFF, and MP3 are most common, but it can also import MP4/M4A files, as long as they are not rights-managed or copy-protected (like some songs purchased through stores such as Apple Music).

    • **Tech tip**: Go into your Apple Music and click and drag the song from Apple Music to Audacity's project window. If the song is not copyright protected, this will work. The best way to know this is to click and drag it to the project window.

- Go to the "Tracks" menu at the top of the screen and scroll down to Add New>Stereo Track. There is now an empty track under the track that includes your music file.
- **To record your voice-over vocal track**:
  - Click on the new empty track.
  - Make sure that the play head is at the beginning of the track.
  - **Microphone**: You can plug in a USB microphone, like one of the Blue microphones found at https://www.bluedesigns.com, or use the computer's internal built-in microphone. I would also suggest a pop screen over the microphone to avoid the popping of "p."
  - **Headphones**: I would suggest wearing headphones that you plug into the headphone jack of the computer when you record your voice-over. It is not required. However, if you record without headphones, then the music file playing in the background of your vocal track will clutter it up and sound messy.
  - **Record**: Once you have your microphone and headphones ready, press the red record button and speak the voice-over you want to include for the movements for Canon in D.
  - Once finished, click the stop button and listen to the recording.
- If you want to delete the recording of the voice-over, highlight the voice-over track and click delete.
- If you like the voice-over track, but would like to record an additional track to see if you can get the recording better, then do the following:
  - Mute the current voice track by selecting the "Mute" button.
  - Add another track by going to the "Tracks" menu at the top of the screen and scroll down to Add New>Stereo Track.
  - Click record to create this additional voice-over track.
  - **Export the track**:
    - When you are happy with the voice-over track and the music track, it is now time to export them mixed together as one track.
    - Go to the "File" menu and scroll down to Export>WAV or AIFF. WAV is a higher quality audio file saved on a PC and AIFF is a higher quality audio file saved on a MAC.
    - Name the file and choose a place to save it on your computer.
    - Click the save button and you now have a music file with a voice-over to use in class.
    - Once finished, you can save the Audacity project if you need to come back and alter the project later on.
    - **Tech tip**: Currently, Audacity will not export directly as an MP3. You would need an outside program to do that. Therefore, I export as a WAV or AIFF. They are higher quality and better sounding files than MP3s. However, if your heart is set on an MP3, you can use Music (formerly iTunes) to convert it by dragging the file into Music, going to the "File" menu and scrolling down to Convert>Create MP3 Version.
- **Soundtrap** (https://www.soundtrap.com)
  - Soundtrap is a cloud-based digital audio workstation (DAW) accessed in any web browser or through a mobile app (Chrome, iOS, and Android). It has digital recording

options, it includes prerecorded loops, multitrack recording, software instruments, voice recording, audio editing, changing of tempos and keys of the track, the ability to connect MIDI devices, and more.

- **Tech tip**: For the purposes of a teacher creating a voice-over to use in the classroom, the free version will work well. If you have the students use Soundtrap, then I highly recommend purchasing the educational (EDU) version.
- Create a free account and launch Soundtrap.
- Click "Enter studio" and then click a blank template.
- To add the Canon in D track, find the file on your computer and drag it onto the project screen. You can also click "Add New Track" and then, "Import file." The file is now on the screen.
- Click "Add New Track" and click on the microphone icon. This track is where you will record your voice-over.
- **To record your voice-over vocal track**:
  - Click on the new empty track.
  - Make sure that the play head is at the beginning of the track.
  - **Microphone**: You can plug in a USB microphone, like one of the Blue microphones found at https://www.bluedesigns.com, or use the computer's internal built-in microphone. It is beneficial to add a pop screen over the microphone to avoid the popping "p" sound.
  - **Headphones**: I would suggest wearing headphones that you plug into the headphone jack of the computer when you record your voice-over. It is not required. However, if you record without headphones, then the music file playing in the background of your vocal track will clutter it up and sound messy.
  - **Record**: Once you have your microphone and headphones ready, press the red record button or the "Start Recording" button and speak the voice-over you want to include for the movements for Canon in D.
  - Once finished, click the stop button and listen to the recording.
- If you want to delete the recording of the voice-over, highlight the voice-over track and click delete.
- If you like the voice-over track but would like to record an additional track to see if you can get the recording better, then do the following:
  - Mute the current voice track by selecting the mute icon.
  - Add another track by clicking "Add New Track" and clicking the microphone icon.
  - Click record to create this additional voice-over track.
- Once finished, title the track at the top of the screen and click the "Save" button. This will begin the process of mixing the file together.
- Click "Exit Studio," which will bring you back to the main project screen.
- **To share or export the file**:
  - Click on the project to see the sharing options. If the file is still mixing, it will take a few minutes before all sharing options are available.
  - To download, click the download button and you will have an MP3 version on your hard drive.
  - You can also share the file via social media like YouTube, SoundCloud, Twitter, etc., or create a temporary link.

Higher Order Thinking Questions to Ask the Students:
With you now free to guide the students who need assistance with the movements, you can also direct them with higher order thinking questions.

- What levels are our movements?
- Is there a pattern to our movements? If so, what movement will come next?

Extensions: On a day when your voice needs rest, but you could not take a sick day, these voice-over tracks work very well. Consider using these programs to create more voice-over tracks or vocal tracks to songs you use daily in your classroom. In addition, these voice-over and vocal tracks help greatly on days you are out and there is a non-music substitute teacher in your classroom.

Creating a Movement Exploration ebook

Curriculum Note: *This is a great activity to do before a school break.*
Objective: The students will create a movement exploration ebook to use during future music classes for step six of the eight-step workout.
Grade Levels: PreK–2
Materials: *First Steps in Music for Preschool and Beyond* (GIA Publications, 2006), and/or *The Book of Movement Exploration* (GIA Publications, 2003) both by Dr. John Feierabend, a projector, a device with internet access, your choice of music for students to move to (suggested: *First Steps in Classical Music: Keeping the Beat* CD by Dr. Feierabend, GIA Publications, 2000), and the Book Creator app for iOS and web-based found at bookcreator.com. This can be done with one device connected to a projector with an adapter (for hard-wire results) or through Airplay, Reflector App, Apple TV (MAC/iOS), Miracast (PC/Android), Chromecast, etc., (for wireless results), or in a classroom with a few devices or a 1:1 classroom.
Standards: Creating: MU:Cr1.1.PKa,   MU:Cr1.1.Ka,   MU:Cr1.1.Kb,
Connecting: MU:Cn10.0.PKa, MU:Cn10.0.Ka, MU:Cn10.0.1a, MU:Cn10.0.2a
Essential Question:

- How do musicians generate creative ideas?

Procedures:
One Device in the Classroom Projected onto the Screen:

- Review movement explorations from *First Steps in Music for Preschool and Beyond* (GIA Publications, 2006), and/or *The Book of Movement Exploration* (GIA Publications, 2003) by Dr. Feierabend.
  - These could include the shapes file from the preceding lesson, the bubbles movement exploration, the room of Jell-O, the star dance, and more.
- Ask the students to create pictures of these movement explorations using paper and crayons, markers, pencils, etc.
- Once finished, launch Book Creator (the iOS app or the web-based app found at bookcreator.com).
  - Book Creator (bookcreator.com) is an iOS app (currently $4.99) or a subscription web-based program (free and up) that allows your students to create and publish ebooks. This can be done with Grades 1 and up.

- If you use the iOS app, your school would purchase it through Apple's Volume Purchase Plan to install on the students' iPads.
- If you use the web-based app, you can create one class with up to 40 ebooks for free. If you pay for the subscription, you can create more classes and more books, along with students collaborating on books.
- Create a new book. You can choose portrait, square, or landscape depending on the device that will view it. Default to square if you are not sure what to choose.
- The cover is the first square that appears; your students can create that during another class, or you can create one after class.
- Click the side + button
- You are now on page 2. Click the top + button (media), and scroll down to the camera.
- Take a picture of the students' pictures.
- Click "Use Photo" to use the photo or "Retake" to retake the photo.
- Do these steps again until the ebook includes all pictures with one picture on each page.
- **Now it is time to record. Record the student telling you about his or her picture and the movement exploration. Use the Higher Order Thinking Questions that follow to guide the students.**
    i. Go to page 2.
    ii. Click the + button at the top (media) and scroll down to the microphone.
    iii. Click the red record button and have the student explain his or her picture and the movement exploration. Accept the recording and go to page 3, unless you need to redo the recording.
    iv. Repeat the steps again until all students have explained their pictures. You will have separate recordings for each page. If a student is too shy to speak, encourage another student to assist or have yourself speak on behalf of the student.
- **Add text to the page**.
    i. Go to page 2.
    ii. Click the + button and scroll down to the text tool.
    iii. Add the title of the movement exploration to the page (for example, "Bubbles").
    iv. You could also use the drawing tool to have the students write the title onto the page.
- **Share the ebook (optional)**.
- Once you or your students have created the cover, your ebook is complete.
- To share the ebook in the iOS version, click the share icon under the book and you will see the following choices: epub (for reading in a ebook app), pdf (for printing), video (for posting to web), and online (for posting on book creator's website). The easiest is video, as most devices can play it and the audio files will be included.
- In the web-based version, click the share icon and publish online. This will create a private link that you can now share.
- Share the book as a video or the private link and you can now post it to students' digital learning portfolios, post it on a music classroom website, post it on the

school's website, or email it to parents. From there, students can tell their parents about the ebook and how they made it, or the music classrooms can share their ebooks with each other. To find a music classroom to connect with, search through the Feierabend Fundamentals Facebook group or at one of their get-togethers to find other music educators to discuss the possibility.

1:1 Devices: This is similar to the procedure in the preceding. The biggest difference is that when the students create their ebook, it would just have a cover and their picture. You can either share numerous small ebooks or combine them into one large ebook, as long as they are all the same shape (i.e., they are all square or portrait or landscape).

Website example: To see an example of an end product using Book Creator, please visit the website that corresponds with this book at www.oup.com/us/utema.⊛

Higher Order Thinking Questions to Ask the Students:

- What movement exploration did you draw?
- Why did you choose that movement exploration?
- Why do you think we perform this movement exploration?

Extensions: In future classes, choose a student to open the ebook and pick a movement exploration for the class to perform. Encourage the student to choose one that he or she did not draw for the ebook. As they perform more movement explorations throughout the school year, have them add to the ebook by drawing a picture in the ebook (or traditionally) and recording themselves explaining the movement exploration.

Movement for Form and Expression

Curriculum Note: *This is step seven in the eight-part musical workout. This part focuses on singing, speaking, and moving with formal structure and expression. The four lessons that follow either enhance or extend the activities with technological tools and manipulatives.*

My Hat It Has Three Corners

Curriculum Note: *Continuing with step seven in the eight-part musical workout, this part focuses on singing, speaking, and moving with formal structure and expression. This lesson provides a digital manipulative to use after the song "My Hat It Has Three Corners" has been introduced and performed for a few classes. It adds another step to learning the song with the actions.*

Objective: To perform the song "My Hat It Has Three Corners," to emphasize the motions in the song.

Grade Levels: PreK–2 (since the digital file has words, the first and second graders could incorporate the file as a cross-curricular lesson in reading)

Materials: The song "My Hat It Has Three Corners" from *First Steps in Music for Preschool and Beyond* (GIA Publications, 2006) by Dr. John Feierabend, a projector, a device with internet access or PowerPoint (PC or MAC), keynote (MAC or iOS app), or Notebook software (SMART Board), the "My Hat It Has Three Corners" file found at the corresponding website: www.oup.com/us/utema.

Standards: Performing: MU:Pr4.2.PKa, MU:Pr4.2.Ka, MU:Pr4.2.1a, MU:Pr4.2.2a, MU:Pr6.1.PKa, MU:Pr6.1.Ka, MU:Pr6.1.1a, MU:Pr6.1.2a, **Connecting**: MU:Cn11.0.PKa, MU:Cn11.0.Ka, MU:Cn11.0.1a, MU:Cn11.0.2a

Essential Question:

- How does connecting music to other subjects affect responding to the music?

Procedures:

- Review the chant, "My Hat It Has Three Corners" from *First Steps in Music for Preschool and Beyond* (GIA Publications, 2006) by Dr. John Feierabend.
- Launch the file "My Hat It Has Three Corners" found at www.oup.com/us/utema.
  - If you are using a device with internet access, you can use the Google Slides link, https://docs.google.com/presentation/d/1aOvaePc-yhudoTpg091vqw VA6KNuFGpAcG5IQ4C8MJY/copy to access this file. This is ideal for music educators who travel on a cart or must use another teacher's device when in their classroom. You must have a Google Drive account, which can be set up for free, to use the file.
  - The link will ask you to copy the file. This is so that you can edit it. If you want the original file, you just use the preceding link and it will bring you back to the original file. The links can be found at www.oup.com/us/utema
  - If you have a device with PowerPoint, Keynote, or Notebook, download the file and launch it on your device.
  - **Tech tip**: If you use Keynote, the link, or PowerPoint, do not put it in "present" mode so that the student leader can move the pictures into the correct place.
- The first slide is a title slide. Click the arrow to go to the next slide.
- On the second slide, the hat, the elbow, the number three, and the smiling face, all can move.
  - Perform the song with the movements found in the book:
  - **Corners**—point to elbow
  - **Three**—hold up three fingers
  - **Hat**—point to head
  - **My**—point to self
  - Assign a student leader or ask the students to assist you with placing the pictures in the correct order of the song (Figure 3.10).
  - If you have a SMART Board, the teacher or the student leader can move the pictures by touching the board.
  - If you are using the PowerPoint, Keynote, or the link, do not place the file in "present" mode so that you or the student leader can move around the pictures in place.
- Perform the song with the pictures in order. For students in Grades 1 and 2, reinforce words by writing the words over the pictures (using the text tool or a SMART Board pen).
- When finished, place the pictures back to the side of the screen or close the file without saving it so the pictures go back to the side of the screen.
- **Tech tip**: The pictures are infinite cloned (in Notebook) or layered on top of each other (in PowerPoint, Keynote, or Google Slides) so that when the teacher or student moves the picture into the song lyrics, there are still pictures left over.

Figure 3.10.
Example of "My Hat it Has Three Corners."

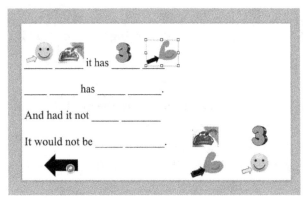

Higher Order Thinking Questions to Ask the Students:

- How do the pictures relate to the song?
- What would happen if we changed around the pictures?

Extensions:

- Sing the song again, and take the hat picture out of the lyrics and move it to the side. Have the children sing without the word "hat," and just perform the movement. Continue to do this for all of the pictures.
- Move around the pictures to create a different version of the song to sing and use the motions.

Action Song and Fingerplays Assessment

Curriculum Note: *This lesson can be done as an extension to step seven of the eight-step musical workout. This can also be used as an assessment tool. Finally, this is a fun activity to perform before a break or on a day where the students are easily distracted due to a class party or the weather.*

Objective: To assess a fingerplay or action song.

Grade Levels: PreK–2

Materials: Any action song or fingerplay from *First Steps in Music for Preschool and Beyond* (GIA Publications, 2006), *The Book of Fingerplays and Action Songs* (GIA Publications, 2003), *The Book of Beginning Circle Games* (GIA Publications, 2004), or a move it activity from the *Move It!* DVDs (GIA Publications, 2003 and 2008), all by Dr. John Feierabend; a device that can be used to take video.

Standards: Performing: MU:Pr6.1.PKa, MU:Pr6.1.Ka, MU:Pr6.1.1a, MU:Pr6.1.2a

Essential Question:

- How is music performed?

Procedures:

- Review an action song, fingerplay, or circle game. For this example, we will use the song, "Eensy Weensy Spider."
- **One Device in the Classroom:**
  - Explain to the students that they will be teaching the action song for others to learn.

- Use a thinking map to help the students plan how they would teach the song. Guide them to include singing the song, showing the actions for each phrase, and performing the entire action song.
- Divide the class into those three groups and have them practice their portion. For the youngest students, plan most of this out with them and have them perform the three portions as one large group. For older elementary, they will most likely be able to rehearse their own portion.
- Take out the device and video their portion to create this tutorial video.
  - Use your own mobile device to video and share via music classroom website, school website, or other venues. Utilize a video editing app to edit the video. These can include iMovie (https://www.apple.com/imovie/, MAC and iOS), WeVideo (www.wevideo.com, web-based), or 123Apps (https://123apps.com/).
  - Use the web-based Seesaw Student Digital Learning Portfolio and Engagement Platform (web.seesaw.me), or a similar app like ClassDojo (classdojo.com), Flipgrid (flipgrid.com), FreshGrade (freshgrade.com), ClassTag (classtag.com), or Bloomz (bloomz.net), to video within the app and to place on the students' digital portfolios/grids for their parents to view. See Appendix, "Links Listed Throughout the Book and Descriptions of Programs," to learn more about these programs.
    - **Tech tip**: Look at the lessons earlier in this chapter or the accompanying website to learn how to use Seesaw and Flipgrid.
- **1:1 Classroom**:
  - Explain to the students that they will be teaching the action song for others to learn.
  - Use a thinking map to help the students plan how they would teach the song. Guide them to include singing the song, showing the actions for each phrase, and performing the entire action song.
  - For older elementary students, have them use a video app to video themselves teaching how to perform the action song "Eensy Weensy Spider" When they create their own tutorial, I explain to them that they are creating a "mock YouTube" video for their "mock YouTube channel."
  - **Chromebooks/web-based devices/laptops/desktops**: The students can use the web-based Seesaw Student Digital Learning Portfolio and Engagement Platform (web.seesaw.me), or a similar app like ClassDojo (classdojo.com), ClassTag (classtag.com), FreshGrade (freshgrade.com), Bloomz (bloomz.net), or Flipgrid (flipgrid.com) to video within the app and to place on the students' digital portfolios/grids for their parents to view. They could also use WeVideo (wevideo.com) or 123Apps's online video recorder that will save to their Google Drives (https://webcamera.io/).
  - **iOS Devices**: Students can also use Seesaw, ClassDojo, FreshGrade, ClassTag, Bloomz, or Flipgrid, as well as iMovie and the camera app.
  - **Troubleshooting technology**: One of the challenging parts about recording in a classroom is the outside noise that gets caught in the video (in addition, when you realize that you have been speaking loudly in a student's video). Some ways to troubleshoot this are to turn a large cardboard box into a recording box where students place their device and upper bodies into to record; if you can trust the

students, to have them quietly record in the hallway; if you can trust the students, to have them quietly record in the classroom's closet; use a Flipgrid portable voice pod (perform a Google search to find where they are sold); or have them sit in a circle when they are ready to record and have each group or student take turns recording.

- **Assessment**:
  - The assessment tool used should be one that works well in your school's grading system and with your students.
  - If they are working in the group setting, you can assess a few individuals on singing and teaching the actions from each group during the class.
  - In a 1:1 setting, you can assess each student by watching the video that they created after class instead of during class.
  - Here is a tool that I use for Grades 2 and above:
    - **Singing**:
      - 4: Sings all notes accurately and started on the correct pitch without a reference to that pitch. This is a consistently competent singer.
      - 3: Sings all notes accurately with a reference to the starting pitch. This is a competent singer.
      - 2: Sings most notes accurately but started on a lower pitch even after begin given the correct pitch to start. This is a developing singer.
      - 1: Spoke the song or would not sing. This is an emerging singer.
    - **Teaching the motions for the song**:
      - 4: The student teaches the motions for the song accurately and with no assistance from the teacher. The student excels.
      - 3: The student teaches the motions for the song accurately and with little assistance from the teacher. The student meets grade level.
      - 2: The student teaches the motions for the song accurately and with much assistance from the teacher. The student is developing.
      - 1: The student cannot teach the motions for the song, but has the capability to do so. The student is emerging.

Higher Order Thinking Questions to Ask the Students:

- What do you think are important skills to have when teaching a song to others?
- What was the most challenging part of making the video?
- What was the best part about making the video?

Extensions:

- Ask the students to go home and teach the song to their caregiver or parent to see if they can successfully learn and perform the song.
- Share the video with the caregivers or parents (either through their digital portfolios or a music classroom website or via email, if you are allowed when there are numerous students shown in one video) and ask them if they learned how to sing and perform the action song.
- Create more video tutorials of action songs, fingerplays, and move it activities from the *Move It!* performances. By the end of the school year, you will have a student-created video library that you could use with future music classes.

Creating a "Groovy" Song Using MusicFirst Junior's Groovy Music

Curriculum Note: *MusicFirst Junior* (https://www.musicfirst.com/musicfirst-junior/) *is a comprehensive, thorough, and interactive online system for teaching elementary music. It includes web-based apps that can easily integrate into any elementary music classroom that has access from limited to full technology resources.*

Groovy Music (https://www.musicfirst.com/applications/groovy-music/) *is a paid app developed by Michael Avery that gives a young student the ability to create a song using building blocks that represent melodies, rhythms, and chords. It can only be found through MusicFirst. There are varying price points to Groovy Music because you can purchase one to multiple subscriptions depending on your use in the classroom. Groovy Music provides music creation for all young students in a very friendly and intuitive way.*

In this lesson, the students are creating a song to a musical form that they experienced during step seven of the eight-part musical workout. This lesson works well before a long break from school or when the students are distracted by a class party or weather.

Objective: To create a song with a musical form.

Grade Levels: PreK–2

Materials: Any movement ideas from *First Steps in Music for Preschool and Beyond* (GIA Publications, 2006), or *First Steps in Classical Music: Keeping the Beat* CD by Dr. Feierabend (GIA Publications, 2000), or a move it activity from the *Move It!* DVDs (GIA Publications, 2003 and 2008), all by Dr. John Feierabend, a device with internet access (can be an iPad or web-based), a subscription to Groovy Music (https://www.musicfirst.com/musicfirst-junior/) through MusicFirst Jr (https://www.musicfirst.com/musicfirst-junior/).

Standards: Creating Standards for PreK–2: Imagine, Plan & Make, and Refine (MU:Cr1, 2, and 3)

Essential Questions:

- How do musicians generate creative ideas?
- How do musicians make creative decisions?
- How do musicians improve the quality of their creative work?

Procedures:

- In this lesson, we will use the Waltz in A-flat, Op. 39, No. 15 by Johannes Brahms found in *First Steps in Music for Preschool and Beyond* (GIA Publications, 2006) and on the *Move It!* DVD (GIA Publications, 2003).
- Have the students perform the movements to the Waltz in A-flat Op. 39, No. 15 by Johannes Brahms.
- For older elementary, ask them about the pattern that they experienced with the movements for the song (ABABA). For younger elementary, guide them to understand that they moved in the form of an ABABA pattern.
- Explain that today, they will create a song with the same pattern using melodies and rhythms. For older elementary, you can add chords and arpeggios if they understand the concepts of these musical elements.
- **Set up Groovy Shapes**:
  - Launch Groovy Shapes.
  - Set up the song to be in the key of F and pentatonic.
  - Choose the meter and the tempo.

- Create a song using Groovy Shapes:
- Using a web-based device or the iOS app, show the students how to create a song by listening to the rhythms first.
- **Create the A section**:
  - Ask them what they hear when they hear the rhythms (drum patterns).
  - Listen to numerous rhythms and have them describe what they hear. Accept any type of answer, as it encourages their listening and descriptive skills.
  - Show them how to click and drag a drum pattern to the first measure.
  - Delete that drum pattern and ask a child to choose a rhythm pattern to drag to the first measure.
  - Ask another child to drag a rhythm pattern to drag to the second measure.
  - Listen to the two drum patterns and ask the students to respond to it through movement.
  - Click on melodies and ask the students to describe the various melodies that you tap. Encourage any answer.
  - Ask a child to click and drag a melody to the first measure.
  - Ask another child to click and drag a melody to the second measure.
  - Listen to the two measures and ask the students to respond to it through movement and then words.
- **Create the B section**:
  - Do the same as the A Section, but encourage the rhythms and melodies to be different or contrasting from the A Section.
- **Finish the piece of music**:
  - Once the A and B sections are created, copy and paste them to form an ABABA piece of music with melodies and rhythms (older elementary can add chords and arpeggios).
- **Create movements**:
  - Have the students listen and create movements to represent the form of their newly created song.
- **Website example**: To see how this was created, please visit the website that corresponds with this book at www.oup.com/us/utema.◉

Higher Order Thinking Questions to Ask the Students:

- How do the melodies move (high to low, low to high, stay the same)?
- What happens to the music and the mood if we change the tempo of the music?
- What can be improved about the song?
- Can you tell me what you liked, what you wonder about the piece of music, and a "what if" about the music? For example, "I like the melodies." "I wonder if the melodies could be louder or quieter." "What if we made them louder. What will happen to the piece of music?"

Extensions:

- Create a Section C to the music.
- Create a very short move it activity like the ones found in the *Move It!* DVDs to the newly created piece of music.
- Add lyrics to the melody and sing with the music.

- Share the music with others by using the web extension Screencastify (https://www. screencastify.com/) in the Chrome browser to video record your screen. If you are using an iPad, use the video screen recording tool in the control panel.

Beat Motion Activities

Curriculum Note: *Beat Motion Activities are step eight in the eight-step musical workout. However, as Missy stated in the introduction of First Steps, the SongTales from step five will be moved to follow the Beat Motion Activities. The following lessons use technology to enhance the child-initiated beat activities.*

Engine, Engine Number Nine

Objective: To assess the steady beat of the student.
Grade Levels: PreK–2
Materials: *First Steps in Music for Preschool and Beyond* (GIA Publications, 2006), or *The Book of Songs and Rhymes with Beat Motions* (GIA Publication, 2004), or *First Steps in Classical Music: Keeping the Beat* CD (GIA Publications, 2000), all by Dr. Feierabend, and the website, http://www.beatsperminuteonline.com/, to assess the student's beat. The website will require internet access. If you do not have access to the internet but have an iOS device, you can use the iOS GarageBand app (https://www.apple.com/ios/garageband/).
Standards: Performing: MU:Pr4.2.PKa, MU:Pr4.2.Ka, MU:Pr4.2.1a, MU:Pr4.2.2a
Essential Questions:

- Why does a lot of music have a steady beat?

Procedures:

- You can use any chant from the resources listed under Materials. For this lesson, we will use Engine, Engine. At this point in the curriculum, the students can perform it by themselves.
- Review Engine, Engine with the students.
- **Launch the website, http://www.beatsperminuteonline.com/.**
  - Have the child come up to the device or to an interactive whiteboard (like a SMART Board) and begin tapping the beat.
  - The students then perform the chant to the student's beat.
  - You can watch the beats per minute (bpm) that the student is using and record in your notes the bpm and if it stayed steady.
- **If you are using the GarageBand iOS app:**
  - Click the + button, find the acoustic guitar instrument (make sure your screen shows instruments and not loops in order to find the guitar), and it will default to a C major tablature.
  - Set the dial to "1" and tap "C." GarageBand is now playing a C chord.
  - Tap the wrench tool and click on Tempo.
  - Have the student click on "Tap to set Tempo" to assess their steady beat. Have the students sing the chant on sol and mi (ssmmssm, ssmmssm) to the student's beat.
  - Assess their beat and the tempo, marking that they perform the beat.

- If you do not like using C major, click the wrench tool>Key Signature> and change the song to a new key.
- Perform this for a few students to assess their beat and to record their bpm.

Higher Order Thinking Questions to Ask the Students:

- Why do most of the chants we perform have a steady beat?
- Why do most of the songs we sing have a steady beat?
- What happens to some songs and chants when we do not perform them with a steady beat?

Extensions:

- Use other chants and songs from the resources listed in the Materials and continue to assess the students' steady beats.

William He Had Seven Sons

Curriculum Note: *Some students have challenges that prevent them from playing traditional instruments. Virtual instruments connected to a decent pair of speakers can help students with special needs perform on instruments during music class.*
Objective: To assess the steady beat of the student.
Grade Levels: PreK–2
Materials: *First Steps in Music for Preschool and Beyond* (GIA Publications, 2006), or *The Book of Songs and Rhymes with Beat Motions* (GIA Publication, 2004), or *First Steps in Classical Music: Keeping the Beat* CD (GIA Publications, 2000), all by Dr. Feierabend, and the website, https://www.apronus.com/music/onlineguitar.htm, to assess the student's beat. The website will require internet access. If you do not have access to the internet, but have an iOS device, you can use the iOS GarageBand app (https://www.apple.com/ios/garageband/) or the Autoharp iOS app (http://www.autoharpapp.com/). The Autoharp app also has a Google Play/Android version. The app currently costs $.99 with more in-app purchases.
Standards: Performing: MU:Pr4.2.PKa, MU:Pr4.2.Ka, MU:Pr4.2.1a, MU:Pr4.2.2a
Essential Questions:

- Why does a lot of music have a steady beat?

Procedures:

- You can use any song from the resources listed under Materials. For this lesson, we will use "William He Had Seven Sons." At this point in the curriculum, the students can sing the song by themselves.
- Review "William He Had Seven Sons" with the students. Encourage them to tap the beat in the group of the meter.
- **Launch the website, https://www.apronus.com/music/onlineguitar.htm, and click on the "Dm" button.**
  - Ask a student to tap the space bar to play the steady beat on the Dm chord.
  - Have the students sing along with the performer.
  - Ask another student to perform, and assess.

- **Tech tip**: This website is a virtual online guitar. Please test it before you use it to see if you are having trouble keeping the steady beat due to a slow internet connection. If that is the case, then use a traditional instrument or the app listed in the following.
- **If you are using the iOS GarageBand app**:
  - Click the + button, find the acoustic guitar instrument (make sure your screen shows instruments and not loops in order to find the guitar), and it will default to a C major tablature.
  - Demonstrate how to strum with the app and strum on the Dm chord.
  - Assign a student to strum the Dm chord while the class sings. If the student is doing very well, show them the Gm chord to switch to during the song.
  - Assign another student to perform on the acoustic guitar.
  - **Tech tip**: If you decide to project the iOS device onto the screen, make sure you hard-wire the device (do not use Airplay). GarageBand works better when it is hard-wired to a projector.
- **If you are using the Autoharp iOS or Google Play app**:
  - Launch the app.
  - You can click the Settings tool to change around touch sensitivity, turn on controls for left-hand setup, stopping strings with multiple fingers, set up a 15- or 21- or custom-string layout (this is nice for multiple learning styles), and more.
  - Click Done when you are finished with the settings.
  - Click the + button to make the screen and chord buttons larger and easier to read.
  - Hold the Dm button and have the student strum the beat of the song. The students sing to the tempo of the performer.
  - Assign another student to perform on the virtual autoharp.
  - **Tech tip**: Have a good set of speakers connected to this app. It makes a world of difference.
- **Assess the steady beat. I use the following rubric**:
  - 4: Student consistently plays the steady beat. The student is consistently competent.
  - 3: Student plays the steady beat accurately for most of the song. The student is competent.
  - 2: Student plays the steady beat accurately for some of the song. The student is developing.
  - 1: Student cannot perform a steady beat at this time. The student is emerging.

Higher Order Thinking Questions to Ask the Students:

- Why do most of the chants we perform have a steady beat?
- Why do most of the songs we sing have a steady beat?
- What happens to some songs and chants when we do not perform them with a steady beat?

Extensions:

- Use other chants and songs from the resources listed in the Materials and continue to assess the students' steady beats.

4, PART A

The Kodály Approach
to Teaching Music

An Overview

Glennis E. Patterson

Zoltán Kodály (1882–1967)

Zoltán Kodály was born in Kecskemét, Hungary, on December 16, 1882. His parents were both amateur musicians who often performed the chamber music of the European masters in their home. He completed studies in teacher education, philosophy, languages, and music at Pazmany University and at the Franz Liszt Academy. In 1906, he received a doctorate after completing a thesis entitled "The Stanzaic (Strophic) Structure of Hungarian Folk Song." Along with Béla Bartók, Kodály collected and classified the folk songs of many regions of the Austro-Hungarian Empire. He taught music for many years at the Liszt Academy in Budapest, beginning in 1907 and continuing to teach even after his official retirement in 1942.[1]

As a composer and author, Kodály's most prolific period was from 1923 to 1939. His most noted compositions of this period were written for opera and chorus. His scholarly works included a number of articles that sought to define the nature of Hungarian folk music. Kodály stated that 1925 was the year that his attention turned to the musical education of children. His former students began the Youth Choral Movement in Hungary, which led to the publication of choral collections for children. Kodály wrote the first volume of *Bicinia Hungarica* in 1937, which discusses the benefits of using relative pitch for ear training. Other textbooks, folk music materials, and collections of classical music followed.[2]

From 1940 until his death in 1967, Kodály worked to improve music education in Hungarian schools. He continued to publish collections of singing exercises and textbooks.[3] He gave lectures discussing the importance of basing Hungarian music education on Hungarian folk music, defended the idea of teaching Hungarian music as a prerequisite to the music of other cultures, and addressed the value of teaching singing before learning to play an instrument. Kodály lobbied Hungarian leaders for better music education in

1   Micheál Houlahan and Philip Tacka, *Kodály Today* (New York: Oxford University Press, 2015), 15–16.

2   Micheál Houlahan and Philip Tacka, *Kodály Today* (New York: Oxford University Press, 2015), 16–17.

3   Margaret L. Stone, "Zoltán Kodály Centennial: 1882–1982," *Kodály Envoy* VIII, no. 4, (1982), 1.

75

Glennis E. Patterson, *The Kodály Approach to Teaching Music* In: *Using Technology with Elementary Music Approaches.* Edited by: Amy M. Burns, Oxford University Press (2020). © Oxford University Press.
DOI: 10.1093/oso/9780190055653.003.0005

the schools. The foreword of the 1964 edition of *Let Us Sing Correctly* contains Kodály's explanation that the proper intonation in singing matches the acoustic, not tempered, intervals, and that the singing teacher should not depend on the piano for pitch. The 1964 Budapest Conference of the International Society for Music Education drew international attention to what was named "the Kodály method," and he was recognized as prominent figure in twentieth-century music education.[4]

Kodály's Philosophy of Music Education

Zoltán Kodály's interest in music education began in the early 1900s, when he was disappointed by the literacy skills of music students entering music schools in Hungary. He worked to develop a system that would teach children to love and have knowledge of music from an early age.

Kodály became interested in the collection and analysis of Hungarian folk songs around 1900. Along with Béla Bartók, he collected around one thousand children's songs, which he analyzed according to mode, scale, and type. This work of collecting, analyzing, and publishing Hungarian folk music, started by Bartók and Kodály, continues today at the Academy of Sciences in Budapest.[5]

All of the pedagogical tools and processes used in the Kodály method were gathered from other sources. Solfege was created by Guido D'Arezzo in the eleventh century. Solfege teaching techniques were borrowed from Jaques-Dalcroze. John Curwen created the hand signs associated with solfege in nineteenth-century England. Rhythm syllables arose from the work of nineteenth-century French theoretician Emile Cheve, and Pestalozzi wrote about the relation of instruction to child development.[6]

Because all of these tools were gathered from existing sources, the attraction to Kodály's methodology did not solely arise from them. Instead, his philosophy of music education was what caught the attention of teachers outside of Hungary. As outlined by Lois Choksy in *The Kodály Method I*, this philosophy can best be stated in six parts:

1. Music should exist at the core of the curriculum, a basic subject alongside math and language, and music is essential to any complete education.
2. Music literacy is as universally possible as linguistic literacy and the development of such literacy is an obligation of the schools.
3. Instruments are not necessary and are counterproductive in the music education of young children. The best possible instrument for instruction is the child's own unaccompanied voice.
4. Begin music education as early as possible.
5. Only the best music is good enough for teaching, and this music must suit the emotional, musical, and intellectual world of the child.
6. Only the well-trained musician should teach music to even the youngest children. To teach any subject well at the simplest levels, it is necessary to understand it at the most complex level.[7]

4 Micheál Houlahan and Philip Tacka, *Kodály Today* (New York: Oxford University Press, 2015), 16.

5 Lois Choksy, *The Kodály Method I* (Upper Saddle River, NJ: Prentice Hall, 1999), 15.

6 Choksy, *The Kodály Method I*, 16.

7 Choksy, *The Kodály Method*, 16.

Kodály noted, "It is the right of every citizen to be taught the basic elements of music; to be handed the key with which he can enter the locked world of music. To open the ears and hearts of the millions to serious music is a great thing."[8]

Kodály Methodology Goals

The principal goals of Kodály musical training are as follows:

1. To develop to the fullest extent possible the innate musicality present in all children.
2. To make the language of music known to children; to help them become musically literate in the music of their own culture . . . to be able to read, write, and create.
3. To make the music of a child's own culture known to him through the folk songs of his own language and culture.
4. To make the great art music of the world available to children through performing, studying, and analyzing music while developing a love and appreciation for all types of music.[9]

Essential Concepts

As outlined on the Organization of American Kodály Educators website (https://www. oake.org/about-us/the-Kodály-concept), the essential concepts of Kodály methodology are as follows:

1. Singing
   - We should first learn to love music as human sound and as an experience that enriches life.
   - The voice is the most natural instrument and one which every person possesses.
   - Kodály called singing "the essence" of this concept.
   - Singing is a powerful means of musical expression.
   - What we produce by ourselves is better learned; and there is a stronger feeling of success and accomplishment.
   - Learning through singing should precede instrumental training.
   - It is in the child's best interest to understand the basics of reading music before beginning the difficult task of learning the technique of an instrument.
   - What do we sing?
     - Folk songs and games of the American culture
     - Traditional children's songs and games
     - Folk songs of other cultures
     - Music of the masters from all ages
     - Pedagogical exercises written by master composers
   - Singing best develops the inner, musical ear.

---

8   Zoltán Kodály, *The Selected Writings of Zoltán Kodály* (London; New York: Boosey & Hawkes, 1974), 77.

9   Ann Eisen and Lamar Robinson, *An American Methodology* (Lake Charles, LA: Sneaky Snake Publications, 2010), x.

2. Folk Music
   - Folk music is the music of the people. There can be no better material for singing than the songs and games used by children for centuries.
   - Folk music has all the basic characteristics needed to teach the foundations of music and to develop a love of music—a love that will last a lifetime.
   - Folk music is the classical music of the people, and, as such, is a perfect bridge leading to and working hand in hand with art music.

3. Solfege
   - Solfege is the best tool for developing the inner ear.
   - It is an invaluable aid in building all musical skills.
     - Sight singing
     - Dictation
     - Ear training
     - Part hearing
     - Hearing and singing harmony
     - Perceiving form
     - Developing memory
   - The movable do system, highly developed in English choral training, was advocated by Kodály as a tool for teaching musical literacy.
   - Use of the pentatone (do, re, mi, sol, la) was recommended by Kodály for early training of children because of its predominance in their folk music.

4. Music and Quality
   - We believe that music enhances the quality of life. So that it may have the impact it deserves, only the best music should be used for teaching:
     - Folk music, which is the most representative of culture
     - The best music composed by the masters.
   - Quality music demands quality teaching:
     - Teachers need to be as well-trained as possible.
     - Teachers' training must be well-rounded.
     - Teachers need to develop their musical and vocal skills to the highest degree possible.

5. Development of the Complete Musician
   - Kodály training is a complete and comprehensive approach to music education which meets the National Standards for Arts Education.
   - The development of all skill areas begins very early with simple tasks required of all the students. As knowledge grows, skills are developed: part-singing, part-hearing, improvisation, intonation, listening, memory, phrasing, and understanding of form.
   - An awareness and knowledge of musical styles develop as skills become more proficient.

6. Sequencing
   - Presentation of materials, concepts, and development of skills can be done in a meaningful way only if curriculum is well-sequenced.
   - A carefully planned sequence, well taught, will result in successful experiences for children and teacher. Success breeds success—and fosters a love of music.

- A Kodály sequenced curriculum is an experience-based approach to learning rather than a cognitive developmental approach.[10]

Teaching Music with the Kodály Approach

Teaching music with the Kodály approach follows a three-step sequence.

1. Preparation
2. Presentation
3. Practice.

Following this sequence, it integrates a step-by-step approach that is developmentally appropriate for children. Musical elements are introduced one at a time in a sequential order that mirrors their appearance in the folk music of the child's culture. Singing is the basis for instruction, and other instruments follow after the students demonstrate mastery of the elements using their voice and bodies.

Implementing the Sequential Approach

As musical elements are introduced to students, Kodály methodology follows a strict sequence of preparation, presentation, and practice. To meet the needs of all students, it is important to address visual, aural, and kinesthetic styles during each step. Let's examine each step and the ways that the musical element is taught.

Preparation

The first step toward learning a new musical element or concept is learning new songs that feature the element prominently. Songs are taught through rote by listening to the teacher, then repeating them back. If there is a play party or game associated with the song, the teacher presents it as part of the preparation process. Playing the game fosters repetition of the song in an engaging way that helps students master the song. For each element, the teacher establishes a repertoire of songs to draw from as the class proceeds through the learning sequence. Work on the song repertoire can begin far in advance of learning the element. Mastery of the songs contributes to a more successful experience as the elements are isolated for introduction.

Once the song repertoire is established, the teacher may begin leading the students through the preparation steps. These steps are designed to address all three learning styles (visual, aural, and kinesthetic). The kinesthetic preparation activities can be employed with known songs even as more songs containing the element are taught. Preparation activities include: indicating melodic contour with hand gestures; tapping the beat or rhythm with hands; moving a parachute or sheet to demonstrate the melodic contour; indicating the melodic contour on one's body; playing the rhythm or beat on

10 "The Kodály Concept," Organization of American Kodály Educators, 2019, https://www.oake.org/about-us/the-kodaly-concept.

an instrument; stepping the beat while clapping the rhythm; and having one-half of the class tap the beat while the other half claps the rhythm.

When all of the song repertoire has been established, preparation continues through aural activities. The aural activities are designed to help the students accurately hear the new element, whether it be rhythmic or melodic. For melodic elements, this takes the form of singing the song with known note names and humming when the students reach a note they do not know. For rhythmic elements, students can sing the song and clap when they reach the new rhythmic element. It is important that the students are able to identify the new element on their own.

After the element has been identified aurally, the teacher leads the students through the visual preparation activities. In this step, students see pictures or icons that represent the element. For melodic elements, the grade level of the students determines what form this takes. Visual preparation for primary grades begins as pictures indicating the shape of the melodic contour. The teacher points to the pictures while the students sing the phrase and students take turns pointing to them independently. Next, the pictures are placed on the lines and spaces, then are replaced with notes. For older students, the phrase is written on the staff with notes with the new melodic element missing.

Visual preparation for rhythmic elements begins by singing the phrase containing the element while pointing to hearts (which represent the beat). The words of the phrase are written over the corresponding beat. Notation is written over the words, with the notation for the new element missing.

The preparation step can vary in length. What is most important is that the students are able to perform and identify the new element in the context of known repertoire before the teacher proceeds to the presentation step. Following the order of kinesthetic, then aural, then visual steps places the students in the best position for the presentation lesson.

Presentation

Unlike the preparation step, the presentation step takes place during only one lesson. During this lesson, the teacher leads the students through a reminder of the preparation steps that have already taken place. For a melodic element, the students would use kinesthetic movement to indicate the new note. The element is identified aurally while the teacher displays the previously used visual cues. Finally, the teacher displays the phrase of the song that contains the new note on a musical staff. The teacher places the new note on the staff, then sings the phrase with the new solfege name while using Curwen hand signs. The students practice singing the new element.

Rhythmic element presentation lessons take a similar form. The teacher leads the students through performing the beat, then the rhythm of the phrase containing the element. The new element is aurally isolated, then the visual prompt is displayed. This prompt includes the words written over hearts (which symbolize the beat) and the known rhythms in the phrase. The teacher writes the new rhythm in the phrase, then claps and sings the entire phrase for the class. The students practice clapping and singing the new element.

Practice

After the presentation lesson, the final step of the sequential approach is practice. Practice can take the form of reading, writing, or practicing inner hearing. Writing does not always have to be with pencil and paper. Students can use popsicle sticks, note and musical staff manipulatives, whiteboards and markers, or even interactive whiteboards to practice writing notes and rhythms. Reading practice can include reading known and unknown songs, flashcards, and rhythmic and melodic exercises. Inner hearing is defined as being able internalize the sound of the element without audibly performing it. The teacher can prompt students to use inner hearing by directing them to "sing in your head." When the students sing before and after the inner hearing, the teacher can assess whether or not the exercise was effective. Giving the students the notation for known songs and asking them to identify them without singing is another method for practicing inner hearing.

Example of the Sequential Approach

To understand the application of the sequence of preparation, presentation, and practice, let's examine it as the new element of sol-mi is introduced in Grade 1. Preparation begins during kindergarten and the beginning of Grade 1. The students learn many songs that include sol-mi patterns. The games and play parties associated with these songs are played and performed many times for reinforcement of the song, long before formal teaching of the musical element begins.

After the students have mastered singing the repertoire for the element, it is time to begin teaching the musical element of sol-mi. For sol-mi, this begins by finding the melodic contour of high and low and practicing it by pointing to pictures and moving hands high and low. Next, the teacher places pictures associated with the song in the spaces (for example, snails for "Snail, Snail"). The students continue to demonstrate high and low with their hands. The pictures are replaced with notes on the staff. Finally, the teacher defines the notes as "sol" and "mi" by singing the pattern and demonstrating the hand signs.

Practice can take many forms. The pattern is reinforced by finding it in other known songs and leading the class to place it on the staff in the same manner as the presentation lesson. Patterns with sol and mi can be written using manipulatives by individual students. Students can practice writing it on paper on worksheets or on whiteboards with markers. Students can create the pattern with students standing and sitting to show sol and mi.

Sequencing introduction of elements overlaps. Classes are typically working on a melodic and rhythmic element simultaneously. They can be practicing a known element while a new element is prepared. Care must be taken not to have more than one presentation in the same lesson. Long-range planning of the introduction of elements over the course of a school year is helpful for the teacher. As in any music methodology, elements continue to be practiced and built upon from year to year.

Planning in the Kodály Classroom

To address all of the musical elements requires planning of the year-long curriculum in the music classroom. Teachers begin by making a list of the musical elements that they plan to teach in each grade level for the year. All three steps of the learning process (preparation, presentation, and practice) must be considered and time allowed for them to be completed in a way that results in mastery of the skills.

Each school year begins with the establishment of repertoire. If a Kodály approach was used during the previous school year, a review of mastered elements is conducted. Depending on the frequency of the class meeting schedule, this review and teaching of new songs lasts for the first month of school.

When the repertoire for the first new elements to be introduced has been mastered, the teacher may begin the preparation steps. As these steps are followed, the teacher continues to introduce and review repertoire for the current element and others that will be addressed later. When the current elements reach the practice stage, the teacher begins the preparation steps for the next element. In this manner, the three stages of teaching an element happen congruently.

For effective planning, it is necessary for the teacher to begin the school year with a list of elements to be addressed during each grade level. Taking into account how long the preparation, presentation, and practice stages will take for each element, the teacher can make a plan for each month of the school year. This will help the teacher to address the elements in a timely manner and create daily lesson plans which reach these learning goals.

Materials

Kodály believed that the folk music of the child's homeland was the best material for teaching children. He compared the development of music from folk song to art music to the development of child from infant to adult. Teachers around the world following the Kodály approach are encouraged to use the music of their own cultures to teach skills while integrating music from other cultures.

Teachers using Kodály methodology gather song repertoire for use in teaching musical elements. They organize the songs into lists of usefulness for teaching the individual elements. This allows teachers to plan the teaching of repertoire far in advance of beginning the steps toward teaching a musical element.

Comprehensive books about Kodály methodology and accompanying materials provide guidelines to teachers using this approach. *The Kodály Method I* by Lois Choksy, *An American Methodology* by Ann Eisen and Lamar Robertson, and *Kodály Today* by Micheal Houlahan and Philip Tacka are all method books that specifically outline the teaching sequences and provide lists of song repertoire to use. Lois Choksy has also written *The Kodály Method II: Folksong to Masterwork*, which addresses the teaching of musical elements in the context of art music. Eisen and Robertson developed a long-range lesson planning tool, sets of student worksheets that accompany their methodology book, and "Directions to Literacy: Teaching the Older Beginner," which suggests a sequence for using the Kodály approach with upper elementary students. Houlahan and Tacka have written grade-level handbooks for kindergarten through Grade 6 that align with *Kodály Today*.

Kodály organizations and ethnomusicologists have created collections of folk songs and their accompanying play parties, games, and dances. These include *150 American Folk Songs* by Peter Erdei and Katalin Komlos, and *Sail Away: 155 American Folk Songs* by Eleanor G. Locke; both are standard collections utilized by Kodály teacher training programs. Other popular collections for teachers incude *120 Singing Games and Dances for Elementary Schools* by Lois Choksy and David Brummitt, Jill Trinka's four collections of folk songs (*My Little Rooster; Bought Me a Cat; John, the Rabbit*; and *The Little Black Bull*), and *My Singing Bird: 150 Folk Songs*, edited by Ida Erdei, Faith Knowles, and Denise Bacon. In addition, the methodology books include appendices of the folk songs mentioned in their curricula. Teachers trained in the Kodály approach create lists of songs for teaching musical elements as part of their educational process and draw from them in their teaching practice.

Training in Kodály Methodology

Teachers wishing to the implement the Kodály approach are best served by seeking training in it. In the United States, the Organization of American Kodály Educators (OAKE) maintains a list of endorsed certification programs, most of which are conducted during the summer at universities. Endorsed programs must meet a set of guidelines set out by OAKE, pay for an annual institutional membership, and submit a yearly report and report fee. This allows the organization to monitor the quality of instructors, structure, and content.[11] Certification programs are two to three weeks in length and require at least three summers to complete. If a training program is not available, following the sequence set out in *The Kodály Method I* by Lois Choksy or *An American Methodology* by Ann Eisen and Lamar Robertsen will provide guidance to teachers. Workshops are offered by local chapters of OAKE, and conferences are held by the regional divisions and the national organization. Teachers may attend these to improve their teaching skills and learn about more aspects of following the methodology.

Resources

Choksy, Lois. *The Kodály Method I: Comprehensive Music Education*. Upper Saddle River, NJ: Prentice-Hall, Inc., 1999.

Choksy, Lois, and David Brummitt. *120 Singing Games and Dances for Elementary Schools*. Upper Saddle River, NJ: Prentice-Hall, 1987.

Eisen, Ann, and Lamar Robertson. *An American Methodology: An Inclusive Approach to Musical Literacy*. Lake Charles, LA: Sneaky Snake Publications, 2010.

Erdei, Ida, Faith Knowles, and Denise Bacon. *My Singing Bird: 150 Folk Songs*. Columbus, OH: Kodály Center of America, 2002.

Erdei, Peter, and Katalin Komlos. *150 American Folk Songs*. New York: Boosey & Hawkes, 1974.

Houlahan, Micheál, and Philip Tacka. *Kodály Today: A Cognitive Approach to Elementary Music Education*. New York: Oxford University Press, 2015.

Kodály, Zoltán. *The Selected Writings of Zoltán Kodály*. London; New York: Boosey & Hawkes, 1974.

11 "What is an Endorsed Certificate Program?," Organization of American Kodály Educators, 2019, https://www.oake.org/about-us/what-is-an-endorsed-certificate-program.

Locke, Eleanor G. *Sail Away: 155 American Folk Songs to Sing, Read, and Play*. New York: Boosey & Hawkes, 1988.

OAKE. "Chapter Workshops." Accessed January 17, 2019. www.oake.org/chapter-workshops.

OAKE. "Chapters and Divisions." Accessed January 17, 2019. www.oake.org/chapters-and-divisions.

OAKE. "Education Programs." Accessed January 17, 2019. www.oake.org/education-programs.

OAKE. "The Kodály Concept." Accessed January 17, 2019. www.oake.org/about-us/the-kodaly-concept.

OAKE. "National Conference." Accessed January 17, 2019. www.oake.org/conferences.

OAKE. "What Is an Endorsed Certificate Program?" Accessed January 17, 2019. www.oake.org/about-us/what-is-an-endorsed-certificate-program.

OAKE. "Who Was Kodály." Accessed January 17, 2019. www.oake.org/about-us/who-was-kodály.

Trinka, Jill. *My Little Rooster and Other Folk Songs, Singing Games, & Play Parties*. Dripping Springs, TX: Folk Music Works, 1987.

Trinka, Jill. *Bought Me a Cat and Other Folk Songs, Singing Games, & Play Parties*. Dripping Springs, TX: Folk Music Works, 1988.

Trinka, Jill. *John, the Rabbit and Other Folk Songs, Singing Games, & Play Parties*. Dripping Springs, TX: Folk Music Works, 1989.

Trinka, Jill. *The Little Black Bull and Other Folk Songs, Singing Games, & Play Parties*. Dripping Springs, TX: Folk Music Works, 1996.

4, PART B
Technology Integration with the Kodály Approach

Amy M. Burns

Important Note: Before you use any tool with your students, please check with your school's administration regarding the technology policies of your school to make sure you can use students' information, including images, and that you have their support.

Tech Resources

There are numerous resources for elementary music educators using the Kodály approach in their classrooms so that one can easily obtain folk songs, manipulatives, connect with others using the approach, and more. Here is a list that I have found helpful:

Accompanying Website for This Book

- Type in any web browser, www.oup.com/us/utema, or click on the link found here.⊚

Organization Websites

- **International Kodály Society (IKS)** (https://www.iks.hu): This site offers information about the worldwide organization and offers scholarships for foreign students to study the Kodály concept at the Zoltán Kodály Pedagogical Institute in Kecskemét, Hungary.
- **Organization of American Kodály Educators** (https://www.oake.org): You can find out about the approach and organization as well as become a member to access numerous resources. Also check out the Chapters and Divisions section to find a local Kodály chapter in your area.
- **Organization of American Kodály Educators Facebook Group** (https://www.facebook.com/oakeorg/): This Facebook group is open to music educators who would like to learn more about the concept and to ask questions of the experts.
- **Perform a Google Search to find Kodály organizations in your country and your local chapter.**

Amy M. Burns, *Technology Integration with the Kodály Approach* In: *Using Technology with Elementary Music Approaches*. Edited by: Amy M. Burns, Oxford University Press (2020). © Oxford University Press.
DOI: 10.1093/oso/9780190055653.003.0006

Some Folk Song Collections

- **Kodály Center—The American Folk Song Collection** (http://kodaly.hnu.edu): This free website provides a collection of songs that may include recordings, games, analysis, sequence, and more. There are great filters in their search tools to assist you in finding a certain song with specific melodic and rhythmic sequences.
- **Kodály Song Analysis Directory** (https://ksadirectory.blogspot.com): This is a free searchable database for teaching songs using the Kodály approach.
- **Kodály Song Website** (http://kodalysongweb.net/): Search their free database to find song notation pdfs of many songs.
- **My Song File—Music Resources for the Classroom** (https://mysongfile.com): This site offers many free resources that involve songs, worksheets, games, and strategies. For a paid membership, you can access all of the resources.
- **The Global Jukebox** (https://theglobaljukebox.org): Listen to authentic recordings from around the world.

Music Educators' Websites

Note: This is a small list of music educators who share the way they use the Kodály approach in their classrooms. Perform a Google search to find more classrooms sharing materials via websites, Teachers Pay Teachers, blogs, and more.

- **Amy M. Burns Website** (https://www.amymburns.com): Amy provides various resources and examples on how to integrate technology into the elementary music classroom.
- **Beth's Notes** (https://www.bethsnotesplus.com): Beth provides free materials and resources on her site. For a membership fee, you can access and download pdfs, monthly bundles, contact her with questions, and more.
- **Kodály Collaboration Board** (https://www.pinterest.com/linzyjo7/kodaly-collaboration-board/?fbclid=IwAR14oD1DfRGj6fPVOJitQF6MSeqPWgJBsef_ZBkIxrnO6syllLIXGT4d4eY): Music educators pin resources and materials for use in a Kodály-inspired classroom.
- **Kodály Corner** (http://kodalycorner.blogspot.com): This website is a collaboration of music educators who share ideas and materials from their Kodály-inspired music classrooms.
- **Kodály Crafts** (https://www.kodalycrafts.com/): Jenny's website from Melbourne, Australia, features lessons and ideas for the Kodály classroom. She also provides links to her social media sites.
- **Kodály Inspired Classroom** (http://www.kodalyinspiredclassroom.com/): Lindsay's website has many wonderful ideas and lessons that revolve around the Kodály approach. You can also access her social media sites and follow her so you can utilize her materials.
- **Katie Wardrobe Midnight Music** (http://www.kodaly.org.au/creating-rhythm-flashcards-in-sibelius/): Katie Wardrobe wrote an article about creating rhythm flashcards using stick notation in Sibelius.
- **Mrs. King's Music Class** (http://mrskingrocks.blogspot.com): Tracy, the Bulletin Board Lady, has great bulletin board materials for a Kodály-inspired classroom. Her site links to her other social media sites.

- **Mrs. Miracle's Music Room** (https://www.mrsmiraclesmusicroom.com/): Aileen's Kodály-inspired website with free lesson plans, ideas, and activities, as well as links to her social media sites.
- **Mrs. Stouffer's Music Room** (https://mrsstouffersmusicroom.com/): This blog has multiple resources for a Kodály-inspired music classroom, as well as a Kodály-inspired recorder curriculum.
- **Music a la Abbott—A Kodály-Inspired Blog** (http://www.musicalaabbott.com/): Amy's website posts ideas and activities as well as links to her social media sites.
- **Yellow Brick Road** (https://yellowbrickroadblog.com/): Jennifer provides lesson ideas, plans, and resources on her blog and her other social media sites.

Interactive Websites to Use in a Classroom with One Device, Multiple Devices, or 1:1 Devices

Note: The following is a short list of interactive websites that can be used in a classroom with one device, multiple devices, or 1:1 devices. Some of these websites still require Adobe Flash (which will be discontinued in late 2020) and might be compatible with the devices in your classroom, or might not. As with any website, I highly encourage you to test the website before you use it in the classroom. Please also check with your administration about technology use in the classroom. In addition, I recommend a decent pair of speakers hooked to the device that you are using to present the website.

Orchestral Websites

- http://www.sfskids.org: The site allows the students to listen to acoustic sound samples, discover and explore instruments, and more.
- http://www.dsokids.com: The Dallas Symphony Orchestra's website is a fantastic doorway into a world of music and learning for students, parents, and teachers.
- http://www.nyphilkids.org: The New York Philharmonic Kidzone is a place for kids to visit and learn about the New York Philharmonic, the instruments of the orchestra, the music, the musicians, and so much more.
- http://listeningadventures.carnegiehall.org/ypgto/index.aspx: This is based on Benjamin Britten's *Young Person's Guide to the Orchestra*. If you click on "Local Game" and then "Practice Round," your students do not need to create a login to use the games of instrument explorations.
- https://www.tso.ca/education/teacher-resources: The Toronto Symphony Orchestra Teacher Resources include study guides and podcasts of the repertoire from their concerts.
- http://www.classicsforkids.com/: Classical music's great composers come to life through music and stories that are age-appropriate for elementary students.

Interactive Websites

- http://www.musictechteacher.com: Karen Garrett, the Technology in Music Education (TI:ME-https://www.ti-me.org) 2006 Teacher of the Year, created this interactive website to assist her elementary students with learning all things music. Click on the games and quizzes to have your students practice their knowledge about rhythms, instruments, and more.

- http://www.themusicinteractive.com: The Music Interactive has numerous free and paid games for download to a laptop or desktop such as Staff Wars, the note-naming game in a Star Wars style. If you are craving these games for devices that can only play apps or websites, then check out their compatible apps that can be accessed from this website.
- http://www.therhythmtrainer.com: The rhythm trainer is a website where the student listens to the rhythm pattern being played and then notates it.
- http://www.philtulga.com: This website has many free activities that are musically based with cross-curricular connections. Some favorites are creating rhythm patterns with the free Counting Music and singing solfege with Sequencing with Simon.

Tech Tools That Enhance the Classroom

- **Audacity** (https://www.audacityteam.org/): Change keys and tempo and remove vocals.
- **Soundtrap** (https://www.soundtrap.com): Change keys and tempo.
- **Class Tools** (https://www.classtools.net/): Gives you a random name chooser, a timer, and more to assist in your classroom.

Assessment Tools

- **Google Forms** (https://www.google.com/forms/about/): *If your school is based around Google (Google Drive, Google Classroom, etc.), then using Google Forms for assessment is intuitive as the students can access it easily.*
- **Kahoot!** (https://kahoot.com/): Great assessment/gaming tool for classes with a few devices to 1:1 devices. You can find numerous pre-made Kahoot! challenges so that you do not have to reinvent the wheel.
- **Plickers** (https://www.plickers.com/): Great to use for multiple-choice or true/false questions when there is only one device in the room because the one device will scan the printout Plickers cards to assess the multiple-choice or T/F answers.
- **Socrative** (https://socrative.com/): Wonderful to use for assessment of multiple-choice questions, exit tickets, short answers, and more, with no email addresses required of the students.
- **iDoceo** (https://idoceo.net): This is a paid iOS app that can be used to manage and organize data collected from assessments. This could involve audio assessments, video assessments, composition files/recordings, and more. In addition, it can be used for attendance charts, seating charts, random picker, quick recordings, and so much more.

Melodic and Rhythmic Sequence Lessons Integrated with Technology

Curriculum Note: *Technology can effectively be used in the preparation, presentation, and practice sequences of the approach. The lessons presented here will give some brief ideas used in preparing and presenting the concepts and then go into more details about how technology can be used for practicing the concepts. Although each lesson involves certain melodic and rhythmic sequences, these lessons are interchangeable for any sequence. When you see the melodic* *sequences listed as "mi-sol-la-do-re" or the rhythmic sequences listed as quarter, half, whole, and eighth notes and their coordinating rests, this is the sequence in which the new pitches and rhythms are taught. In the lesson, the pitches and rhythms are varied and in numerous combinations.*

Preparation for Low and High Sounds (Mi-Sol) and Rhythms of Quarter and Eighth Notes and Quarter Rests

In the preparation sequence for high and low sounds (in various combinations like mi-sol, sol-mi, mi-sol-sol, etc.), students can listen to numerous musical examples and create movements for high sounds that have them reaching upward and create movements for low sounds that have them bending downward. A few musical examples and songs that contain high and low sounds, or two pitches of mi and sol, are:

- Tchaikovsky's Chinese Dance from "The Nutcracker"
- Lemonade
- One, Two, Tie My Shoe
- Seesaw.

Presentation: Creating Presentation Slides with Google Slides, PowerPoint, Keynote, Notebook, and PDF Versions

When presenting the pitches mi and sol and the rhythm values of quarter and eighth notes, you can present them with multiple modalities, such as hands-on as well as digitally. Using a hands-on approach is beneficial as the students are touching the manipulatives, which help the students recall what they are learning. Using a digital manipulative helps enhance the presentation for a large class of students to see and focus on the concept. Here are some ideas to assist in creating a digital manipulative for presentation.

Google Slides (https://www.google.com/slides/about/):
I begin with Google Slides because it is cloud-based, free, and many schools are providing Google's apps for teachers and students to use daily. Google Slides is a part of the Google Drive service and is comparable to PowerPoint. It requires internet access, but can be worked on offline.

Melodic Sequence:

- Launch Google Slides (https://www.google.com/slides).
- Click on a blank slide.
- There is a "Themes" tab that lets you change the theme of the slide. Choose a theme. For this example, we will use a blank theme with a white background.
- Remove the title and text boxes by clicking on them and then clicking delete. This needs to be done as those preset boxes will not group and we will need to group them later.
- Click on the text box icon (the letter T with a box around it) and type the word "Mi." Feel free to change the font.
- Move the "Mi" around the slide by clicking and dragging it. You can also reshape the "Mi" box by clicking on the box and making it bigger, smaller, etc.

- Add the Curwen hand sign of Mi to the slide:
  - Click on "Insert" and scroll down to "Image," then "Search the web."
  - A Google Images search tool now appears on the side of the screen.
  - In the search box, type "Mi Curwen hand sign" or "Mi hand sign."
  - This search is producing images that are labeled for reuse and can be used commercially.
  - Select an image and click insert. It will now appear on your slide.
  - Click on the image to drag the corners to make the image larger or smaller.
  - If there is only an image of all the hand signals, you can crop it by inserting the image onto the screen. Then, select the crop tool (Figure 4.1a) and move the edges of the picture so that only the "Mi" appears. Then click outside the picture box and only the "Mi" signal is left.
  - Figure 4.1b is a very basic slide to introduce "Mi." Feel free to change the background, add more images, change the font, etc.
- Add the next slide where we will add the sign "Sol."
  - Click the + sign to add a new slide.
  - Follow the previous steps, but use "Sol" instead of "Mi."

Figure 4.1a.
Crop tool.

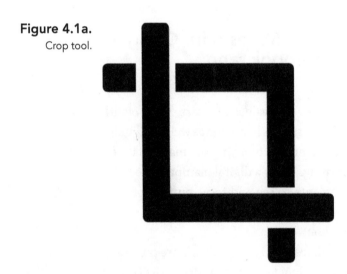

Figure 4.1b.
Presenting mi in
Google Slides.

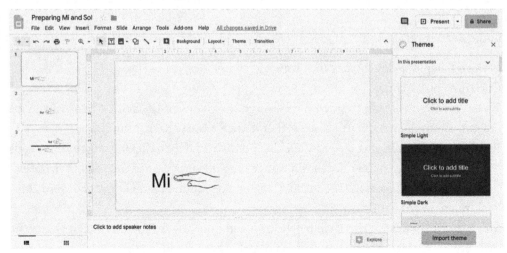

- Add the third slide, which will be a one-line staff. Some music educators begin with a five-line staff instead of starting smaller and progressing up. I tend to begin with a five-line staff as that it is the staff the students will use when they read music. However, you should use what works best in your classroom with your students.
  - Copy and paste the "Mi" and the "Sol" hand signs from the first two slides. To do this, select the hand signal, go to "Edit," and scroll down to "Copy." Or Control C on PC/Chromebook or Command C on MAC. Then, click into the third slide, go to "Edit," and scroll down to "Paste." Or Control V on PC/Chromebook or Command V on MAC.
  - If you want the words "Mi" and "Sol" to appear on their respective hand signals, copy and paste all of them to the third slide. You can group "Mi" and "Sol" with their respective hands signs by clicking on "Mi" and clicking on the "Mi" Curwen hand sign, right-clicking or control clicking on them, and scrolling down to "Group." Now the "Mi" text box and the Curwen hand sign are grouped together and can move as one image. You can do the same for "Sol."
- Click the line tool and draw a line across the slide. You now have a one-line staff.
  - If you want a thicker line, click on the line you created, then click the "Line Weight" tool, and choose the level of thickness for the line. For this example (Figure 4.1c), I used 12 point.
- You can continue to add slides with more lines, like a two-line staff, then a three-line staff, using the same steps listed in the preceding. You could also duplicate the original slide with the one-line staff by clicking on the slide, go to "Edit," and scroll down to "Duplicate" (or Control D on PC and Command D on MAC), and then add the lines using the "Line Weight" tool.
- Click on the title at the top of the screen to title your file.
- Hook your device to a projector and present the melodic concept.
- **Tech tip**: In Google Slides, if you want to move items around the screen to show the students (like moving mi and sol around the staff lines), then do not place the slides in presentation mode. Items cannot currently be moved around in presentation mode.
- **Website example**: There is a video of how to create this file on the accompanying website for this book, found at www.oup.com/us/utema.⊚

91

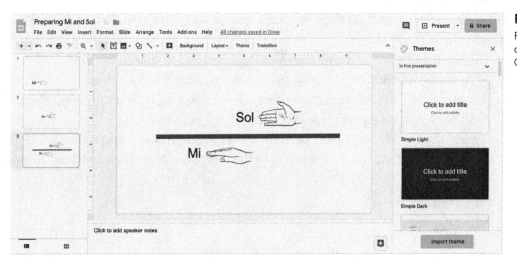

Figure 4.1c.

Presenting mi and sol on a one-line staff in Google Slides.

Rhythmic Sequence:

- Using a blank slide, click on the line tool.
- Draw a quarter note stem.
  - If you want a thicker line, click on the line you created, then click the "Line Weight" tool, and choose the level of thickness for the line. For this, I like to use 12 point.
  - Use the pointer tool to move the tool around the screen.
  - Copy and paste the line to create more movable quarter note stems.
- Use the line tool to create two eighth note stems. Use the "Line Weight" tool to set the thickness of the lines to 12 point.
- Highlight the eighth note stems. Right-click on the eighth note stems (PC) or Control-click (Mac) to bring up the editing window and scroll down to "Group." If "Group" does not appear, then try this again and make sure to right-click or control-click directly on the eighth note stems. Once grouped, you have movable eighth note stems.
- For quarter rests, add a text box, type the letter Z, shape the text box to fit around the Z, change the font to 144 point (click on the font size and type "144"), and then use the pointer tool to move it around the screen (Figure 4.1d).
- **Tech tip**: There are stick notation rhythm fonts sold on Teachers Pay Teachers that you purchase, download, and follow the instructions from the seller to add into your font collections accessed from most apps and software programs like Word, PowerPoint, Docs, Slides, etc.
- **Tech tip**: In Google Slides, if you want to move items around the screen to show the students (like moving rhythmic notation around to create different patterns), then do not place the slides in presentation mode. Items cannot currently be moved around in presentation mode.
- **Website example**: There is a video of how to create this file on the accompanying website for this book, found at www.oup.com/us/utema.⊚

PowerPoint:

PowerPoint, a Microsoft program for presentations, has been around for years. It requires the software to be purchased and installed onto a computer. It can be installed on a PC or MAC.

Melodic Sequence:

- Launch PowerPoint
- Click on blank presentation (though you can explore the themes and use one of them)
- Click in the title box and type the word "Mi." Feel free to change the font.
  - To remove the other text boxes, click on them and then click delete.
- Move the "Mi" around the slide by clicking and dragging it. You can also reshape the "Mi" box by clicking on the box and making it bigger, smaller, etc.
- To add the Curwen hand sign, perform a Google image search and right-click (PC) or control-click (MAC) to save the image to the computer. Then, click and drag the image

Figure 4.1d.
Creating stick notation with Google Slides.

to the slide. If you are using this commercially, perform a Google image search with the tools set to "Labeled for reuse." This will probably produce images that will have to be cropped so you can just use "Mi." When cropping in PowerPoint, you must insert the image, click on the image so that it is highlighted, and then click the "Picture Format" tab at the top of the page. That is where the crop tool can be found.

- **Activity tip**: If you will be moving items around on the slide, pictures move easier than text boxes. I would suggest using the pictures of the hand signs.
- Add a new slide (+ button) and perform the same steps for Sol.
- Add the third slide. Copy and paste the Mi and Sol from the first two slides. You can do this using the "Edit" menu at the top of the screen or Control C (PC)/Command C (MAC) for copy and Control V (PC)/Command V (MAC) for pasting.
- Add a line by clicking the "Insert" menu or tab, clicking the "Shapes" menu, and scrolling down to "Line."
- Double click on the line to increase the width and make the line thicker.
- Ask the students where "Mi" and "Sol" should go in relation to the one-line staff (Figure 4.1e).
- You can continue to add slides with more lines, like a two-line staff, then a three-line staff, using the same steps listed previously. You could also duplicate the original slide with the one-line staff by clicking on the slide, go to "Edit," and scroll down to "Duplicate" (or Control D on PC and Command D on MAC), and then add the lines using the "Line Weight" tool.
- Save and title your presentation file.
- Hook your device to a projector and present the melodic concept.
- **Tech tip**: In PowerPoint, if you want to move items around the screen to show the students (like moving a melodic sequence around to create different patterns), then do not place the slides in presentation mode. Items cannot currently be moved around in presentation mode.
- **Website example**: There is a video of how to create this file on the accompanying website for this book, found at www.oup.com/us/utema.⊙

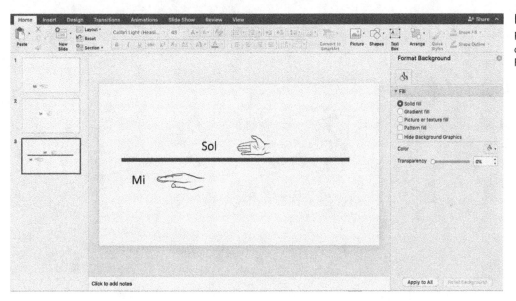

Figure 4.1e.
Presenting mi and sol on a one-line staff in PowerPoint.

Rhythmic Sequences:

- Add a blank slide.
- Click on the "Insert" tab, then the "Shapes" tool, and scroll down to the "Line" tool.
- Create a vertical line.
- Change the thickness of the line by going to the "Shape Outline" tool and scrolling down to "Weight," and then to 6 point.
- To create eighth note stems, do the same thing but create two vertical lines and one horizontal line.
- To group the eighth note stems, highlight all three stems, right-click (PC) or control-click (MAC) and scroll down to "Group." Click on "Group" and the eighth note stems are now grouped.
- To create a rest, click on the insert menu, then click on the text box, click on the slide where you want to add the text box, add the letter Z into the text box, click the "Home" tab, and increase the font size to 144 (you will have to type the number into the font size box) (Figure 4.1f).
- You now have movable stick notation and a rest.
- Save and title your presentation.
- Hook your device to a projector and present the rhythmic concept.
- **Tech tip**: There are stick notation rhythm fonts sold on Teachers Pay Teachers that you purchase, download, and follow the instructions from the seller to add into your font collections accessed from most apps and software programs like Word, PowerPoint, Docs, Slides, etc.
- **Tech tip**: In PowerPoint, if you want to move items around the screen to show the students (like moving rhythmic notation around to create different patterns), then do not place the slides in presentation mode. Items cannot currently be moved around in presentation mode.
- **Website example**: There is a video of how to create this file on the accompanying website for this book, found at www.oup.com/us/utema.⊚

Figure 4.1f.
Creating stick notation with PowerPoint.

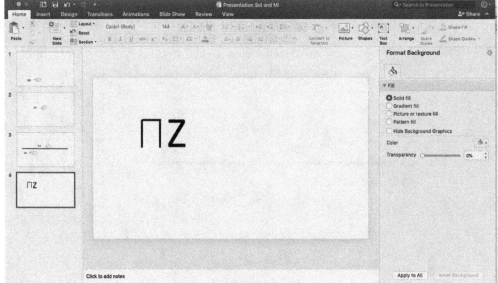

Keynote (MAC only):

Keynote, an Apple program for presentations, has been around for years. It requires the software to be purchased and installed onto a computer. It can only be installed on a MAC. There is an iOS app as well.

Melodic Sequence:

- Launch Keynote
- Follow the steps for PowerPoint.
- When adding the lines, use the Shape Tool.
- When you want to format the lines, click "Format" to make them thicker.
- **Tech tip**: I do find that dragging textboxes or images works well in Keynote.
- **Tech tip**: Keynote has image transparency, which means that you can delete the background of an image. This is a wonderful item included in Keynote.
  - For example, to get rid of the background in this image of hand signs (Figure 4.1g), click on the image.
  - The Format menu appears on the side of the screen.
  - Click on the "Image" tab.
  - Click on "Instant Alpha."
  - Click around the hand to get rid of the background.
  - Click "Done."
  - Your image now has no background.
- **Tech tip**: To crop an image in Keynote, you would click on the image and in the formatting menu, click on the "Image" tab. Then, click "Edit Mask." This will allow you to crop the image. When finished cropping, click "Done."
- Save and title your presentation file.
- Hook your device to a projector and present the melodic concept.
- **Tech tip**: In Keynote, if you want to move items around the screen to show the students (like moving a melodic sequence around to create different patterns), then

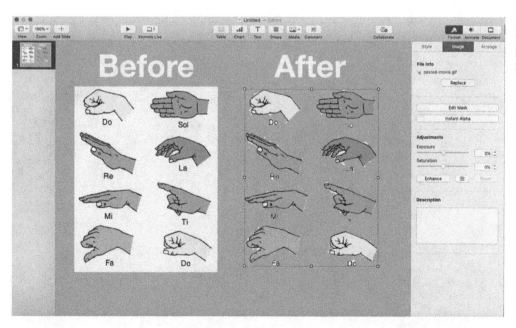

Figure 4.1g.

Removing the background from an image with Keynote.

do not place the slides in presentation mode. Items cannot currently be moved around in presentation mode.

- **Website example**: There is a video of how to create this file on the accompanying website for this book, found at www.oup.com/us/utema.⊚

Rhythmic Sequence:

- Launch a blank slide.
- Click the "Shape" tool and scroll to a line.
- Click on the line and it will be added to your slide.
- Reshape the line to make it vertical.
- Increase the thickness to 6 point. The tools to do this automatically appear on the side of the screen.
- You now have a movable quarter note stick notation.
- To create eighth note stems, create three lines (two vertical and one horizontal), move them into position, highlight them, and right-click or control-click on them to bring up the menu that will group them.
- You now have movable eighth note stems.
- To add a quarter rest, click on the textbox and type "Z." Click out of the textbox to bring up the formatting menu on the side of the screen.
- Click on the "Text" tab to bring up the font size and increase it to 144 point. You now have a movable quarter rest (Figure 4.1h).
- Save and title your presentation.
- Hook your device to a projector and present the rhythmic concept.
- **Tech tip**: There are stick notation rhythm fonts sold on Teachers Pay Teachers that you purchase, download, and follow the instructions from the seller to add into your font collections accessed from most apps and software programs like Word, PowerPoint, Docs, Slides, etc.

Figure 4.1h.
Creating stick notation with Keynote.

- **Tech tip**: In Keynote, if you want to move items around the screen to show the students (like moving rhythmic notation around to create different patterns), then do not place the slides in presentation mode. Items cannot currently be moved around in presentation mode.
- **Website example**: There is a video of how to create this file on the accompanying website for this book, found at www.oup.com/us/utema.⊚

Notebook/Interactive Whiteboard (IWB) Applications:

Though I hear that many schools are moving away from IWB, I still find some great uses for the applications.

Melodic Sequence:

- Launch the IWB application. For this example, we will use Smarttech's Notebook software.
- Click on the text box tool and type "Mi."
- Click the pointer tool to move "Mi" around the slide.
- To reshape "Mi," click on the word and then drag the corners to make the word larger or smaller.
- To change the font, click on "Mi" and then change the font from the menu that appears.
- To add the Curwen hand sign, perform a Google image search and right-click (PC) or control-click (MAC) to save the image to the computer. If you are using this commercially, perform a Google image search with the tools set to "Labeled for reuse."
- Click and drag the image to the slide.
- **Tech tip**: To delete the background of the "Mi" image, click on the image that is on the slide, click the arrow that appears, and scroll down to "Set Image Transparency. . . ." Then, in the new window, click around the hand until you have deleted the background. Then click the "Set Transparency" tab and you have an image with a deleted background (Figure 4.1i).

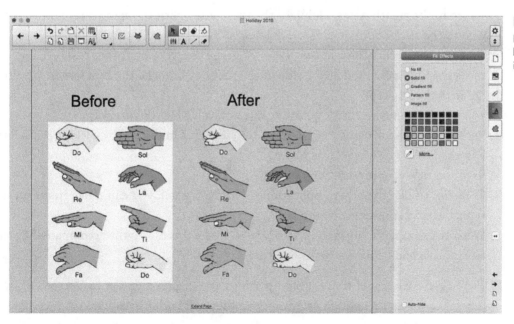

Figure 4.1i.

Removing the background from an image with Notebook.

- **Tech tip**: To save the image so you can use it with other files you create in Notebook, click the "Gallery" Tab and find the folder labeled "My Content." Click and drag the image to that folder. The image will bounce back to the screen, but also will be saved in that folder so you can access it at any time you create files in Notebook.
- **Tech tip**: To crop the image, click on the image, then click the arrow, and scroll down to "Mask." Move the corners around until you have the image cropped in the way that you want. Then click outside of the image and it is now cropped.
- Add a new slide (+ button) and perform the same steps for "Sol."
- Add a third slide. Copy and paste the "Mi" and "Sol" from the first two slides. You can do this using the "Edit" menu at the top of the screen or Control C (PC)/Command C (MAC) for copy and Control V (PC)/Command V (MAC) for pasting.
- To add a line, click on the "Lines" tool and draw the line onto the slide. To change the width of the line, click on the line, then click on the "Line Style" menu, and choose the width of the line.
- Ask the students where "Mi" and "Sol" should go in relation to the one-line staff.
- You can continue to add slides with more lines, like a two-line staff, then a three-line staff, using the same steps listed in the preceding. You could also duplicate the original slide with the one-line staff by clicking on the slide, go to "Edit," and scroll down to "Duplicate" (or Control D on PC and Command D on MAC), and then add the lines using the "Line Weight" tool.
- Save and title your presentation file.
- Hook your device to a projector and present the melodic concept.
- **Tech tip**: Unlike the other applications, with Notebook, you can move items on the screen when in presentation mode.
- **Website example**: There is a video of how to create this file on the accompanying website for this book, found at www.oup.com/us/utema.◉

Rhythmic Sequence:

- Use the line tools mentioned previously to draw and create stick notation.
- To group the eighth notes, highlight the three lines, click the arrow that now appears next to the stick notation, and scroll down to "Group."
- To create a rest, click the text tool, type "Z" in the box, click out of the text box, and use the reshaping tool found at the side of the text box to make the font larger. Or, draw "Z" with the line tool.
- You now have movable stick notation and a movable rest (Figure 4.1j).
- **Tech tip**: Notebook has traditional notation included in the app by clicking on Gallery Essentials>Arts>Music>Music Notes.
- Save and title your presentation file.
- **Tech tip**: Unlike the other applications, with Notebook, you can move items on the screen when in presentation mode.
- **Website example**: There is a video of how to create this file on the accompanying website for this book, found at www.oup.com/us/utema◉

PDF: You can save any of these files as pdf files and display them onto a screen using a document camera such as an ELMO, however, they will not be interactive.

Figure 4.1j.
Creating stick notation
with Notebook.

Practice Lessons for Mi-Sol and Low/High Enhanced with Technology

Assessing Students' Understanding of High and Low Sounds Using Plickers (https://www.plickers.com)

Curriculum Note: *Plickers is a free app for iOS and Android (there is a paid version as well) that is a wonderful assessment tool to use in a one-device classroom and with younger elementary students. The teacher creates a free account at plickers.com. The teacher adds questions that can be true/false, yes/no, multiple-choice, or a survey. You add your class lists by copying and pasting them into Plickers' class roster. You then print out your class roster and the free cards (up to 63 cards) and use these as an assessment tool and an exit ticket. The teacher launches the questions from his or her account and projects the questions onto the screen. When a question is asked, the student holds up the card with the letter on top that corresponds to the answer. The letters are small so it is difficult for the students to look at each other's cards. The teacher has the app launched on his or her device. The teacher presses the scan button and the device scans the answers and immediately records the responses. The teacher can later go into his or her account to review the students' answers and to print or export the data.*

Objective: To assess the students in identifying high and low sounds.

Grade Levels: PreK–1

Materials: Set up a Plickers account at plickers.com. Plickers cards that can be downloaded from plickers.com. One device with a Plickers app that can be Android or iOS.

Standards: MU:Cr1.1.PreKa, MU:Cr1.1.Ka, MU:Cr1.1.a, **Performing**: MU:Pr4.2.PreKa, MU:Pr4.2.Ka, MU:Pr4.2.1a

Essential Question: What is a high sound and what is a low sound?

Procedures:

- To set up this assessment, I perform movement activities that emphasize high and low movements with high and low sounds. I might perform high and low music on the piano. Or, I might play Tchaikovsky's Chinese Dance from *The Nutcracker*, or

Prokofiev's *Peter and the Wolf* (Bird for high sounds and Grandfather for low sounds) and have the students create movements for high and low sounds.

- We then sing songs with mi and sol, such as Lemonade, Seesaw, and One Two Tie My Shoe, and play their corresponding games.
- Once completed, we assess their ability to recognize high and low sounds. This could be an exit ticket, a pre-test, a post-test, or an assessment.
- Launch Plickers.com.

- Before class, the account is set up, the class lists are inputted and printed so you know which Plickers card to give to the students, and the questions are inputted as well.
- Pass out the Plickers Cards to the students.
- Open Plickers app on a device to be ready to scan the cards.
- An example of the questions would be:
  - Are you in kindergarten? (This question is so that the children understand how to use the cards to answer the question. They must hold the letter A so that it is on top of the card for the answer to be "yes".)
  - Is my name Mrs. Burns? (Again, another question to see if the students understand how to use the cards to answer the questions. A = yes and B = no).
  - Does a bear make a high or low sound? (A = high and B = low)
  - Does the bird make a high or low sound? (A = high and B = low)
  - Does the whistle make a high or low sound? (A = high and B = low)
  - Which sound/pitch is higher? Mi or sol? (A = mi and B = sol)
- **To create the questions in Plickers**:
  - You can create a "Set" of questions. The advantage of this is that when you launch the questions in the app, you can easily transition to the next question. The con is that you can only create five questions in a set with the free version. If you have more than five questions in your assessment and you are using the free version, then do not create a set and just create individual questions. The pro is that you can create more questions. The con is that you will be clicking a lot when giving the assessment with your device.
  - Click "Your Library" and create a new folder for the grade level.
  - Click on that grade level and the arrow (or double-click on the grade level).
  - Click "New Set in Folder" if you want to create five questions with the free version or click on the " . . . " if you know you are creating more than five questions by adding the questions individually.
  - Type a question into the box and then type possible answers into the A–D boxes. Click on the letter that is the correct answer and it will turn green. Add a picture if you want the visual to project onto the screen.
  - Type more questions and title your set. Plickers saves automatically.
  - Plickers does not allow audio files at this current time. However, you can play audio files from your other audio sources to enhance the questions.
  - Have plickers.com launched and project it onto the screen. This is a visual for the students to see each question. It is optional but very helpful is you are using pictures.
  - Pass out the Plickers cards (Figure 4.2) with the corresponding number to the student's name on the Plickers class list.

Figure 4.2.
Plickers cards.

- Launch the iOS or Android app and click on "Library" (this is just one way to launch a Plickers assessment).
- Click the grade level that you created.
- This will show questions, folders of questions, or a set of questions, depending on what you created. Click on what you want to display. For this example, we will click on the question, "Are you in kindergarten?"
- Click the play button and then click the class that is in the room with you.
- Your app now shows the question and your laptop is now projecting it onto the screen.
- Have the students hold up their Plickers cards with what they believe to be the correct answer's letter on top of the card (A = yes, B = no).
- Press the circle button in the app. It will launch a camera-type screen where you point it at the cards. You will be able to see the answers they are giving you.
- Move the device around the room until you see the screen read that everyone has answered (you will see green and red answers, corresponding with the correct and incorrect answers). You will also be able to click the graph button to see a graph of correct and incorrect answers, as well as a square button to show a class grid of who has answered and who has not.
- **Tech tip**: If a child is holding up an answer and the app is not scanning it, aim the device at the Plickers card again until it reads it. Sometimes the students need to hold the Plickers cards flat with no crease or glare on them. In addition, their hands cannot be touching the black portion of the Plickers card.
- **Tech tip**: Mount the Plickers cards on construction paper so that they last and hold up longer with elementary students.

- **Tech tip**: You can laminate them, but unless you have a matte laminator, sometimes regular laminations produce a glare that can be challenging for the app to read. You can also find matte laminated Plickers cards on Amazon.
- When the app has recognized that everyone has answered, click the red stop button.
- Once finished, collect the cards.
- You can go back into your account later to view your data and export it if you would like.
- **Website example**: There is a video of how to create a Plickers account, questions, and an example of the tool be used for assessment on the accompanying website for this book, found at www.oup.com/us/utema.⊛

Higher Order Thinking Questions to Ask the Students:

- What makes a sound high?
- What makes a sound low?
- *Some of these questions will be challenging for younger students to answer. However, it helps them to begin to experience the concept of high and low pitches and opposites.*

Extensions: If you are using this as a pre-test, then do this activity again in the near future to track their progress.

Placing Mi and Sol on a Staff

Curriculum Note: *There are variations to this activity depending on whether you begin with a reduced staff or a traditional five-line staff. For young students, such as PreK, this would be done with one device in the classroom and for a very short period of time as they will need to move on after a couple of minutes.*

Objective: The students will place the pitch mi on the staff for the song "Seesaw," while the teacher places the pitch sol.

Grade Levels: PreK–1

Materials: The song "Seesaw" can be found at http://kodaly.hnu.edu/song.cfm?id=863. For this lesson, you can use the file created for Google Slides, PowerPoint, Keynote (MAC only), Notebook (SMART Board), and project them onto a screen or an interactive whiteboard. The files for this lesson titled "Placing Mi and Sol on the Staff" can be found at www.oup.com/us/utema, the supplemental website to this book. This lesson can be achieved in a one-device classroom or 1:1 classroom.

Standards: Creating: MU:Cr2.1.PreKa, MU:Cr2.1.PreKb, MU:Cr1.1.Ka, MU:Cr1.1.Kb, MU:Cr2.1.Ka, MU:Cr2.1.Kb, MU:Cr1.1.1a, MU:Cr1.1b, MU:Cr2.1.1b

Essential Question:

- How do we see high and low on a staff in relation to how we hear it?

Procedures:

- Review the song "Seesaw" through singing and performing a partner game of "Seesaw" while singing together.
- Review high and low sounds through movement.
- Review placement of mi and sol on a one/two/five-line staff. If sol is on a space, then mi is on the space below sol. Use traditional manipulatives to review this concept.

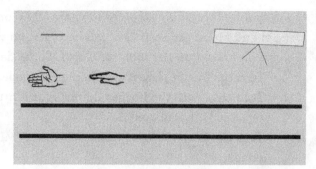

Figure 4.3.
Placing mi and sol on the staff.

103

- Launch the file "Placing Mi and Sol on the Staff" to assess the students' understanding of mi and sol on the staff.
  - **Google Slides:** The Google Slides file can be found at this link: https://docs.google.com/presentation/d/1XnWitQl34lr7c7D-4Q_RKrQixHSO7RwSxMrTqNuyRJo/copy (Figure 4.3). You can use this link on any device with internet access. This is ideal for a teacher on a cart, continuously changing devices, or 1:1 devices.
    - Copy the link to launch the file or find the link at www.oup.com/us/utema to click on it. This file will ask you to make a copy so you can edit it if you would like. Once you use the file, the hand signs will be everywhere. To use the file again, either click the link above or save the file as a copy before you start the lesson.
    - **Tech tip**: Do not place it in presentation mode, or the shapes will not move.
    - The mi and sol hand signals have been cloned several times.
    - The teacher places the sol above the one-line staff and sings, "See." The teacher asks the students to sing the next syllable in the song, "saw."
    - Ask the students: If "See" (which is the sol hand sign) is above the line, then where does "saw" (which is the mi hand sign) go? (below the line).
    - Ask a student to come to the board to place "saw" (which is the mi hand sign) in the proper place.
      - If your student needs assistance, give him or her a pointing tool or mallet to help move the mi hand sign.
      - If you do not have an interactive board, have the student use the device you are using to project onto the screen.
    - Continue for the rest of the song, with the teacher placing the "see" (which is the sol hand sign) and the students placing the "saw" (which is the mi hand sign).
    - In slides 4 and 5, there is a two-line staff. Do the same as described earlier, but with the two-line staff.
    - In slides 6 and 7, there is a five-line staff. Do the same as described earlier, but with the five-line staff.
  - **PowerPoint**: If you have access to PowerPoint, the PowerPoint file titled, "Placing Sol and Mi on the Staff.pptx" can be found on www.oup.com/us/utema. Download the file and follow the steps for Google Slides described earlier.
  - **Tech tip**: Do not place it in presentation mode, or the shapes will not move.
  - **Tech tip**: The shapes will not lock on the screen. Therefore, when you use the file, either make a copy or do not save it, so it goes back to the original file. You can always download the file again at www.oup.com/us/utema.

- **Keynote**: If you have access to Keynote (MAC only), the Keynote file titled, "Placing Sol and Mi on the Staff.key" can be found on www.oup.com/us/utema. Download the file and follow the steps for Google Slides described earlier.
  - **Tech tip**: Do not place it in presentation mode, or the shapes will not move.
  - **Tech tip**: Since the images do not move intuitively in Keynote, the images are replaced with "Sol" and "Mi."
  - **Tech tip**: With the exception of "Sol" and "Mi," all other shapes are locked on the screen.
- **Notebook**: If you have access to Notebook software (for SMART Boards), the Notebook file titled, "Placing Sol and Mi on the Staff.notebook" can be found on www.oup.com/us/utema. Download the file and follow the steps for Google Slides described earlier.
  - **Tech tip**: This file has the words "Sol" and "Mi" to move around the staff.
  - **Tech tip**: You can put this in presentation mode.
  - **Tech tip**: The other items are locked on the screen.
  - **Tech tip**: Once finished, go to the Edit Menu, and scroll down to Reset Page. This will reset the page back to its original look.
- **1:1 Devices**:
  - Though I would not advise doing this in a 1:1 classroom with PreK or K, you could try it with Grades 1 and 2. The easiest tool to use would be the Google slide file to share to their devices or to use the Chrome extension of Peardeck (found at https://chrome.google.com/webstore/detail/pear-deck/dnloadmamaeibnaadmfdfelflmmnbajd?hl=en), where your presentation shares directly to their devices.
  - **Website example**: To see how to share this Google Presentation with their 1:1 devices in multiple ways, go to the accompanying website found at www.oup.com/us/utema.⊙
  - **Tech tip**: If your students use the digital learning journal of Seesaw (found at web.seesaw.me), this template can be found in the Seesaw Activities.

Higher Order Thinking Questions to Ask the Students:

- When the pitch "sol" is on the space, where is "mi" (referencing the staff with two or more lines)?
- When the pitch "sol" is on the line, where is "mi" (referencing the staff with two or more lines)?
- How do we see the pitches on the staff in relation to how we hear it?

Extensions: Add the rhythm sequence to this by drawing the rhythm onto the screen or file.

Creating a Rhythm Composition with the Song "Seesaw"

Curriculum Note: *In this lesson, the students will create a rhythm composition from the rhythm patterns used in the song "Seesaw."*

Objective: The students will create and perform a rhythm composition with the rhythm patterns found in the song "Seesaw."

Grade Levels: PreK–2

Materials: The song "Seesaw," found at http://kodaly.hnu.edu/song.cfm?id=863. For this lesson, you can use the file created for Google Slides, PowerPoint, Keynote (MAC only), Notebook (SMART Board), and project them onto a screen or an interactive whiteboard. The files for this lesson, titled "Creating a Rhythm Composition with Seesaw," can be found at www.oup.com/us/utema, the supplemental website to this book. This lesson can be achieved in a one-device classroom or 1:1 classroom.

Standards: Creating: MU:Cr2.1.PreKa, MU:Cr2.1.PreKb, MU:Cr1.1.Ka, MU:Cr1.1.Kb, MU:Cr2.1.Ka, MU:Cr2.1.Kb, MU:Cr1.1.1a, MU:Cr1.1b, MU:Cr2.1.1b, MU:Cr1.1.2a, MU:Cr1.2b, MU:Cr2.1.2b

Essential Question:

- How do musicians generate musical ideas?

Procedures:

- Review the song "Seesaw."
- Launch the file "Creating a Rhythm Composition with Seesaw."
- **Google Slides**: https://docs.google.com/presentation/d/17E14sMrfdyWJgondEPg9g vbrGYBZzWLNj2M3ZhOruAU/copy (Figure 4.4),
  - This link can be used on any device with internet access. It can be used in a classroom with one device or a 1:1 classroom.
  - This link is a copy so that you can come back to it and download it fresh when needed.
  - The students review the rhythms of "Seesaw" with the syllables used in the classroom to count rhythms.
  - The students click and drag a rhythm pattern to an empty box. (Cannot be in present mode to click and drag.)
  - Once the empty boxes are filled, the students perform the new rhythm composition.
  - Add instruments and a drumbeat (playing one on classroom instruments or using one from a digital audio workstation (DAW) like Soundtrap or GarageBand, or using a track like Herbie Hancock's Chameleon's backtrack (https://www.youtube.com/ watch?v=8IdBAmJmlK0) and have them perform their new rhythm composition.
  - Go to the next slide and create another one.
  - The patterns are cloned so that students can choose the same rhythm pattern more than once.
- **PowerPoint: "Creating a Rhythm Composition with Seesaw.pptx"**
  - Do the same as in described earlier for the Google Slides file.

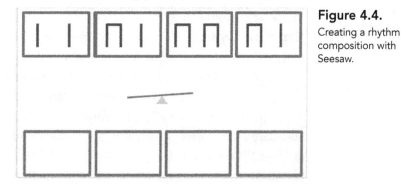

Figure 4.4.
Creating a rhythm composition with Seesaw.

- **Keynote: Creating a Rhythm Composition with Seesaw**
  - Do the same as described earlier for the Google Slides file.
- **Notebook: Creating a Rhythm Composition with Seesaw.Notebook**
  - This file will work on a SMART Board, an interactive whiteboard, or SMART Interactive Suite.
  - Follow the steps listed in the preceding.
  - **Tech tip**: Since this program can infinite clone, the rhythm patterns are set up to do that. In addition, after you complete the activity, you can reset the page by going to the Edit menu scrolling down to "Reset Page."
- **1:1 Devices**:
  - Though I would not advise doing this in a 1:1 classroom with PreK or K, you could try it with Grades 1 and 2. The easiest tool to use would be the Google slide file to share to their devices or to use the Chrome extension of Peardeck (found at https://chrome.google.com/webstore/detail/pear-deck/dnloadmamaeibnaadmfdfelflmmnbajd?hl=en), where your presentation shares directly to their devices.
  - **Website example**: To see how to share this Google Presentation with their 1:1 devices in multiple ways, go to the accompanying website, found at www.oup.com/us/utema.⏵
  - If your students use the digital learning journal of Seesaw (found at web.seesaw.me), this template can be found in the Seesaw Activities.

Higher Order Thinking Questions to Ask the Students:

- How do musicians create music?
- When is a creative work ready to share?

Extensions: Video the students performing their rhythm compositions and share it with their parents/caregivers using a music website, school website, social media, email, or a student digital portfolio like Seesaw (web.seesaw.me).

Recording and Assessing Students' Singing Voices Using "Mi" and "Sol"

Curriculum Note: *Assessing students' singing skills of high and low has great value. It assists the teacher in seeing how the class is comprehending the musical concepts being taught. It also helps the teacher to gauge each student's progress. A great resource for pre- and post-testing is Dr. Edwin E. Gordon's* The Primary Measures of Music Audiation (PMMA) *from GIA Publications. However, if this resource is not available, there are some beneficial tech resources that can work.*

Objective: To encourage and assess the students to practice sol and mi patterns.

Grade Levels: PreK–1

Materials: Any songs that you might be using to present high and low pitches, or specifically, sol and mi pitches. For this lesson, we will use "Lemonade," found at http://kodaly.hnu.edu/song.cfm?id=746. A device used to record singing voices such as a smartphone, iOS device, tablet, digital voice recorder, laptop, or desktop. This can be done with one device in a classroom or a 1:1 classroom.

Standards: Performing: MU:Pr4.2.PKa, MU:Pr4.2.Ka, MU:Pr4.2.1a, MU:Pr6.1.PKa, MU:Pr6.1.Ka, MU:Pr6.1.1a

Essential Understanding: Music has high and low sounds.

Procedures:

- As the students practice sol-mi pitch patterns through songs, movement, games, and dances, when the time is right, it is beneficial to assess their progress.
- Have the students practice the song "Lemonade" through singing and playing the game.
  - There are many variations to the game that is used for "Lemonade." You can check the resources listed under Materials or your resources from your Kodály certification.
  - One game that we have used in music class and physical education is the following:
    - Divide the classes into two groups. If it is a larger class, divide the class into more groups.
    - The students work together to decide a trade. If your students will need guidance in deciding a trade together, give them guidelines such as reducing the number of choices for the trade.
    - The students then work together to decide where they are from and the movements for the trade. Again, guide the students with choices if they have challenges working together.
    - Once ready, the group sings the solo together and the guessing group sings the group part together. The solo group then pantomimes their trade and the other group can give up to three guesses before the solo group reveals the answer. Then switch, so the other group gets to solo and pantomime.
    - When using games in this way, my shyest of singers will project their singing voices because a lot of times, they do not realize that they are singing. They feel that they are playing a fun game.
- Using one of the following devices, set up the device to record in the classroom:
- **Laptop/Desktop/Chromebook:**
  - Sit the students in assigned seating in a circle formation.
  - On the laptop, use the 123Apps online voice recorder found at https://online-voice-recorder.com/, and place it in the middle of the circle. For a desktop, depending on where it is located in the room, you can try this website and the internal microphone to see if it would pick up the voices.
    - **Tech tip**: I tend to use the laptop's built-in microphone as it will pick up the singing voices in the circle better. However, you can plug an external USB microphone into the laptop. When you launch the website, click on the settings button and scroll down to the external microphone listed. The site will usually default to the built-in microphone.
  - Press record. This free online voice recorder will begin recording using the built-in microphone found in the laptop (see previous tips about microphones).
  - You sing the solo part first and the class sings the group part. During the next solo part, have the student next to you sing the solo and the class again sings the group part. Continue around the circle until all students have sung the solo part.
  - **Activity tip**: I will begin the activity by stating all of the students' names in the order that they are sitting so that I can make it easier for me to assess later when I listen to the recording.
  - When the recording is finished, click the stop button (there is a stop button and a pause button). Then click the "Save" button.

- Your recording will now download to your hard drive. Label the name and revisit it later to assess the students. If you are using a Chromebook, it will save to the Google Drive that is currently logged in at that time.
- **Activity tip**: If not every student would sing a solo, then continue on and make a note that with the assessment rubric described in the following.
- **Tech tip**: At this current time, the website will record for a good length of time and is free to use.
- **Website example**: To see an example of this, go to the accompanying website, found at www.oup.com/us/utema.⊛
- **Chromebook (1:1 classroom)**:
  - You can utilize the website listed earlier (https://online-voice-recorder.com) and press record.
  - Allow the website to access the Chromebook's microphone.
  - Press record and have the students sing the song. When finished, click the stop button and then the "Save" button. It will save to the students' Google Drives.
  - **Tech tip**: Since the children are younger elementary, to do this in a 1:1 atmosphere on a Chromebook might not be ideal because they will need to share the file from their Google Drive to you. If your classroom is set up to do this and the young children can do this successfully, then it should work well. If the classroom is not set up this way, I would suggest doing this with one device.
- **iOS Device or Tablet**:
  - You can use the device's camera app to video record the students.
  - Sit the students in assigned seating in a circle formation.
  - If the students are uncomfortable with being video recorded, place the device in the middle of the circle so that the video app collects audio, and the video does not matter.
  - There are also other great apps that can audio record. Two that work well are GarageBand (iOS only) and Soundtrap.
    - GarageBand is a free iOS app found at https://www.apple.com/ios/garageband/. Once you launch the app, find and click on the "Audio Recorder" (microphone icon), and then press the "voice" button.
    - Click the + button on the far-right side of the screen.
    - Set the measures from "8 bars" to "Automatic" by moving the slider to the right and clicking "Back." This is so that the recording does not end until you press the stop button.
    - Click the blue metronome so that the metronome turns off, or it will play for the recording.
    - Sit the students in assigned seating in a circle formation and place the device in the middle of the circle.
    - Click the red record button and place the device in the middle of the circle.
      - **Tech tip**: GarageBand will use the built-in microphone unless you plug in an external microphone. I have used the built-in mic because it is able to pick up all of the children in the classroom when they sing the solo.
      - **Tech tip**: Do a sound check before you record with the class.
    - You sing the solo part first and the class sings the group part. During the next solo part, have the student next to you sing the solo and the class again sings

the group part. Continue around the circle until all students have sung the solo part.

- **Tech tip**: I will begin the activity by stating all of the students' names in the order that they are sitting so that it will be easier for me to assess later when I listen to the recording.
- When done, click the stop button.
- To view the file, click the "Tracks View" button.
- To save, click "My Songs." You can rename the file by clicking on the title (which usually defaults to "My Song. . . ."
- **To share the file**
  - If you want this file stored somewhere other than the iOS device you used to record it, click "See All."
  - Then click "Select."
  - Select the file.
  - If you click "Move," you can move it to cloud-based storage systems like Google Drive, iCloud, Dropbox, etc. Once you choose the storage device, click "Copy."
  - If you click "Share," you can send your song as an audio file, create a ring tone, or send the file as a GarageBand project, which will contain all of the multitrack recordings, if you used more than one track.
- **Website example**: To see an example of this, go to the accompanying website, found at www.oup.com/us/utema.⊚

- **Soundtrap** (https://www.soundtrap.com)
  - If you have a later iOS mobile device (currently iOS8 or later) or an Android mobile device, then Soundtrap will be an excellent and free tool to use.
    - Soundtrap is like the love child of Google Docs and GarageBand. It is a cloud-based online digital audio work station (DAW), where it saves your music-making so you can access it from multiple devices, invite people to collaborate, and revert back to previous revisions.
  - By setting up a free account at soundtrap.com, you, the music educator, can access your account through the mobile device.
  - Once the app is launched and you are logged in, you have two choices: Create a quick recording or setting up a new file to record.
  - **To create a quick recording** (this is for when you want to record the students quickly and have no need for additional tracks or loops):
    - In the main screen, click on "Make Music."
    - Click "Quick Record."
    - **Tech tip**: Do a test before you use this with the students.
    - Have the students sit in assigned spots in a circle formation.
    - Place the device in the middle of the circle.
    - Click "Start Recording."
    - You sing the solo part first and the class sings the group part. During the next solo part, have the student next to you sing the solo and the class again sings the group part. Continue around the circle until all students have sung the solo part.
    - **Activity tip**: I will begin the activity by stating all of the students' names in the order that they are sitting so that it will be easier for me to assess later when I listen to the recording.

- Click the stop button when finished and then click "Save".
- Closeout the screen and click the "Profile" icon. It will be saved as "Quick Recording".
- **To set up a new file to record instead of a quick recording** (I usually set up files over quick recordings so I can add to the file later on. Either way works well.):
  - Click on "Create New Project."
  - Click "Blank" template.
  - Click "Add New Track."
  - Click the microphone icon.
  - **Tech tip**: Soundtrap will default to the device's built-in microphone. You can add an external microphone. My experience has been that the built-in microphone picks up the students' singing voices when they are further away from the microphone.
  - **Tech tip**: Do a test before you use this with the students.
  - Have the students sit in assigned spots in a circle formation.
  - Place the device in the middle of the circle.
  - Click "Start Recording" and click on the answers to the questions of whether you are using headphones or not. Since you are assessing the voices in a large class, you are probably not using headphones.
  - You sing the solo part first and the class sings the group part. During the next solo part, have the student next to you sing the solo and the class again sings the group part. Continue around the circle until all students have sung the solo part.
  - **Activity tip**: I will begin the activity by stating all of the students' names in the order that they are sitting so that it will be easier for me to assess later when I listen to the recording.
  - Click the stop button to end the recording.
  - Click "Save" at the top of the screen.
  - Click the "Exit the Studio" icon.
  - In the main screen, rename your song by clicking on the file, then ". . . " and then "Change name."
  - In this screen, you can also share this file as a link or audio file when you click on the share icon.
  - Since Soundtrap can be accessed from most devices, you can easily listen to this file later to assess the singing voices.
- **Website example**: To see an example of this, go to the accompanying website found at www.oup.com/us/utema.⊙
- **Assessment Rubric**:
  - Feel free to use, adapt, or create your own assessment rubric that works well for your teaching atmosphere.
  - 4: Sings solo on pitch with no assistance from the teacher.
  - 3: Sings solo on pitch with the starting pitch given the teacher.
  - 2: Sings the sol mi pitches in a different, most likely, lower key.
  - 1: Speaks the solo or does not participate.

Higher Order Thinking Questions to Ask the Students:

- Which sound (pitch) is higher, sol or mi?
- Which sound (pitch) is lower, sol or mi?

- How do you make your voice sound high and low?
- *Some of these questions will be challenging for younger students to answer. However, it helps them to begin to experience the concept of high and low pitches.*

Extensions: Use this audio file and rubrics of assessments to help you assess their future progress.

Preparation of Three Pitches (Mi-Sol-La)

To prepare for the sequence with Mi-Sol-La pitches (in various combinations like msl, sml, etc.), students can listen to, move to, play games, and sing songs with the pitches mi-sol-la. Look at the Holy Names University's Kodály Center American Folk Song Collection found at http://kodaly.hnu.edu/collection.cfm for more ideas. Here are some songs with variations of the mi-sol-la tone set:

- We Are Dancing in the Forest
- Rain Rain
- Doggie Doggie
- Bounce High Bounce Low
- Acka Backa.

Presentation of Three Pitches (Mi-Sol-La)

To present the pitches mi, sol, and la, please look at how to create the presentation slides with mi and sol using Google Slides, PowerPoint, Keynote (MAC only), and Notebook (interactive whiteboard software) found earlier in this chapter. In addition, look at how to create lines in all of the apps listed earlier. Finally, use an image of a dog (for the song "Doggie Doggie," with mi, sol, and la pitches) to move around the staff lines. By performing a Google image search, clicking on "Tools," clicking on "Usage rights," and then scrolling down to "Labeled for reuse," you can commercially use an image of the penny for this lesson.

Practice Lessons for Mi-Sol-La Enhanced with Technology

- The lesson titled "Recording and Assessing Students' Singing Voices Using Mi and Sol" can be used for the pitches mi-sol-la.

Practicing "La" Using a Student Digital Learning Portfolio: For Assessing by the Teacher and for Having Their Parents Hear Them Sing a Solo in Their Music Class

Curriculum Note: *There are many student digital learning portfolios that teachers can use for free in their classrooms. The paid versions give many more options, but for this lesson, this can be done with the free versions. Currently, Seesaw (https://web.seesaw.me/), ClassDojo (https://www.classdojo.com/), Flipgrid (https://www.flipgrid.com), FreshGrade (freshgrade. com), Bloomz (https://www.bloomz.net/), and ClassTag (https://www.classtag.com/) are* *popular student digital learning portfolios. For this lesson, we will use Seesaw. As with any new technology, please get approval from your administration before you install and use the technology in your classroom.*

Objective: The students will draw and record the melodic direction of "Doggie Doggie."

Grade Levels: PreK–2

Materials: A printed version of "Doggie Doggie," which can be found in many sources such as http://kodaly.hnu.edu/song.cfm?id=694. I have also included one in the resources for this book, which is found at www.oup.com/us/utema. Seesaw, a student digital learning journal found at web.seesaw.me. This lesson can be used with one device in a classroom or in a 1:1 classroom.

Standards: Performing: MU:Pr4.2.PKa, MU:Pr4.2.Ka, MU:Pr4.2.1a, MU:Pr4.2.2a, MU:Pr6.1.PKa, MU:Pr6.1.Ka, MU:Pr6.1.1a, U:Pr6.1.2a

Essential Questions:

- How does the sound of a melodic direction correlate with the sight of the melodic direction?
- How does a student listening to her recording help her understand melodic direction?

Procedures:

- Review the song "Doggie Doggie" by singing and playing the game.
- Practice the melodic direction of the song.
- **One Device with Seesaw (PreK-2)** (For a more detailed look at Seesaw, please visit Appendix, "Links Listed Throughout the Book and Descriptions of Programs"):
  - Create a free account at web.seesaw.me
  - Create a class and add names to that class.
  - Pass out the printed versions of the song.
  - Ask the students to use their fingers to follow the melody as they sing.
  - In Seesaw, tap the post icon (currently a + sign) and click on the video camera.
  - Ask a child to sing and trace the song as you video record him or her in Seesaw.
  - When finished, click the stop button.
  - Click the check button to submit, then click on the student's name so that it appears on his or her journal. With Seesaw, the program defaults so that you must approve the posts before they will post.
  - **Activity tip**: If it is a large class, try this with a few students during one class. Then, do this again with another few students during the next class.
  - **Tech tip**: You can always hit the back button (usually an arrow or "x") to delete the recording and to start again.
  - **Tech tip**: Since you are doing this with your teacher account, once you submit it, the recording automatically appears on the child's journal.
  - **Tech tip**: Level up this activity and use Seesaw's premade email and printouts to invite parents to view their child's journal. When you or the child posts to their journals, their parents will receive a notification and can now see any post in which their child is tagged and the teacher has approved. They cannot see other children's posts unless they are tagged with their child.

- **1:1 Classroom**: Seesaw and many other student digital learning portfolios can work on multiple devices found in classrooms such as Chromebooks, iOS devices, tablets, laptops and more. This would work for Grades 1 and above.
  - Create a free account at web.seesaw.me
  - Create a class and add the students' names to that class.
  - Ask students to join the class via a QR code, text code, or their school email addresses. When they do this, they will click on their names and join the class.
  - Have the students click the posting icon, which is currently a +.
  - Have them click the camera icon and take a picture of the music.
  - Click the check button to approve the picture.
  - Then click the drawing tool to draw the melodic direction onto the picture of the music that they just took.
  - Click the check button to approve the picture with the drawing.
  - Click the record button or microphone and have the students record themselves singing the song. Sometimes it helps the students to trace the line that they drew while they sing and record the song.
  - When finished, click the check button to approve the recording.
  - Click the check button again to submit it to the teacher to approve.
  - **Tech tip**: It can get loud when the recordings all happen at once. Find places and corners in the room to record. In addition, have a box in which they can place their device and lean into (like a cardboard air conditioning box) to record. This will dampen the background sound and focus their sound. Finally, make sure that the students know where the internal microphone is located on their devices so that they can sing closely to it. If you have a more advanced microphone or a headset with a microphone attached, that would be more ideal.
  - **Tech tip**: You can always hit the back button (usually an arrow or "x") to delete the recording and to start again.
  - **Tech tip**: Since the students are submitting it to you, you have the final say on whether it appears in their journals. Nothing can appear without your approval. The settings in Seesaw default to this option, but you can turn it off.

Higher Order Thinking Questions to Ask the Students:

- What does your voice do when the line goes up?
- What does your voice do when the line goes down?
- How do you make your voice sing higher and lower?

Extensions: Use Seesaw's video tool to video the students singing the song with hand signs.

Creating a New Melody Using the Pitches Mi-Sol-La

Curriculum Note: *In this lesson, technology will be used to create a melody to the rhythm found in "Bounce High." This lesson can be done with traditional manipulatives. However, the files included in the lesson and the recording features help level up this lesson so that it can be shared with an audience and allows the student to reflect.*

Objective: The student will create a new melody using the pitches mi-sol-la.

Grade Levels: PreK–2; technology will be varied for the younger students versus the older students

Materials: Bounce High file in the format of Google Slides (https://docs.google.com/presentation/d/1lqTJnfbIE-rmDlwCetZHMeoXGDppV0EkTqjj0C0iK-k/copy), PowerPoint, Keynote, and Notebook found at the corresponding website for this book, www.oup.com/us/utema. You will need a device that can access the internet for Google Slides, or a device that has PowerPoint, Keynote, or Notebook installed. An interactive whiteboard is not required for this activity. This activity can be run from the device. The device should be connected to a screen so the students can see better. In addition, to record the students, use a device with recording capabilities like a smartphone, a tablet, or an online audio recording website like https://online-voice-recorder.com/ (Figure 4.5).

Standards: Creating Standards for PreK through Grade 2.

Essential Questions:

- How do musicians make creative decisions?
- How do musicians improve on their creative work?
- How do musicians know when to share their work?

Procedures:

- Review the song "Bounce High" by singing, playing the game, and/or movements.
- **Google Slides**:
  - Launch the Google Slides file https://docs.google.com/presentation/d/1lqTJnfbIE-rmDlwCetZHMeoXGDppV0EkTqjj0C0iK-k/copy
  - This will ask you to make a copy. This is good because if the file gets used many times, you can click the original link and make another copy that starts fresh.
  - Display the file onto the screen.
    - **Tech tip**: Do not go into presentation mode or the items will not drag, which is required for this activity.
  - Go to the second slide and show the students the basketballs.
  - Ask the students why the basketballs are high and low (to reinforce the pitches of the song).
  - Show how the "s" ball is sol, the "l" ball is la, and the "m" ball is mi.
  - Ask the students to help you create a new melody using mi-sol-la.
  - Ask a student to drag a black box to an orange box. Once four students have done this, a new melody is created.

Figure 4.5.
Bounce High, Bounce Low.

- **Tech tip**: Either drag the box for them or ask them to drag the box by the black lines as opposed to the basketballs.
- Have the students sing the new melody.
- Use a recording device such as a smartphone, or a tablet, or an online recording website like https://online-voice-recorder.com/ to record them singing their new song.
- After class, share the recording with the parents either through their digital learning portfolio like Seesaw (web.seesaw.me), or the school's website, or email the parents, or a music web page that you have created. If you cannot use the students' faces, record the audio, take a picture of the new melody, and place them together using iMovie, WeVideo (wevideo.com), or some other app that places audio and pictures together that you are comfortable using.
  - **Website example**: To see this done in iMovie, go to www.oup.com/us/utema to see a tutorial video of this.⊚
- Use the duplicate slides to have more students create new melodies and follow the steps listed in the preceding.
- **Tech tip**: Since the original file forces you to make a copy, click the file link to download a fresh copy of the file when you want to use it again with a new class.
- **PowerPoint**: Download the file "Bounce High.ppt" from www.oup.com/us/utema. Follow the directions for the Google Slides. The "tips" also apply, as you are to show the students how to drag the item from the black lines or drag it for them. In addition, do not put the file into presentation mode or the boxes will not drag, which is required for this activity.
- **Keynote**: Download the file "Bounce High.key" from www.oup.com/us/utema. Follow the directions for the Google Slides. The "tip" does not apply, as you can drag the boxes by the basketballs in Keynote. The "tip" to not put it in presentation mode does apply for this program.
- **Notebook**:
  - Download the file "Bounce High.notebook" from www.oup.com/us/utema.
  - Launch the file.
    - **Tech tip**: You can place this file in full-screen mode if you would like.
    - **Tech tip**: The boxes are "infinite cloned" so you can use one box more than once.
  - Ask the students to help you create a new melody using mi-sol-la.
  - Ask a student to drag a black box to an orange box. Once four students have done this, a new melody is created.
  - Have the students sing the new melody.
  - Follow the recording instructions for the Google Slides if you would like to share the melodies with an audience.
  - Use the duplicate slides to have more students create new melodies and follow the steps listed in the preceding.

Higher Order Thinking Questions to Ask the Students:

- Depending on the outcome of the melody, you can ask the students who helped in creating the melody, why did you want the melody to go higher? Lower?
- What did you like about the new melody?

- Did you wonder anything about the melody after you sang it? Like what it would be like if it always went higher or lower?
- What if you try to improve your melody?
- When did you know you were ready to share your melody?

Rhythm Sequence Extension: Identify the rhythm patterns in the song "Bounce High." Use one of the duplicated slides to create a rhythm composition with the rhythm patterns found in the song. For example, in one box, write two quarter note stems. In the next, write two pairs of eighth note stems. Use a line tool/scribble tool/drawing tool found in the program, or create this rhythm composition with traditional methods of popsicle sticks or paper and pencil.

Recording and Assessing an Improvisational Conversation using Mi-Sol-La

Curriculum Note: *In this lesson, you are asking the students a question using mi-sol-la, and they are improvising an answer using mi-sol-la in various melodic combinations. There are some recording suggestions for this lesson so that you can record and assess the pitch accuracy after the lesson.*

Objective: The students will improvise a short musical phrase using the pitches mi-sol-la.

Grade Levels: PreK–2 (if PreK is not ready for the three pitches, then just use one or two pitches.

Materials: For this lesson, we will use a variety of recording tools. These are just suggestions. Choose one, or use one you feel most comfortable using to record singing voice. For this lesson, https://online-voice-recorder.com/, a mobile device's voice recorder, Soundtrap (https://www.soundtrap.com), GarageBand (iOS/MAC only), iDoceo (iOS Only, https://www.idoceo.net) will be used. Only one device is needed for this lesson.

A microphone, such as the Blue Line of microphones (https://www.bluedesigns.com/), will help and enhance the sound quality of the recording but is not necessary for this activity.

Standards: Creating: MU:Cr1.1.PKA, Mu: Cr2.1.PKa, MU:Cr2.1.PKb, MU:Cr1.1.Ka, MU:Cr1.1.Kb, MU:Cr2.1.Ka, MU:Cr1.1.1a, MU:Cr1.1.1b, MU:Cr2.1.1a;
Performing: MU:Pr4.1.PKa, MU:Pr4.2.PKa, MU:Pr4.3.PKa, MU:Pr5.1.PKa, MU:Pr4.1.Ka, MU:Pr4.2.Ka, MU:Pr4.3.Ka, MU:Pr5.1.Ka, MU:Pr4.1.1a, MU:Pr4.2.1a, MU:Pr4.3.1a, MU:Pr5.1.1a

Essential Questions:

- How does understanding melodic sequences influence performance?
- How do performers interpret musical motives?
- How do musicians generate musical ideas?

Procedures:

- Before the class begins, I have the device ready to record and either placed near me or in the center of the circle.
- Welcome your students and have them sit in their assigned seats or in a circle in an assigned spot.
- Begin the class with your usual welcome routine.

- I then tell the students that we are playing a game. The game is that I sing the question to them using the pitches mi, sol, and la, and they sing the answer back to me using the pitches.
- I give them an example: "What's your favorite sport?" on s-s m-l s m, with the rhythm ti-ti ti-ti ta ta. I then give them an example of an answer and sing, "basketball and hockey" imitating the same melody.
- I give them the same question with the same melodic sequence and give them the same answer, but using a different combination of mi, sol, la in the answer. I ask them if the answer had the same melody and why it did not. I tell them that this is OK and to encourage it as long as they are using mi-sol-la. They might only respond with echoing the same melodic pattern. That is fine. I also try to encourage improvising as well.
  - **Activity tip**: When doing this activity as a practice for the pitch "la," the students will have challenges using it comfortably when improvising. Please keep encouraging them to use "la."
- I tell the students that the goal is to sing the answer, so if they do not like any sports, they can sing, "I don't like any sports." If they like every sport, you might ask them to limit it to two sports.
- Questions can vary from "What's your favorite sport?" to "What's your favorite candy?" When you ask them for their favorite, their minds shift away from having to sing a solo to letting everyone in the room know about their favorite things. I use one question per activity, as opposed to one question per child. This helps greatly.
- **Using https://online-voice-recorder.com/**
  - Launch https://online-voice-recorder.com/ on a device with internet access.
  - Click the record button.
  - Sing the question with the child's name in the question. For example, "Mikayla, what's your favorite sport?"
  - They sing the answer.
    - **Activity tip**: If the student will not sing, move on. The student is not ready to improvise at this time.
    - **Activity tip**: If you know that the student can sing and needs a little encouragement, encourage once. If the student does not sing, then move on. They are not ready.
    - **Activity tip**: If the student speaks the answer, remind them to use their singing voice and sing the question again. If they speak the answer again, move on and make a note in your assessment after class.
  - When done, click the "Save" button. The file is now downloaded to your hard drive (on a Chromebook, it will save to your Google Drive).
- **Using Your Mobile Device's Voice Recorder**:
  - Currently, if you are using an iOS device, there are native voice recording/memo apps such as Voice Recorder and Voice Memos.
  - Launch Voice Memos.
  - When ready, press record.
  - Sing the question with the child's name in the question. For example, "Mikayla, what's your favorite sport?"
  - The student sings the answer.

- See the "Activity Tips" listed in the preceding for students who will not sing or who need encouragement.
- When finished, click "Done." (If you click the pause button, you will have to click resume to continue recording or click "Done" to finish the recording.)
- The recording will automatically save with the file either named after the day and time of the recording, or the area where the recording is taking place, or both. It is now saved to the device.
- To share this recording to another app (app-smash), click on the file, click the share icon, and then click where you would like to share it (i.e., Seesaw, iDoceo, email, text message, add to notes, Google Drive, Dropbox, to name a few).
  - **Tech tip**: It is currently reported that the app can record up to 30 minutes pretty well.
  - **Tech tip**: You could use the device's video recorder as well.
  - **Tech tip**: Samsung Voice Recorder would be an equivalent app on an android device.
- **Using Soundtrap** (https://www.soundtrap.com):
  - Soundtrap is a free digital audio workstation (DAW) where you can make music online by recording, using loops, editing audio files, inviting others to collaborate, and more. You can create a free account for you to use as a teacher to do all of the preceding. If you have students using Soundtrap, look at the pricing for the educational (EDU) version, which you can use through Soundtrap or a music education platform like MusicFirst (https://www.musicfirst.com).
  - Since you are using this and not your students, create a free account and launch Soundtrap. You can launch it through a web browser or the app.
  - Click "Enter Studio" and then click "Blank" to set up a blank studio.
  - Click "Add New Track" and click on the microphone icon.
  - You can attach a more professional mic and change the mic input directly in Soundtrap on the same screen. However, using the laptop's internal microphone will work well for this activity.
  - Place the laptop in the middle of the circle.
  - When ready, press the red record button and answer the prompts for using headphones or not. I do not use headphones for this activity. Soundtrap will give you a few seconds before it begins recording.
  - Sing the question with the child's name in the question. For example, "Mikayla, what's your favorite sport?"
  - The student sings the answer.
  - See the "Activity Tips" listed earlier for students who will not sing or who need encouragement.
  - When finished, click the stop button.
  - Title the file at the top of the screen to something that you will recall later, like "Kindergarten Petrie October 2020." If you do not title it, Soundtrap will give it a default title.
  - Click the save button at the top of the screen.
  - To download the file, you can click the download icon at the top of this screen. To go back to the main screen that lists all of your audio files and projects, click the "Exit Studio" button or the Soundtrap icon.

- When you are in the main screen, you have more options than downloading, as you can share it to YouTube, SoundCloud, Facebook, Twitter, and more.
- **Tech tip**: When using the Soundtrap app on a mobile device, click "Make Music" and then click "Quick Record." Click the record button and you can make a quick recording from your mobile device that you can access from your account later.
- **Website example**: You will find examples of how to use Soundtrap on the accompanying website, found at www.oup.com/us/utema.◉

- **Using GarageBand (iOS only)**:
  - Launch the GarageBand app.
  - Depending on if you have used this before, you are looking for the "+" button.
  - In the "Tracks" tab, scroll to find the microphone icon ("Audio Recorder") and tap the microphone.
  - GarageBand defaults to recording only eight measures. To correct this, click the "+" button, click "8 bars", and turn on "Automatic." Click out of the box to remove that menu from the screen.
  - Click the blue metronome to turn it off.
  - Click the red record button when you are ready to record the students singing.
  - Sing the question with the child's name in the question. For example, "Mikayla, what's your favorite sport?"
  - The student sings the answer.
  - See the "Activity Tips" listed earlier for students who will not sing or who need encouragement.
  - When finished, click the stop button.
  - Click "My Songs," which brings you back to the screen with the saved files. You can retitle it here.
  - To share or export, from the main screen:
    - Click the "Browse" folder at the bottom of the screen. Click "Select," click the file you want to share, and click "Share."
    - I usually choose "Song" for this activity, as it is not a project with a lot of tracks.
    - Choose the quality. I have used its default of "High Quality" or "Uncompressed AIFF or WAV" if I would like a great-sounding file with no compression (meaning not an MP3-quality file).
    - Click "Share" and then choose where you want to share it, i.e., email, Seesaw, iDoceo, social media, etc.
    - **Website example**: You will find website examples of how to use Soundtrap on the accompanying website, found at www.oup.com/us/utema◉
- **Using iDoceo (iOS Only, https://www.idoceo.net)**:
  - iDoceo is a paid app that currently, you only pay once to own. It is an internal app, so no internet needed. This app is like a big digital gradebook where you can add unlimited students, create attendance charts, assessment charts, seating charts, import data, export data, input plans in its internal planner, and so much more.
  - Launch iDoceo and create a class. You can input a class, or attach an Excel file with a list of students to an email. Open the email on your iOS device. Click and hold the

Excel attachment until the "open with" screen appears. Open the file using iDoceo and it will automatically create your class.

- On the right side, label the tab assessments.
- Click on the + button to add a column. Label the column "mi-sol-la." I also add the date as well.
- Have the device in your lap as you begin to record.
- Click and hold on the cell next to the student's name that you are recording. A new menu appears. Click the microphone. Tap the red record button and sing your question.
- When the student sings the response, click the red stop button and then click the green check button. The recording is now saved in that child's cell.
- See the "Activity Tips" listed earlier for students who will not sing or who need encouragement.
- Continue to do this for each child.
  - **Tech tip**: Using iDoceo takes a little time to get used to and takes a little longer for this activity. However, once you begin using it to hold all of your assessments, data, charts, etc., you love how intuitive it is and how everything is organized in one place.
  - **Tech tip**: Go into the Seating Chart and record from there. If the column is selected, you can record a bit faster this way.
  - **Tech tip**: You will not need to share or export the recordings because they are all in this one place for you to access and easily assess.
- **Assessment**:
  - Once finished, you will want to revisit the recordings to assess them.
  - Your assessments should be based on your school's or state's standards. Here is a basic rubric to get you started:
    - 6: Student answered question creating his or her own melody with the pitches mi-sol-la.
    - 5: Student answered question creating his or her own melody using two out of the three pitches.
    - 4: Student answered question singing back the same melody as the question.
    - 3: Student answered question creating his or her own melody using one pitch.
    - 2: Student spoke the answer.
    - 1: Student did not respond or participate.

Higher Order Thinking Questions to Ask the Students:

- Did you realize that you can create a song about anything? What else could we sing about?
- When you sang your answer, did your melody end up or down? What would happen if you did the opposite?

Extensions: This can be done with every melodic sequence. When you use this with older elementary, and they have their own devices, have them use their devices to record themselves singing the answer to share with you.

If you used Soundtrap or GarageBand to record, add some loops at the beginning and the end and turn this assessment into a podcast to share (if all students participated and wanted to share this activity).

Extensions:

- With the younger students, use a drawing and recording tool like Seesaw (web.seesaw.me), ShowMe (showme.com), or Explain Everything (explaineverything.com) to have the students draw and sing a melody. If they do not have the pitches yet, have them record a pitch exploration that varies from high to low and low to high (begin with high first).
- With the older students, have them create and record a new melody using the pitches mi-sol-la by writing the words or letters.
- Share these recordings with parents and/or use them as assessments.

Rhythm Sequence Extension: Sing the question, have the students clap the rhythm of the words, and have them decode the rhythm.

Preparation of Four Pitches (Mi-Sol-La-Do)

To prepare for the sequence with mi-sol-la-do pitches (in various combinations like msld, mlsd, etc.), students can listen to, move to, play games, and sing songs with the pitches mi-sol-la-do. Look at the Holy Names University's Kodály Center American Folk Song Collection found at http://kodaly.hnu.edu/collection.cfm for more ideas. Here are some songs with variations of the mi-sol-la-do tone set:

- I See the Moon
- Ickle Ockle
- My Owlet
- Ring Around the Rosey.

Presentation of Four Pitches (Mi-Sol-La-Do)

To present the pitches mi, sol, la, and do, please look at how to create the presentation slides with mi and sol using Google Slides, PowerPoint, Keynote (MAC only), and Notebook (interactive whiteboard software) found at the beginning of this chapter.

Practice Lessons for Mi-Sol-La-Do Enhanced with Technology

All practice lessons from the previous melodic sequences can be used for this sequence as well. You will need to adjust some of the manipulatives to accommodate more pitches.

Using the Flashnote Derby App to Practice Naming Do, Mi, Sol, and La on the Staff

Curriculum Note: *This lesson has the students practicing naming the pitches do, mi, sol, and la on the treble clef staff using the Flashnote Derby app. With this particular app, you can set it up in any key, but "do" is always middle C. This lesson can be done with one device in a classroom or in a classroom with 1:1 devices. For 1:1 devices, this is a paid app that can be played on iOS devices, Android, Chromebooks that have access to Google Play apps, and Kindle Fire Tablets. Many of these apps have volume purchasing programs and it might be worthwhile to check with* *your tech department or administration to see if they have a budget to purchase software/apps/ tech. This app cannot currently be played on a laptop or desktop.*

Objective: The students will name the notes do, mi, sol, and la on the staff using solfege and the Flashnote Derby app.

Grade Levels: Grades 1 and above

Materials: This lesson uses the Flashnote Derby app. This is a paid app available for iOS devices (https://itunes.apple.com/us/app/flashnote-derby-musical-note/ id453126527?mt=8&at=11l4BL), devices that support Google Play/Android (https:// play.google.com/store/apps/details?id=com.lukedbartolomeo.flashnotederby), and Kindle Fire Tablets (http://www.amazon.com/Flashnote-Derby-learn-music-notes/dp/ B00BF4EL1E). If you have Chromebooks and your Chromebooks have access to Google Play, then you have the school purchase the app for the Chromebooks. For more information about Flashnote Derby and to view their video lessons, you can visit their website here: https://flashnotederby.com/.

Standards: Performing: MU:Pr4.2.1b, MU:Pr4.2.2b, MU:Pr4.2.3b, MU:Pr4.2.4b, MU:Pr4.2.5b

Essential Questions:

- What do leaps and skips mean in relation to pitch on a staff?
- How does the way a pitch looks on the staff relate to the sound that is played? For example, if a pitch is high on the staff, is its sound high or low?

Procedures:

- **One Device in a Classroom**:
  - Before class, purchase, install, and launch Flashnote Derby on your iOS device, Android, Chromebook with access to Google Play, or Kindle Fire Tablet. You might need to go through the tutorial first, so leave some time to do so.
  - If you can, project your device onto the screen. This will make it easier for your entire class to see Flashnote Derby.
    - If your school has a device set up so that you can airplay your laptop/desktop to a screen, that will work well. If not, a program such as Reflector (found for a fee at https://www.airsquirrels.com/reflector) will mirror most devices onto the screen.
    - In addition, you can use a VGA/HDMI adapter to connect your device to the projector/TV Screen/etc. Perform a Google search to determine which adapter your device will need.
  - Click the settings and set them to the following:
    - How Many Questions: 10
    - Race Speed: Walk
    - Answer Method: Choose>Letter Buttons. On the bottom of the list, also choose "Do, Re, Mi. . . ." Tap the back button.
    - Theme: Currently, there are four themes of "Fresh Air," "Pretty Pegasus," "Ecliptic Encounter," and "Reindeer Race." "Fresh Air" is the original theme with the two derby racers. "Pretty Pegasus" is a Pegasus theme with two of them racing. "Ecliptic Encounter" is two spaceships that try to blow each other up. "Reindeer Race" is another original theme with reindeer racing. Choose the theme that would work well for your class and grade level.

- Clefs to Use: Treble (you can choose from all clefs).
- Accidentals and Key Signatures: This shows the circle of fifths with a fixed do on middle C. Use middle C fixed do for this lesson. However, feel free to move it to another key if you would like. Tap the back button.
- The other items will not be needed but are helpful for teachers or if you want to use a grand staff (iPads only).
- Tap back into the main screen and choose the notes middle C (do), E (mi), G (sol), and A (la).
- Click the icon on the bottom left-hand side of the screen. The icon changes depending on the theme. Click this icon when the class is present and you are ready to begin the activity.
- Review the pitches do, mi, sol, and la with the students through song and activities (Figure 4.6).
- There are a few ways to perform this activity with an entire class.
  - Tell the students that they will be playing a game together as a class. When they recognize the pitch, call it out. The pitch called out the most is the pitch that you will tap.
  - Line the students up and have each student identify the pitch that appears on the screen. If you have a class of 29, go back in the settings and change the number of questions.
  - Divide the class into smaller groups. Each group takes turns naming pitches.
  - Set this game up at a station and use it as one of the stations in a rotation. The students using it at the station must write down their score at the end of the game.
  - Perform the activity and make a note to how many questions they answer correctly. For a game with 10 questions, they need to answer at least seven correctly for them to win the game.
- **1:1 Devices**:
  - If you have a class with 1:1 devices, and the school has purchased the app, then they can play it on their devices.
  - To set up the game, there are two ways:

Figure 4.6.
Flashnote Derby.

- The students can launch the app and go into the settings to set it up to the way that you would like.
- On the main screen of your device, set up the activity then click the settings and go to "Teacher Login." Here, you can set up yourself as the teacher and provide your school email address. This will allow you to assign the activity to the students.
  - Once you are logged in, you click on the icon at the top of the screen that looks like a flag.
  - Click + and name the activity "dmsl."
  - Once it appears on the screen, click the email icon next to it. You can then add the students' email addresses and have them open the activity from their email.
  - **Tech tip**: Test this by sending it to yourself first. In my teaching situation, I cannot send an email from the app to a student.
- Perform the activity and have them write down their scores each time.
- **Activity tip**: 1:1 can work well if you can monitor the students and their devices. If that is not the case, then I would suggest using this activity with one device projected onto the screen.

Higher Order Thinking Questions to Ask the Students:

- Where did you find leaps in the pitches do, mi, sol, and la?
- Where did you find steps in the pitches do, mi, sol, and la?
- What are the differences between steps and leaps?

Extensions: Use this activity as a pre- and post-test to assess the skills of your class.

"Sol-Mi" Poison Game for Practicing Singing the Melodic Sequence of "Sol-Do"

Curriculum Note: *This game isolates the melodic sequence of sol-do. This game can be found at the supplemental website for this book: www.oup.com/us/utema. Use the game to adapt it to any melodic sequence. Though it is named the "Sol-Mi Poison Game," the pitch sequence sol-mi is the poison melodic sequence, which means that they do not sing it. The melodic sequence of sol-do appears often in the game to help the students to practice that sequence numerous times in a fun activity.*

Objective: The students will practice the melodic sequence of sol-do with this fun "Poison" game/activity.

Grade Levels: Grade 1 and up

Materials: A song that has the sol-do combination in it, like the traditional folk song, "Sweetly Sings the Donkey" (the notated melody is found on the supplemental website to this book: www.oup.com/us/utema). The Sol-Mi Poison Game for Google Slides (https://docs.google.com/presentation/d/13SyeQ-hjWq9lBkz1oe18kNqxhrBrFNqEeNylPAXi8Ts/copy), PowerPoint, Keynote, Notebook (for the Interactive SMART Board), and a pdf version. All of these can be found at the supplemental website for this book: www.oup.com/us/utema. This lesson requires one device connected to a projector/TV screen so that the students can see the activity projected onto a big screen (Figure 4.7).

Figure 4.7.
Sol-Mi Poison Game.

Standards: Performing: MU:Pr4.2.1a, MU:Pr4.2.1b, MU:Pr4.2.2a, MU:Pr4.2.2b, MU:Pr4.2.3a, MU:Pr4.2.3b, MU:Pr4.2.4a, MU:Pr4.2.4b, MU:Pr4.2.5a, MU:Pr4.2.5b

Essential Questions:

- Why does the combination of sol-do feel like a musical answer more than a musical question?

Procedures:

- Review the traditional folk song "Sweetly Sings the Donkey," with the students using the hand signals on the phrase, "Hee haw! Hee haw! Hee haw! Hee haw! Hee haw!"
- Ask the students about how far their hand signals have to be to go from sol to do.
- Ask the students: When they sing that phrase, does it sound like a musical question or a musical answer? (It should sound like an answer as the song ends on do and do is the tonic.)
- Review other combinations of melodic sequences such as m-s, s-m, m-s-s, s-m-m, m-s-l, s-l-m, m-m, s-s, s-l, l-s-m, m-l-s, and s-d.
- Out of all of those sequences (or use three sequences, with one being s-d), ask the students which sequence sounds like a musical answer. (The s-d sequence should sound like the one that is the musical answer.)
- Tell the students that we will be playing a game called "Poison." This game will have all of those musical sequences in it. The poison sequence today is s-m. If s-m appears on the screen, they are not to sing it. If they do, they must sit down. Play the game until the end of the file or until one student is standing. I did not make sol-do the poison sequence because we are purposely practicing singing that interval.
  - **Tech tip**: If you want to make the file longer, copy and paste more slides into the file.
  - **Tech tip**: If you want to change the poison sequence to a different interval, then copy the original file. Open the new file and change the poison emoji and the red background to the slide with the poison interval of your choice.
  - **Tech tip**: When in Google Slides, Keynote, or PowerPoint, use presenter mode and use the computer keyboard to progress through the slides, or tap the board if the board is interactive. When using the Notebook file, place it in full-screen and use the computer to progress or use the controls that come with the Notebook software.
- **Google Slide/PowerPoint/Keynote/Notebook/PDF Files**: Go to www.oup.com/us/utema to access a copy of Sol-Mi Poison Game for all of the versions listed.⊚

Higher Order Thinking Questions to Ask the Students:

- When you sing sol-mi and then you sing sol-do, why does sol-do sound like an answer to a question?
- If sol-do sounds like an answer and sol-mi sounds like a question, what does sol-la or la-sol sound like? A question or answer? *The answers can vary. These questions help the students to think about musical phrases and their purpose when singing melodies.*

Extensions: Edit the file to mix around the slides so that they can play again. In addition, create another copy of the file (File>Save As) and cut and paste the sad emojis from the sol-mi slide to a different slide. Make that slide the new poison interval/sequence.

Preparation of Five Pitches (Mi-Sol-La-Do-Re)

To prepare for the sequence with mi-sol-la-do-re pitches (in various combinations like mlsrd, drmsl, etc), students can listen to, move to, play games, and sing songs with the pitches mi-sol-la-do-re. Look at the Holy Names University's Kodály Center American Folk Song Collection found at http://kodaly.hnu.edu/collection.cfm for more ideas. Here are some songs with variations of the mi-sol-la-do-re tone set:

- Billy, Billy (Billy, Bolly)
- Bow Wow Wow
- Great Big House in New Orleans
- Sally Goes Round the Sun
- Star Light, Star Bright.

Presentation of Five Pitches (Mi-Sol-La-Do-Re)

To present the pitches mi, sol, la, do, and re, please look at how to create the presentation slides with mi and sol using Google Slides, PowerPoint, Keynote (MAC only), and Notebook (interactive whiteboard software) found at the beginning of this chapter.

Practice Lessons for Mi-Sol-La-Do-Re Enhanced with Technology

Creating an ebook to Teach the Movements to "Bow Wow Wow"

Curriculum Note: *This is one of my students' favorite songs and games. The game I use is adapted from the original. I teach the game this way so the students can feel the rest. Please feel free to use this version or any other version you know for this game.*

Objective: The students will review the song and create an ebook of how to play the game so that other classes can use the ebook to learn the game and song.

Grade Levels: Grades 1–4

Materials: The song "Bow Wow Wow" (you can find the song at http://kodaly.hnu.edu/collection.cfm) or at the supplemental website www.oup.com/us/utema and the app Book Creator, which can be used on iOS devices (https://itunes.apple.com/us/app/book-creator-for-ipad/id442378070?mt=8) or as a web-based program found at https://bookcreator.com. This lesson can be done in a classroom with one device projected onto a screen or in a class with 1:1 devices. If you are using the Book Creator iOS app, your device does not need internet access. If you are using the web-based app, your device does need internet access.

Standards: Creating: MU:Cr3.2.1a, MU:Cr3.2.2a, MU:Cr3.2.3a, MU:Cr3.2.4a, **Performing**: MU:Pr6.1.1a, MU:Pr6.1.1b, MU:Pr6.1.2a, MU:Pr6.1.2b, MU:Pr6.1.3a, MU:Pr6.1.3b, MU:Pr6.1.4a, MU:Pr6.1.4b

Essential Questions:

- When is creative work ready to share?
- How does the audience influence the content of the creative work?

Procedures:

- Before class, create a Book Creator account at https://bookcreator.com or download the iOS version of the app at https://itunes.apple.com/us/app/book-creator-for-ipad/id442378070?mt=8.
  - The price for the web-based app ranges from free and up. The free version gives you one library with 40 books to use in your classroom.
  - The free iOS app gives you one book to create. The paid iOS app, currently priced at $4.99, gives you unlimited books to create.

One Device in the Classroom
- Review the song "Bow Wow Wow" on solfege and lyrics. Sing and use hand signals to show the melodic direction and to review the new pitch, re.
- Review the game.
- Assign students partners and then create a circle.
- Students face their partners.
- "Bow wow wow!" Students clap their partners' hands together.
- "Whose dog art thou?" Students wag their right fingers at each other.
- "Little Tommy Tucker's dog." Students hold hands and perform a half turn so that they switch places.
- "Bow wow wow (rest)!" Students clap their partner's hands together and then jump and turn on the rest. When they jump and turn, they will turn 180 degrees and face a new partner.
- Perform this game slowly so that they can learn the game successfully. Then, increase the tempo.
- Launch Book Creator on a device connected to a screen so that the students can see the app.
  - Explain to the students that they need to create an ebook together that will be used to teach the song and game to the other classes.
  - Begin with a Brainstorm or Circle Thinking Map (see Figure 4.8). Have the students brainstorm ideas about what to include in the book. The will vary from pictures or stick figures of each phrase of the game to a recording of them singing the song. Remind the students of the goal: to create an ebook so that the other classes can learn the game.
  - Using the web-based app (the iOS app is very similar), click the "+ New Book" and select the format of portrait, square, or landscape. I tend to default to square mode. Since this is a tutorial ebook, I do not offer the comic book option.

127

Figure 4.8.

Example of thinking map for "Bow Wow Wow."

- The first page is the cover. Click the + tool and scroll down to "Text." Add the title of the ebook. In this example, we call the ebook, *How to Perform Bow Wow Wow!* and click "Done."
- With the title highlighted (it has a blue outlines box around it), click the *i* tool to change the font, color, size, background, and order of the text. Click out of the tool when you are finished.
  - **Activity tip**: When asking the students to help you choose a font, color, size, etc., give them two or three choices and take the consensus. Or, ask a group of students to choose a font and another group to choose a text color.
- To change the color of the cover, make sure the text box is not highlighted. Then click the *i* tool and you will see the options for changing the color of the cover.
- Once finished with the cover, click the ">" and you will now see page two.
- Use the students' thinking map of their ideas to decide what will go on this page. Here is one idea that you can use:
  - Page two: Add a picture and recording of the song.
    - To add a picture of the song within the app:
      - Click the + tool and scroll down to "Camera."
      - Allow the device to access your camera if you have not already done so.
      - Hold up a copy of the song and take a picture.
      - Click "Use Picture" or "Delete" and take another picture until you have one you can use.
      - The picture now appears on page two. When you click on it, you can resize it or turn it to appear on an angle.
    - To add a picture by performing a Google search, accessing a file from your hard drive, accessing a file from your Google Drive, or embedding a picture with an embed code, click the + tool and scroll down to import. Find the picture file and add it to the page.
  - Page two: Add a recording.
    - With the picture now on page two, let's add the recording.
    - Click the + tool and scroll down to the microphone icon.

- Click "Start Recording." You might need to allow the app to access your device's microphone the first time you do this.
- The app will give you three seconds before the microphone begins recording. Record the students singing and then either accept the recording or delete and try again.
- Once accepted, a sound icon will appear on the screen.
- **Tech tip**: My students like to add a text box that reads, "Turn your volume up and tap here →" to remind the reader to click on the sound icon.
- Pages three through six: Add pictures of the game.
  - Use the camera tool or upload pictures of your students performing the games.
  - Use the text tool to add the lyrics. Use a separate text box to add the directions of the dance in italics and smaller font from the lyrics.
  - Each page has a phrase.
  - **Tech and activity tip**: If you cannot use pictures of the students, use the drawing tool to add stick figures. To find the drawing tool, go to + and scroll down to the pen icon.
- Once finished, share the book with other classes by displaying it from the app directly, or sharing it by exporting it as a video (iOS version—this keeps all sound intact) or publishing it online at bookcreator.com, which will give you a private link so that you can share with others (see Figure 4.9).
- **Website example**: You can see a website example of the ebook on the accompanying website found at www.oup.com/us/utema⊙

Higher Order Thinking Questions to Ask the Students:

- What did you like about the ebook?
- What did you wonder about the book that could be improved?
- What if we tried that during our next class?

Extensions: Take some of the suggestions from the higher order thinking questions and add them to the ebook. In addition, use the camera tool in Book Creator that you used to take the pictures, but use it to take a video. Have the students perform the dance and add the video to the last page of the ebook.

Rhythmic Sequence Extension: Using the drawing tool in Book Creator, have the students draw the rhythm pattern to the words listed on the page.

Figure 4.9.
Example of an ebook created with Book Creator.

Creating a Melody with DoReMi 123 (Singing Simon Game)

Curriculum Note: *The free version of the app DoReMi 123 can be found at the iOS app store (https://itunes.apple.com/us/app/doremi-1-2-3-music-for-kids/id479692413?mt=8) and on Google Play (https://play.google.com/store/apps/details?id=com.creativity.doremi.lite&hl=en_US). There are also paid versions with in-app purchases that can be found for both systems.*

Objective: The students will create a melody using the pitches do, re, mi, sol, and la for the rest of the class to sing while performing the game Singing Simon.

Grade Levels: Grades 1–4

Materials: One device connected to a screen. I would suggest using an adapter so that when the students tap a pitch, the app responds quickly. You can mirror your device's screen through Airplay/Chromecast/etc., but there might be a delay when the student taps a pitch and when the app plays the sound. You will need the free version of the app DoReMi 123 for iOS or Google Play. Google Play versions of the app can play on Android devices, as well as Chromebooks.

Standards: Creating: MU:Cr1.1.1a, MU:Cr1.1.2a, MU:Cr1.1.3a, MU:Cr1.1.4a, **Performing**: MU:Pr4.2.1a, MU:Pr4.2.1b, MU:Pr4.2.2a, MU:Pr4.2.2b, MU:Pr4.2.3a, MU:Pr4.2.3b, MU:Pr4.2.4a, MU:Pr4.2.4b

Essential Questions:

- How does the understanding of musical concepts shape how a melody is improvised by a performer?
- How do musicians generate musical ideas?

Procedures:

- Before class, launch the app DoReMi 123.
  - Press play.
  - **Tech tip**: If you are using the Google Play version on the Chromebook, it will tell you that the page is missing. Press the back arrow and click on guest user. It will then continue as listed in the following.
  - Press the rainbow button.
  - Press Rockin' River (the one with the dragon).
  - Press the panda bear to make music.
  - In the upper right-hand corner, change the pointer so it points at the eighth notes.
  - The pandas will now sing in their head voices using solfege.
- Greet the students and review songs that include the pitches do, re, mi, sol, and la using solfege.
- Introduce the game Singing Simon.
- Singing Simon is based on the electronic game Simon. In this game, Simon had four colors: red, green, blue, and yellow. The game would begin with Simon flashing one color that coordinated with a pitch. The player would play that pitch. If the player performs the correct pitch, Simon then added another pitch. The player would then have to copy the two pitches in the correct order. If the player was correct, Simon continued adding a pitch to the sequence. This happened until the player messed up the sequence.
- Assign a student to come up to the device. The student can be Simon, and begin with one pitch. The pitches that the student can use are do, re, mi, sol, and la. The student is encouraged to repeat pitches.

- The student begins with one pitch, "sol." The class echoes "sol."
- The student then adds a pitch to make a pattern of two pitches, "sol mi." The class echoes, "sol mi." The student continues to add one pitch to the sequence.
- Getting out in Singing Simon: You can vary this to what works best for your class.
  - Since the class is singing the echo together, the teacher should be the referee and determine when the class has not followed the pattern accurately. If most of the students are singing the pattern correctly, with a couple of students singing wrong pitch names, then the teacher can give a warning and continue the game.
  - If the majority of the class is singing the wrong pitches, whether the names of the pitches or the intervals, then the class is out. Have the leader go one more time until the class or leader gets out. If the class gets out again, assign a new leader so other students get a turn to be the leader.
  - If the leader messes up their own pattern, meaning they were using "sol mi mi do," and then did "sol mi la do," then the leader is out and chooses another leader.
  - If the leader uses the pitches "fa," "ti," and/or "do," the leader is out and must choose another leader. However, use the opportunity to showcase these new pitches.

Higher Order Thinking Questions to Ask the Students:

- How do the musical ideas from the game turn into melodies?
- Was it easier to echo the pattern back when a leader played the patterns with a steady beat? Why or why not?

Extensions: Use a staff on a felt board with music notes (or create a staff in a program like Google Slides, PowerPoint, Keynote, Notebook) and have the students drag the same pitches to the staff to create a melody that they can sing and record themselves to share with others.

Preparation of Six Pitches (Mi-Sol-La-Do-Re-Do')

To prepare for the sequence with mi-sol-la-do-re-do' pitches (in various combinations like d'mlsrd, drmsld', etc.), students can listen to, move to, play games, and sing songs with the pitches mi-sol-la-do-re-do'. Look at the Holy Names University's Kodály Center American Folk Song Collection found at http://kodaly.hnu.edu/collection.cfm for more ideas. Here are some songs with variations of the mi-sol-la-do-re-do' tone set:

- Brick Yard
- Liza Jane or Lil' Liza Jane
- Shady Grove
- Steal Liza Jane
- Do Let Me Out.

Presentation of Six Pitches (Mi-Sol-La-Do-Re-Do')

To present the pitches mi, sol, la, do, re, and do' please look at how to create the presentation slides with mi and sol using Google Slides, PowerPoint, Keynote (MAC only), and Notebook (interactive whiteboard software) found at the beginning of this chapter.

Practice Lessons for Mi-Sol-La-Do-Re-Do' Enhanced with Technology

Using Flashnote Derby to Practice Naming Do, Re, Mi, Sol, La, Do' on the Staff

Follow the directions to the lesson, "Using Flashnote Derby to Practice Naming Do, Mi, Sol, and La on the Staff" found earlier in this chapter and add the pitches re and do' in the app.

Preparation of Seven Pitches (Mi-Sol-La-Do-Re-Do'-Low La)

To prepare for the sequence with mi-sol-la-do-re-do'-low la pitches (in various combinations like d'mlsrd low l, low l drmsld', etc.), students can listen to, move to, play games, and sing songs with the pitches mi-sol-la-do-re-do'-low la. Look at the Holy Names University's Kodály Center American Folk Song Collection found at http://kodaly.hnu.edu/collection.cfm for more ideas. Here are some songs with variations of the mi-sol-la-do-re-do'-low la tone set:

- Circle Round the Zero
- The Colorado Trail
- Fare Thee Well, Oh Honey.

Presentation of Seven Pitches (Mi-Sol-La-Do-Re-Do'-Low La)

To present the pitches mi, sol, la, do, re, do', and low la, please look at how to create the presentation slides with mi and sol using Google Slides, PowerPoint, Keynote (MAC only), and Notebook (interactive whiteboard software) found at the beginning of this chapter.

Practice Lessons for Mi-Sol-La-Do-Re-Do'-Low La Enhanced with Technology

Creating an ebook of Dance Videos

Curriculum Note: *One school year, I decided to create an ebook of dance videos so that I could share it with other students in future years to show them how the dance is performed. In addition, I could share it with their parents to show them the importance of dance in the classroom. These factors include learning about various cultures to social emotional learning (SEL).*

Objective: The students will create an ebook of dance videos throughout their school year to share with an audience.

Grade Levels: Grade 2 and up

Materials: For this lesson, we will use the song "Circle Round the Zero" (which can be found at http://kodaly.hnu.edu) and the iOS and web-based app, Book Creator (https://www.bookcreator.com). Book Creator has free versions where you can create one ebook in the iOS app or 40 ebooks with one library in the web-based app. The paid versions give you more ebooks and libraries, as well as real-time collaboration with the web-based version.

Standards: Responding Standards Grade 2 and up: MU:Re7.1.2a to MU:Re8.1.2a

Essential Questions:

- Why is learning dance important?
- What life skills can be learned through dance?

Procedures: *As with any activity in which you will film the students' faces, please make sure you have permission from the school to do so.*

- Review the song "Circle Round Zero."
- Teach the dance:
  - Stand in a circle formation.
  - One student is the leader.
  - The students in the circle clap the beat and sing the song.
  - The leader walks around the circle.
  - On the words "Back, back zero," the leader chooses a student and stands back-to-back with them.
  - On the words, "Side, side zero," the leader stands to the side of the student.
  - On the words, "Front, front zero," the leader stands in front of the student.
  - On the words, "Tap your lovin' zero," the leader taps the student on the shoulder and the student follows the leader, so that now there are two leaders.
  - Continue until everyone is a leader and they are all circling and finding someone to back, side, front, and tap.
  - When someone cannot find a partner at the end of the dance, have the student go to the middle of the room and raise her hand. These students are to partner with others who have their hands up.
- Creating an ebook of dances:
  - Launch the Book Creator app.
  - Create a new ebook in landscape mode.
  - Click the + tool at the top of the screen. Scroll down to the text tool.
  - Add the title to the ebook.
  - Click the > or + button on the side of the screen to advance to the next page.
  - Click the + button at the top of the screen and scroll down to the camera icon.
  - Let the app access the device's camera and film the dance.
  - Approve the video or record it again.
  - Once finished, click the + tool and scroll down to the text tool and write a caption to the dance.
- Throughout the school year, continue to add dances to this ebook to share at the end of the school year.
- Once completed, the ebook created in Book Creator can be shared by publishing it to the web and sharing the private link (iOS and web-based app) or by exporting it as a video (iOS).

Higher Order Thinking Questions to Ask the Students:

- What SEL skills can you learn from dancing together?
- How is dancing together a lot like performing as a band or orchestra?

Extensions: Instead of the teacher writing the captions of the dance, have the students write the captions to the dance and include them in the ebook.

Creating a Melody in Minor Mode within 6/8 Meter

Curriculum Note: *When introducing the pitch low la, it is great to reinforce minor mode. In this lesson, technology is used to reinforce the pitch low la through composition. This lesson uses the web-based composition program, Noteflight (https://www.noteflight.com). Noteflight is free to use with limitations of creating 10 scores. To have the students use it in a classroom of a few devices or a 1:1 classroom, I would highly suggest purchasing a subscription for Noteflight for each student either through Noteflight's website or through a learning management music system like Music First (https://www.musicfirst.com).*

Objective: The students will compose a four-measure melody starting and ending on the pitch low la.

Grade Levels: Grades 2–5

Materials: This lesson can be done with one device in a classroom projected onto a screen, TV, or interactive whiteboard, or in a classroom with 1:1 devices. If the classroom has one device, then set up a free account to Noteflight (https://www.noteflight.com) for the class to work on together. For a 1:1 classroom, create a music classroom website in Noteflight Learn and give the students the website/login/password and give them the guidelines to compose their melody. A song based in low la, like "Skin and Bones," can be found on the supplemental website to this book: www.oup.com/us/utema.⊚

Standards: Performing: MU:Pr4.2.2a, MU:Pr4.2.2b, MU:Pr4.3.2a, MU:Pr5.1.2a, MU:Pr5.1.2b, MU:Pr6.1.2a, MU:Pr6.1.2b, MU:Pr4.2.3a, MU:Pr4.2.3b, MU:Pr4.3.3a, MU:Pr5.1.3a, MU:Pr5.1.3b, MU:Pr6.1.3a, MU:Pr6.1.3b, MU:Pr4.2.4a, MU:Pr4.2.4b, MU:Pr4.3.4a, MU:Pr5.1.4a, MU:Pr5.1.4b, MU:Pr6.1.4a, MU:Pr6.1.4b, MU:Pr4.2.5a, MU:Pr4.2.5b, MU:Pr4.3.5a, MU:Pr5.1.5a, MU:Pr5.1.5b, MU:Pr6.1.5a, MU:Pr6.1.5b

Creating: MU:Cr1.1.2a, MU:Cr1.1.2b, MU:Cr2.1.2a, MU:Cr2.1.2b, MU:Cr3.1.2a, MU:Cr3.2.2a, MU:Cr1.1.3a, MU:Cr1.1.3b, MU:Cr2.1.3a, MU:Cr2.1.3b, MU:Cr3.1.3a, MU:Cr3.2.3a, MU:Cr1.1.4a, MU:Cr1.1.4b, MU:Cr2.1.4a, MU:Cr2.1.4b, MU:Cr3.1.4a, MU:Cr3.2.4a, MU:Cr1.1.5a, MU:Cr1.1.5b, MU:Cr2.1.5a, MU:Cr2.1.5b, MU:Cr3.1.5a, MU:Cr3.2.5a

Essential Questions:

- How do musicians generate creative ideas?
- How do musicians make creative decisions?
- How do musicians improve the quality of their creative work?
- When is a creative work ready to share?

Procedures:

- Before class, log into Noteflight (noteflight.com) and create the first verse's melody of "Skin and Bones" in A minor; however, only use the rhythm of the melody. The pitches of the melody will only be low la, or A below middle C. Use the 6/8 meter or transpose it to a 3/4 meter, depending on the skill level of your students.
  - **Website example**: Check the supplemental website to this book, www.oup.com/us/utema, to watch a tutorial video on how to create a melody in Noteflight.⊚
- Sing the song "Skin and Bones" on solfege and lyrics.
- Review the mode as minor and the song is based around the pitch low la.

One Device in the Classroom:

- Launch Noteflight (https://www.noteflight.com).
- Open the Noteflight file you created with the "Skin and Bones" melody all on the pitch of low la or A below middle C.
- Play the melody and ask the students what is not accurate about the "Skin and Bones" melody (it has the correct rhythm, but an inaccurate melody).
- Identify that the melody is only low la or A below middle C.
- Ask the students what they need to create a melody: notes, rhythms, melodic direction, steps (notes next to each other), skips (notes not next to each other), patterns, and a starting and ending pitch.
- For this melody, they will compose a new melody, but it must end on the pitch low la or A below middle C, and they can only use the pitches low la, do, re and mi.
- Highlight the second pitch of the melody and ask a student to move the pitch to a different pitch or do, re, mi, or they can leave it on low la.
- Continue until each student has changed the pitches in the song or until we run out of pitches in the song (if you want to make sure that all students receive a turn, copy and paste the melody so that there are enough turns).
- Listen to the newly composed melody and ask them if there are any patterns found in their melody. Ask them if it is easy or challenging to sing. Ask them what they like about the newly composed melody and if they wished it had anything else in it. If they make suggestions for improvement, guide them through the changes so that no students have hurt feelings if their notes are changed.
- Once finished, have them sing the new melody on solfege.

1:1 Classroom:

- Follow the same steps as in the preceding; assign the file to their Noteflight accounts.
  - **Tech tip**: We use MusicFirst (https://www.musicfirst.com) to subscribe to our Noteflight Learn (paid subscription) account. Once we subscribed, they created a school website specifically for us where the students could easily login and compose.
- When they are finished composing their new melodies, save the compositions.
- Ask the students to reflect on whether there are any patterns found in their melodies. Ask them if it is easy or challenging to sing. Ask them what they like about the newly composed melodies and if they wished the melodies had anything else in them. If they make suggestions for improvement, guide them through the changes.
- Once finished, save the melodies.

Share the melodies:

- In Noteflight, export the melody as an MP3 file. Though this is not the best quality sounding audio file format, it is easily shareable.
- Share the MP3 file on the school website, on a music website created in Weebly or Google Sites, or on a student digital learning portfolio like Seesaw, Bloomz, ClassDojo, ClassTag, FreshGrade, Flipgrid, etc.

Higher Order Thinking Questions to Ask the Students:

- When did you feel like your melodies were ready to share?
- If you did not feel that they were ready to share, what would you need to get them there?

Extensions: Use the iOS and web-based app Book Creator to create an ebook of compositions by exporting the Noteflight melodies as pdf files and MP3 files. Create a page with each student's pdf file with its MP3 file.

Preparation of Eight Pitches (Mi-Sol-La-Do-Re-Do'-Low La, Low Sol)

To prepare for the sequence with mi-sol-la-do-re-do'-low la, low sol pitches (in various combinations like d'mlsrd low la and low sol, low sol-low la drmsld', etc.), students can listen to, move to, play games, and sing songs with the pitches mi-sol-la-do-re-do'-low la low sol. Look at the Holy Names University's Kodály Center American Folk Song Collection found at http://kodaly.hnu.edu/collection.cfm for more ideas. Here are some songs with variations of the mi-sol-la-do-re-do' low la, low sol tone set:

- Gypsy Davy
- Train is a-Coming
- Sourwood Mountain
- Willie Reilly.

Presentation of Eight Pitches (Mi-Sol-La-Do-Re-Do'-Low La, Low Sol)

To present the pitches mi, sol, la, do, re, do', low la, and low sol, please look at how to create the presentation slides with mi and sol using Google Slides, PowerPoint, Keynote (MAC only), and Notebook (interactive whiteboard software) found at the beginning of this chapter.

Practice Lessons for Mi-Sol-La-Do-Re-Do'-Low La, Low Sol Enhanced with Technology

Assessing the Pitches Low La and Low Sol Using Kahoot!

Curriculum Note: *In this lesson, students will be assessed using their devices and the free game-based assessment tool of Kahoot!* (https://www.kahoot.com). *This assessment has five questions* (https://create.kahoot.it/share/low-la-and-low-sol-review/b048121a-084d-40a1-90fd-eb2fd738856a). *You can use this assessment or create your own to assess your students on the pitches low la and low sol.*

Objective: The students will be assessed on their knowledge of the pitches low la and low sol.

Grade Levels: Grades 2 and up

Materials: Your students will need devices, ideally a 1:1 classroom. However, you can use this in a team mode with a few devices or as a station. You will need the link, https://create.kahoot.it/share/low-la-and-low-sol-review/b048121a-084d-40a1-90fd-eb2fd738856a

Standards: Responding Standards Grade 2 and up: MU:Re7.1.2a to MU:Re8.1.2a

Essential Understanding:

- Melodies are created with various melodic motives and intervals.

Procedures:

- Students will review the song "Train is A-Coming" to review the low la-do interval.
- Launch https://create.kahoot.it/share/low-la-and-low-sol-review/b048121a-084d-40a1-90fd-eb2fd738856a to assess the students' knowledge of melodic motives.
- You click the play button and choose the classic mode or the team mode.
  - Click on Game Options.
  - Turn on the "Display Game Pin Throughout" so that if a student's device quits during this short game, she can log back in.
  - Turn on "Name Generator" so that Kahoot! will generate funny names instead of the students submitting inappropriate names. If you do this, the team mode will be discontinued.
- Click classic and the game will launch.
- The students launch the Kahoot! app or go to kahoot.it and input the code into their device.
- The students' names will appear on the screen. Once all of the students have logged in, play the game.
- Kahoot! will score the students' answers as they submit them in a fun, game-like way.
- Once finished, the game will show who came in first, second, and third. You can turn this off in the Game Options.
- Your email will receive a data report of the answers.
- My students love playing this game. If you have consistently good devices, this is a fun way to assess and collect data on any topic.
- **Creating a Kahoot!**
  - Create a free account and use the free version.
  - Type in questions. The questions are multiple-choice.
  - You can add images, search their image library, or add a YouTube link. When you add a YouTube link, you can state when you want the video to start and stop.

Higher Order Thinking Questions to Ask the Students:

- Why are these melodic motives so important when creating music?

Extensions: Use the Noteflight lesson titled "Creating a Melody in Minor Mode within 6/8 Meter," earlier in this chapter, to have the students create a melody that includes the pitches low la and low sol.

Preparation of Eleven Pitches (Mi-Sol-La-Do-Re-Do'-Low La, Low Sol, Low Ti, Fa, and Ti)

To prepare for the sequence with mi-sol-la-do-re-do'-low la, low sol, low ti, fa, and ti pitches (in various combinations like d'mflsrtfd low l, low t, and low sol, low sol-low la, low ti, drmfsltd', etc.), students can listen to, move to, play games, and sing songs with the pitches mi-sol-la-do-re-do'-low la, low sol, low ti, fa, and ti. Look at the Holy Names University's Kodály Center American Folk Song Collection found at http://kodaly.hnu.edu/collection.cfm for more ideas.

Presentation of Eleven Pitches (Mi-Sol-La-Do-Re-Do'-Low La, Low Sol, Low Ti, Fa, and Ti)

To present the pitches mi, sol, la, do, re, do', low la, low sol, low ti, fa, and ti, please look at how to create the presentation slides with mi and sol using Google Slides, PowerPoint, Keynote (MAC only), and Notebook (interactive whiteboard software) found at the beginning of this chapter.

Practice Lessons for Mi-Sol-La-Do-Re-Do'-Low La, Low Sol, Low Ti, Fa, and Ti Enhanced with Technology

Using Flashnote Derby to Practice Naming Do, Re, Mi, Sol, La, Do', Low La, Low Sol, Low Ti, Fa, and Ti on the Staff

Follow the directions to the lesson "Using Flashnote Derby to Practice Naming Do, Mi, Sol, and La on the Staff," found earlier in this chapter, and add the additional pitches.

5, PART A

Orff Schulwerk

An Approach to Possibilities

Ardith Collins

What is most exciting about the Orff Schulwerk approach?
The abundance of creative, interconnected possibilities.

What is most challenging about the Orff Schulwerk approach?
The abundance of creative, interconnected possibilities.

Orff Schulwerk is an approach that originated out of the composer Carl Orff's curiosity about the interconnected nature of movement, drama, and music, and the enthusiasm of gymnastics teacher, artist, and author Dorothee Günther to begin a new type of music and movement training center in Munich. Orff named his vision for unified movement and music teaching "elemental music."

> What then is elemental music? Elemental music is never music alone but forms a unity with movement, dance and speech. It is music that one makes oneself, in which one takes part not as a listener, but as a participant. It is unsophisticated, employs no big forms and no big architectural structures, and it uses small sequence forms, ostinato and rondo. Elemental music is near the earth, natural, physical, within the range of everyone to learn it and experience it and suitable for the child. (Orff 1963)

Elemental music flourished as a community of kindred spirits interested in invoking the Greek spirit of *mousike*, the unity of dance, music, and text. Influenced by the work of Émile Jaques-Dalcroze, Rudolf Laban, and Mary Wigman, notable people in the genesis of elemental music included Curt Sachs, Karl Maendler, and later, Maja Lex and Gunild Keetman. This first incarnation of Orff Schulwerk began in 1924 as a training program for young women at the Güntherschule, where Lex and Keetman met as students in 1926.

Orff wrote, "In the beginning was the Drum" (1976, p. 17). The initial experimentations of the Güntherschule arose from the most ancient of sounds: body percussion, rattles, drums, sticks, and speech, as advised by the musicologist Curt Sachs. Reflecting on the conception of the Schulwerk, Orff noted, "The drum induces dance. Dance has the closest relationship to music. My idea and the task that I had set myself was a regeneration of music through movement, through dance" (1976, p. 17).

Recognizing the need for melodic instruments in the elemental movement and percussion ensemble, Sachs suggested the addition of recorder consort, instruments which

Ardith Collins, *Orff Schulwerk* In: *Using Technology with Elementary Music Approaches*. Edited by: Amy M. Burns, Oxford University Press (2020).
© Oxford University Press.
DOI: 10.1093/oso/9780190055653.003.0007

fit in both the historical context of music development and permitted freedom for movement while performing. This desire for readily playable melodic instruments also led to the creation of xylophones based on the Indonesian gamelan and African xylophone developed by harpsichord builder Karl Maendler. As Güntherschule teachers and students continued to venture into music and dance, accompaniment techniques coalesced, beginning with the drone and forms of ostinato, which gave the foundation for exploration and improvisation with the new melody instruments:

> A particular kind of improvisation resulted from the use of the pentatonic scale. Over an ostinato bass several melodies could be improvised simultaneously or in question and answer phrases. . . . Since there were no semitones in this exercise, and therefore no dissonance tensions, the different voices came together in a kind of oscillation. Once the structure of the pentatonic scale had been grasped, the improvisations arose of their own accord, with question and answer phrasing and imitation emphasising formal relationships. (Orff 1976, p. 29)

The improvisatory work of the Güntherschule was first published in 1930 under the title *Rhythmisch-melodische Übung*. The intention was not for the pieces to be practiced and performed precisely as written, but rather to be used as elemental examples of models for creation. Additional books were published between 1931 and 1938. The Güntherschule continued operation for 10 years and trained 650 students until the building and contents were confiscated in 1944 due to political turmoil and the onset of World War II.

It was not until 1948, when Orff received a request to feature elemental music in radio broadcasts, that the second incarnation of the Schulwerk was sparked. This inquiry prompted Orff and Keetman to reunite for the creation of 14 broadcasts that lasted through 1953. It also inspired Keetman and another former Güntherschule student, Traude Schrattenecker, to collaborate in teaching elemental classes for children between the ages of 8 and 10 at the Mozarteum Conservatory in Salzburg, as well as the publication of the ideas and arrangements used with the children in the five-volume series *Music for Children*. Orff wrote, "I am not exaggerating when I say that without Keetman's decisive contribution through her double talent, 'Schulwerk' could never have come into being" (1976, p. 67).

While Orff never wrote about how to teach using the Schulwerk, Keetman provided a detailed handbook, *Elementaria*, dedicated to their 40-year collaboration. *Elementaria* is a rich text filled with succinct ideas to approach rhythmic speech, listening exercises, arrangements, form, recorder, movement, and musicianship training for students of all ages and levels.

Elementaria opens with examples of "rhythmic building bricks" (Figures 5.1 and 5.2), the distilled rhythms extracted from children's rhymes in both two-four and three-four meter (Keetman 1984, p. 17).

Rhythm is set to speech, with attention to prosody.

Music for Children, Volume I, by Orff and Keetman, edited by British musician and educator Margaret Murray, it is not a sequential text, but rather is written in three

Figure 5.1.
Two-four meter.

Figure 5.2.
Three-four meter.

parts: "Nursery Rhymes and Songs," "Rhythmic and Melodic Exercises," and "Instrumental Pieces." The sections were designed to be used in tandem, providing opportunity to focus on speech and rhythm, progressing to singing and playing instruments. As with Orff's original publications, the material is meant to be taught by rote, and to inspire the creation of new elemental works. Improvisation is meant for not only the students, but also the teacher. The teacher should be open to the possibilities of noticing student ideas, giving students permission to set their ideas in motion.

Tonal development in Orff Schulwerk:

> s-m: call
> s-m-l: chant
> drm sl: pentatonic and modes
> drmfsl: hexatonic
> diatonic scale

Forms: AB, ABA, canon, binary, ternary, rondo

Meter

Question–Answer

Improvisation

Because the myriad ways in which Orff Schulwerk–inspired teaching can unfold, it is left to the teachers to determine what content will best suit the needs of their students, and what type of lesson design will spark student curiosity and engagement. Steven Calantropio's supplement book, *Lessons in Elemental Style*, offers this advice in lesson design:

> Movement and improvisation are encouraged in every experience. Each lesson begins with a simple idea which is then developed through process teaching technique into a larger form. . . . Each lesson offers suggestions for divergent development based on ideas, skills or concepts found in the lesson flow. Each experience will help both teacher and student further define elemental music and style by affirming the natural, organic music-making possibilities inherent in all (Calantropio 2015, p. 4).

Just as the Orff Schulwerk approach grew out of a community, the work with students is meant to be a collaborative experience, not instruction for isolation. Rondo is one of the most ubiquitous forms utilized in an Orff Schulwerk lesson, allowing students of all ages to experience a sense of self and community, providing an opportunity to find meaning and purpose in their world.

Process teaching is an often-used phrase in Orff Schulwerk, referring to a playful, child-centered approach through which understanding and discoveries are guided toward achieving a goal in an active, joyful manner. A lesson might begin with a poem, a rhythm, a melody, artwork, or a movement experience that sets the course for a musically satisfying experience for all. In order to accomplish this, students must be willing to listen and respond to the prompts, and to trust the journey set by the teacher. Orff Schulwerk places a higher value on the learning process, rather than the final product or performance.

The four avenues of Orff inspired teaching are the four learning media:
Play, Sing, Speak, Move; and well as four activities to awaken the media:
Explore, Imitate, Improvise, Create. (Orff 1983, pp. 21–22)

Orff-inspired teaching seeks to embrace these media and activities with the teacher as model for creativity. These activities mirror Bloom's taxonomy, as well as the research of Piaget and Pestalozzi, and current trends in neuroeducation. Plato said, "Leave the children free and play so you'll see the natural bent" (Block, 2018). Orff Schulwerk is a playground of possibilities, as Avon Gillespie, noted Orff educator, commented:

I have always been fascinated with Orff Schulwerk because in Orff nothing is ever finished. In Orff we are not involved in problem solving but in possibility seeking. In curriculum we have a prescription, but lifelong work of Orff Schulwerk must be built on roots of wonder (Goodkin, 2017).

Carl Orff's concept of elemental music and movement has grown into an approach that embraces the limitless possibilities in the world around us.

Resources

Block, J. (2018). Danai Gagne and Orff Schulwerk: Ever Growing, Ever Flowing. *The Orff Echo, Spring*, 40–45.

Calantropio, S. (2015). *Lessons in Elemental Style*. Mainz: Schott.

Carley, I. M. (1977). *Orff Re-echoes: Selections from the Orff Echo and the Supplements*. Cleveland Heights, OH: American Orff-Schulwerk Association.

Frazee, J., & Kreuter, K. (1997). *Discovering Orff: A Curriculum for Music Teachers*. Mainz: Schott.

Goodkin, D. (2013). *Play, Sing, & Dance: An Introduction to Orff Schulwerk*. Mainz: Schott.

Goodkin, D. (2017). *The National American Orff-Schulwerk Association Conference. The National American Orff-Schulwerk Association Conference*. Fort Worth.

Hall, D., Keetman, G., Walter, A., & Orff, C. (n.d.). *Music for Children*, Volumes 1–5. London: Schott.

Keetman, G. (1984). *Rhythmische Ubung (Rhythmic Exercises): For Orff Instruments*. Mainz: Schott.

Keetman, G., Frick, O., Keetman, P., & Murray, M. (1974). *Elementaria: First Acquaintance with Orff-Schulwerk*. London: Schott.

Orff, C. (1963). "Orff Schulwerk: Past and Future." Speech. *Opening of the Orff Institute in Salzburg*, October 25. Trans. Margaret Murray.

Orff, C. (1978). *The Schulwerk*. New York: Schott Music.

Orff, C. (1983, October 25). *Orff-Schulwerk—Past and Future*. Speech presented at the opening of the Orff Institute in Salzburg.

Shamrock, M. E. (2007). *Orff Schulwerk: Brief History, Description and Issues in Global Dispersal*. Cleveland, OH: American Orff-Schulwerk Assoc.

Steen, A. (1992). *Exploring Orff: A Teachers' Guide*. New York: Schott.

Warner, B. (1991). *Orff-Schulwerk: applications for the classroom*. Englewood Cliffs, N. J.: Prentice-Hall.

5, PART B

Technology Integration with the Orff Schulwerk Approach

Amy M. Burns

Important note: Before you use any tool with your students, please check with your school's administration regarding the technology policies of your school to make sure you can use students' information, including images, and that you have their support.

Tech Resources

There are numerous resources for elementary music educators using the Orff Schulwerk approach in their classrooms, so that one can easily obtain "orffestrations" (Orff arrangements of songs), folk songs, manipulatives, connect with others using the approach, and more. Here is a list that I have found helpful:

Accompanying Website for This Book

Type in any web browser, www.oup.com/us/utema, or click on the link found here.⊙

Organization Websites

- **International Orff Schulwerk Forum Salzburg (IOSFS)** (http://www.orff-schulwerk-forum-salzburg.org/): This network collects, documents, and publishes international material about Orff Schulwerk. It also communicates and answers questions about the approach and initiates events.
- **American Orff Schulwerk Association (AOSA)** (https://aosa.org/): This site offers information about the approach, history, chapters, workshops, access to the *Orff Echo* periodical, resources, and more.
- **American Orff Schulwerk Association (AOSA) Facebook Group** (https://www.facebook.com/americanorffschulwerkassociation/): This group is open to music educators who have questions about the approach and want to network with others who use it in their classrooms. When questions are asked, many experts in the field will give advice and suggestions.
- **The American Center for Elemental Music and Movement** (https://acemm.us/): This organization promotes the teaching and understanding of elemental music and movement.

Amy M. Burns, *Technology Integration with the Orff Schulwerk Approach* In: *Using Technology with Elementary Music Approaches*. Edited by: Amy M. Burns, Oxford University Press (2020). © Oxford University Press.
DOI: 10.1093/oso/9780190055653.003.0008

- Perform a Google Search to find Orff Schulwerk organizations in your country and your local chapter.

Music Educators' Websites

Note: This is a small list of music educators utilizing and sharing the way they use the Orff Schulwerk approach in their classrooms. Perform a Google search to find more classrooms sharing materials via a website, Teachers Pay Teachers, blogs, and more.

- **AOSA Resource Page** (https://aosa.org/resources/useful-links/): AOSA lists great resources on this page, including music educators' websites. Some highlights from the list are:
  - **O For Tuna Orff** (https://ofortunaorff.blogspot.com/)
  - **Mama Lisa's World** (https://www.mamalisa.com/)
  - **David Row's Make Moments Matter** (https://makemomentsmatter.org/)
- **Amy M. Burns Website** (https://www.amymburns.com): Amy provides various resources and examples on how to integrate technology into the elementary music classroom.

Interactive Websites to Use in a Classroom with One Device, Multiple Devices, or 1:1 Devices

Note: The following is a short list of interactive websites that can be used in a classroom with one device, multiple devices, or 1:1 devices. Some of these websites still require Adobe Flash (being discontinued in late 2020) and might be compatible with the devices in your classroom, or might not. As with any website, I highly encourage you to test the website before you use it in the classroom. In addition, I recommend a decent pair of speakers hooked to the device that you are using to present the website.

Orchestral Websites

- http://www.sfskids.org: The site allows the students to listen to acoustic sound samples, discover and explore instruments, and more.
- http://www.dsokids.com: The Dallas Symphony Orchestra's website is a fantastic doorway into a world of music and learning for students, parents, and teachers.
- http://www.nyphilkids.org: The New York Philharmonic Kidzone is a place for kids to visit and learn about the New York Philharmonic, the instruments of the orchestra, the music, the musicians, and so much more.
- http://listeningadventures.carnegiehall.org/ypgto/index.aspx: This is based on Benjamin Britten's *Young Person's Guide to the Orchestra*. If you click on "Local Game" and then "Practice Round," your students do not need to create a login to use the games of instrument explorations.
- https://www.tso.ca/education/teacher-resources: The Toronto's Symphony Orchestra Teacher Resources that include study guides and podcasts of the repertoire from their concerts.
- http://www.classicsforkids.com/: Classical music's great composers come to life through music and stories in a language that is age-appropriate for elementary students.

Interactive Websites

- http://www.musictechteacher.com: Karen Garrett, the Technology in Music Education (TI:ME-https://www.ti-me.org) 2006 Teacher of the Year, created this interactive website to assist her elementary students with learning all things music. Click on the games and quizzes to have your students practice their knowledge about rhythms, instruments, and more.
- http://www.themusicinteractive.com: The Music Interactive has numerous free and paid games for download to a laptop or desktop such as Staff Wars, the note-naming game in a Star Wars style. If you are craving these games for devices that can only play apps or websites, then check out their compatible apps that can be accessed from this website.
- http://www.therhythmtrainer.com: The rhythm trainer is a website where the student listens to the rhythm pattern being played and then notates it.
- http://www.philtulga.com: This website has many free activities that are musically based with cross-curricular connections. Some favorites are creating rhythm patterns with the free Counting Music and singing solfege with Sequencing with Simon.

Tech Tools That Enhance the Classroom

- **Audacity** (https://www.audacityteam.org/): Change keys and tempo and remove vocals.
- **Soundtrap** (https://www.soundtrap.com): Change keys and tempo.
- **Class Tools** (https://www.classtools.net/): Gives you a random name chooser, a timer, and more to assist in your classroom.

Play-Along Videos

- **Musication Play-Along YouTube Video Channel** (https://www.youtube.com/channel/UCuNYP6sYWgjAddNo534PEKQ)
- **Professor Pedro Morales Rhythm Videos**: Search YouTube to find rhythm play-along videos with Minions, Mario Brothers, Angry Birds, and more.

Assessment Tools

- **Google Forms** (https://www.google.com/forms/about/): *If your school is based around Google (Google Drive, Google Classroom, etc), then using Google Forms for assessment is intuitive as the students can access it easily.*
- **Kahoot!** (https://kahoot.com/): Great assessment/gaming tool for classes with a few devices to 1:1 devices. You can find numerous pre-made Kahoot! challenges so that you do not have to reinvent the wheel.
- **Plickers** (https://www.plickers.com/): Great to use for multiple choice or true/false questions when there is one device in the room.
- **Socrative** (https://socrative.com/): Wonderful to use for assessment of multiple-choice questions, exit tickets, short answers, and more, with no email addresses required of the students.
- **iDoceo** (https://idoceo.net): This is a paid iOS app that can be used to manage and organize data collected from assessments. This could involve audio assessments,

video assessments, composition files/recordings, and more. In addition, it can be used for attendance charts, seating charts, random picker, quick recordings, and so much more.

How Technology Can Include Students with Special Needs and Enhance an Underfunded Elementary General Music Classroom

Using Timothy Purdum's Xylophone Orff App to Supplement an Instrument in the Music Classroom

Curriculum Note: *This app is currently $.99 for iOS devices, only found at https://itunes. apple.com/us/app/xylophone-orff/id1092959126?mt=8. This app can be set up in diatonic, pentatonic, and hexatonic scales with pitch names and solfege syllables presented on each bar.*

Objective: To perform in an ensemble that will include all students making music.

Grade Levels: Grades K–5

Materials: An iOS mobile device with the Xylophone Orff App connected to a decent pair of speakers. Any song with an arrangement for Orff and classroom instruments. For this lesson, we will use "Doggie Doggie" pitched in C. The Orff arrangement to this song can be found on the supplemental website, www.oup.com/us/utema⊚

Standards: Performing Standards for Kindergarten and up

Essential Questions:

- If you do not have enough instruments for all of the students to play, how can we remedy this?
- What is the difference in sound between an acoustic instrument and a virtual instrument?

Procedures:

- Review the song "Doggie Doggie" and play the game.
  - There are a variety of ways to play this game. My students like having the one who is the dog put his head down in the middle of a circle. I choose another student to hide the bone (this can be any inanimate object) in the classroom that is not too difficult to find. We sing the song while I assess the student who is the dog while he sings the solo portion. Once finished, the student who is the dog has to find the bone (we play hot and cold) and then gets three guesses of who hid the bone. The one who hid it is now the dog.
- Teach the Orffestration (vary this per grade level by taking out parts that are too complex for that grade level).
  - **Website example**: Go to the supplemental website, www.oup.com/us/utema to find the Orffestration.⊚
  - Begin with singing the song and tapping the steady beat on their laps.
  - Then alternate the steady beat on each lap.
  - Once mastered, add snaps on the fourth beat, so it is "pat pat pat snap."
  - Teach the ostinato pattern of ti-ti ti-ti t-ti ta (use your rhythmic syllable preference).
  - Assign the Orff instruments to the students.

- Using the Orff Xylophone App, set the app to C Pentatonic and assign an instrument that would be successful to the student playing the app and one that is potentially missing from the ensemble. The student can play the app with her fingers.
- All play the steady bordun on C and G.
- Once mastered, alternate the bordun on C and G and have the basses play this.
- Everyone else plays the "pat pat pat rest" pattern on C and G together. Have the alto xylophones play this.
- While the basses and altos are playing their parts, have the glockenspiels and the metallophones play octave Gs on the rest.
- Finally, have the soprano xylophones play the ti-ti ti-ti ti-ti ta ostinato on G-G E-E G-G E.
- If it is an older class, teach the melody on recorder.
- When finished, ask the students the higher order thinking questions.
- **Tech tip**: I like connecting virtual instruments into a little mixing board (I have the Samson Expedition) so that I can control the volume. This is nice when giving instructions.
- **Tech tip**: If you do not have an iOS app, but have a laptop or Chromebook with internet access, you can use these sites for virtual xylophones:
  - If you subscribe to Denise Gagne's Musicplay Online, there is a virtual xylophone included on the website (https://musicplayonline.com/xylophone/). There are free trials to this wonderful program.
  - http://www.buttonbass.com/Xylophone.html: This will not let you take out the bars, but you can use this free site if your device has internet access and still runs Adobe Flash (which is being discontinued in late 2020). Please test this site before you use it.

Higher Order Thinking Questions to Ask the Students:

- When you heard the Orff instrument app, what sounded the same and what sounded different from the acoustic Orff instrument? Create a comparison thinking map to record the answers.
- For older students: What are some advantages to having virtual instruments in your ensemble?

Extensions: Give every student a chance to play the virtual Orff instrument and chart a comparison in the playing similarities and differences.

Using Acoustic and Virtual Recorders in Music Class

Curriculum Note: *The free iOS recorder apps by AtPlayMusic (PlayAlong Recorder—https:// itunes.apple.com/us/app/playalong-recorder/id600713930?mt=8 and AtPlayMusic Recorder—https://itunes.apple.com/us/app/atplaymusic-recorder-free/id580567733) can provide a virtual recorder for students who have special needs and lack the fine motor abilities to play a traditional recorder. Both of these apps are currently free with add-ons that can be purchased. An iPad connected to speakers would be beneficial for these to run well in the classroom. There is also a paid version of AtPlayMusic PlayAlong Recorder in Google Play for Chromebooks and Android Devices found at* https://play.google.com/store/apps/details?id=com.AtPlayMusic.PlayAlongRecorder&hl=en_US.

Objective: To perform in an ensemble that will include all students making music.

Grade Levels: Grades 3–5

Materials: The free AtPlayMusic iOS recorder apps of PlayAlong Recorder (https://itunes.apple.com/us/app/playalong-recorder/id600713930?mt=8) or AtPlayMusic Recorder (https://itunes.apple.com/us/app/atplaymusic-recorder-free/id580567733) or the paid Google Play version (https://play.google.com/store/apps/details?id=com.AtPlayMusic.PlayAlongRecorder&hl=en_US) downloaded onto an iPad or Chromebook that is connected to speakers. The speakers can be optional. However, it will assist the students in hearing the app better. You could also provide headphones for the students to use to hear the app, especially if they are sensitive to sounds. For this lesson, we will use the traditional beginning recorder song of "Hot Cross Buns." The notation for this song can be found on the supplemental website, www.oup.com/us/utema.⊚

Standards: Performing Standards: MU:Pr4.1.3a, MU:Pr4.2.3a, MU:Pr4.2.3b, MU:Pr4.2.3c, MU:Pr4.3.3a, MU:Pr5.1.3a, MU:Pr5.1.3b, MU:Pr6.1.3a, MU:Pr6.1.3b, MU:Pr4.1.4a, MU:Pr4.2.4a, MU:Pr4.2.4b, MU:Pr4.2.4c, MU:Pr4.3.4a, MU:Pr5.1.4a, MU:Pr5.1.4b, MU:Pr6.1.4a, MU:Pr6.1.4b, MU:Pr4.1.5a, MU:Pr4.2.5a, MU:Pr4.2.5b, MU:Pr4.2.5c, MU:Pr4.3.5a, MU:Pr5.1.5a, MU:Pr5.1.5b, MU:Pr6.1.5a, MU:Pr6.1.5b

Essential Questions:

- If you do not have enough instruments for all of the students to play, how can we remedy this?
- If your school lacked traditional instruments, how could we still make music?
- What is the difference in sound between an acoustic instrument and a virtual instrument?

Procedures:

- Have students take out their recorders. For those using the app, have them launch the PlayAlong Recorder app or AtPlayMusic Recorder app.
  - Launch PlayAlong Recorder app.
  - Scroll down to the free song, "Hot Cross Buns."
  - The screen will show the first two bars of the music.
  - Click the settings button at the top of the screen so that the display mode reads "Smart Charts."
  - Click OK.
  - Your student now has the notes and a fingering chart on the screen. The student can tap the fingering chart to play the song.
  - **Activity and tech tip**: If you are using another song that has the notes B, A, and/or G, use this screen to play the other songs. The screen will not advance unless they are playing the song exactly. Therefore, the student can play numerous recorder songs with the notes B, A, and/or G with their classmates.
- Review the notes B, A, and G on the recorder. You could use the interactive recorder chart found at https://www.musick8.com/rkdojo/rkchart.php.
- Review the rhythms by clapping them.
- Review the pitches by singing the song on pitches and/or words.
- Count off and have the students play the melody together.
  - If they cannot stay together, review each measure one at a time.
  - Also, break into small groups and perform the song.

- **Activity tip**: I use the phrase, "rest position" to stop the class from playing when I want to give a direction. I use interactive modeling to teach them rest position. I will explain the concept. I then play and ask a student to call out "rest position." I stop playing the recorder. That student will now play and I will assign another student to call out rest position. This goes on for a few turns with the students reflecting on what is happening when rest position is called. I then ask one student to not rest position when a student calls it out. Once this occurs, I ask the students what the consequence should be. We go through that a few times and then they are ready to play and stop when rest position is called. Though this process takes a while at first, the students catch on quickly and then you use less time throughout the school year waiting for them to rest when you ask.
- **Activity tip**: Have the students try the app as well and ask them the higher order thinking questions. Chart the answers in a comparison thinking map.

Higher Order Thinking Questions to Ask the Students:

- When you heard the recorder instrument app, what sounded the same and what sounded different from the acoustic recorder? Create a comparison thinking map to record the answers.
- For older students: What are some advantages to having virtual instruments in your ensemble?

Extensions: Share the performance: If you use a student digital learning portfolio like Seesaw (web.seesaw.me), ClassDojo (classdojo.com), ClassTag (classtag.com), FreshGrade (freshgrade.com), Bloomz (bloomz.net), or the social learning video platform of Flipgrid (flipgrid.com), you can share videos of these performances with other classmates and family members. See Appendix, "Links Listed Throughout the Book and Description of Programs," for more information about these portfolio programs.

Using Virtual Boomwhackers in Music Class

Curriculum Note: *Using the website* https://www.musick8.com/boomwhackers/playboomwhackers.php?bwswitch=TRUE, *you can add a diatonic set of boomwhackers to your classroom. If you need a chromatic set, the website has a link to a virtual chromatic set. This set can be played from a device with internet access or projected onto an interactive whiteboard.*

Objective: To perform in an ensemble that will include all students making music.

Grade Levels: Grades K–3

Materials: A device with internet access that can access the website https://www.musick8.com/boomwhackers/playboomwhackers.php?bwswitch=TRUE. It would be beneficial to hook the device to speakers so that the student playing the boomwhackers can hear them. The song "Hop Old Squirrel" will be used for this lesson. The notation for this song can be found on the supplemental website, www.oup.com/us/utema.◉

Standards: Performing Standards: MU:Pr4.1.Ka, MU:Pr4.2.Ka, MU:Pr4.3.Ka, MU:Pr5.1.Ka, MU:Pr5.1.Kb, MU:Pr6.1.Ka, MU:Pr6.1.Kb, MU:Pr4.1.1a, MU:Pr4.2.1a, MU:Pr4.2.1b, MU:Pr4.3.1a, MU:Pr5.1.1a, MU:Pr5.1.1b, MU:Pr6.1.1a, MU:Pr6.1.1b, MU:Pr4.1.2a, MU:Pr4.2.2a, MU:Pr4.2.2b, MU:Pr4.3.2a, MU:Pr5.1.2a, MU:Pr5.1.2b, MU:Pr6.1.2a, MU:Pr6.1.2b, MU:Pr4.1.3a, MU:Pr4.2.3a, MU:Pr4.2.3b, MU:Pr4.2.3c, MU:Pr4.3.3a, MU:Pr5.1.3a, MU:Pr5.1.3b, MU:Pr6.1.3a, MU:Pr6.1.3b

Essential Questions:

- If you do not have enough instruments for all of the students to play, how can we remedy this?
- If your school lacked traditional instruments, how could we still make music?
- What is the difference in sound between an acoustic instrument and a virtual instrument?

Procedures:

- The teacher introduces the song, "Hop Old Squirrel."
- The students talk about what they know about squirrels.
- The teacher sings it again as the students tap the steady beat in groups of two.
- The teacher sings it again, and the students hop like a squirrel, or "squirrel hop" (since hopping is one foot, the students are technically jumping) on the words "Hop old squirrel" and freeze on the words "Eideldum eideldum" and "Eideldumdee."
- The teacher asks how many times they "squirrel hop" when they hear the words "Hop old squirrel"? (3 "squirrel hops").
- Teacher sings again and the students "squirrel hop" and say "hop hop hop" on the words "Hop old squirrel" and freeze on the words "Eideldum eideldum" and "Eideldumdee."
- Assign the students instruments to play the pitch A. For this lesson, assign boomwhackers. In addition, Orff instruments, tone chimes, handbells, piano, keyboards, recorders, etc., can be used. Assign a student to play the boomwhackers on the website, https://www.musick8.com/boomwhackers/playboomwhackers. php?bwswitch=TRUE.
- Have some play the pitch "A A A (rest)" on the words "Hop old squirrel (rest)" and freeze on the words "Eideldum eideldum" and "Eideldumdee," while other students "squirrel hop" and say "hop hop hop (rest)" on the words "Hop old squirrel (rest)" and freeze on the words "Eideldum eideldum" and "Eideldumdee."
- Switch the students around so the ones that were playing are moving and vice versa.

Higher Order Thinking Question to Ask the Students:

- When you heard the boomwhacker instrument app, what sounded the same and what sounded different from the acoustic recorder? Create a comparison thinking map to record the answers.

Extensions: Search YouTube, or revisit the links at the beginning of the chapter, for boomwhacker playalong videos and have the students perform to them. For those students who are challenged to play traditional boomwhackers, have them use a separate device to access the website https://www.musick8.com/boomwhackers/playboomwhackers. php?bwswitch=TRUE, to play along with the YouTube boomwhacker playalong video.

Using a Virtual Autoharp in Music Class

Curriculum Note: *This lesson utilizes the Autoharp app for iOS or Android/Google Play devices found at http://www.autoharpapp.com/.*
Objective: To perform in an ensemble that will include all students making music.
Grade Levels: Grades 2–5

Materials: An iOS or Google Play Device such as an iPad, an Android device, or a Chromebook connected to speakers that has the Autoharp app from http://www.autoharpapp.com/. The folk song "Long Legged Sailor," along with recorders and Orff instruments, will be used. To see the Orff arrangement, go to the supplemental website for this book, found at www.oup.com/us/utema.⊛

Standards: Performing: MU:Pr4.1.2a, MU:Pr4.2.2a, MU:Pr4.2.2b, MU:Pr4.3.2a, MU:Pr5.1.2a, MU:Pr5.1.2b, MU:Pr6.1.2a, MU:Pr6.1.2b, MU:Pr4.1.3a, MU:Pr4.2.3a, MU:Pr4.2.3b, MU:Pr4.2.3c, MU:Pr4.3.3a, MU:Pr5.1.3a, MU:Pr5.1.3b, MU:Pr6.1.3a, MU:Pr6.1.3b, MU:Pr4.1.4a, MU:Pr4.2.4a, MU:Pr4.2.4b, MU:Pr4.2.4c, MU:Pr4.3.4a, MU:Pr5.1.4a, MU:Pr5.1.4b, MU:Pr6.1.4a, MU:Pr6.1.4b, MU:Pr4.1.5a, MU:Pr4.2.5a, MU:Pr4.2.5b, MU:Pr4.2.5c, MU:Pr4.3.5a, MU:Pr5.1.5a, MU:Pr5.1.5b, MU:Pr6.1.5a, MU:Pr6.1.5b

Essential Questions:

- If we do not have a certain instrument in our music classroom, how can we find alternatives for that instrument?
- If we do not have enough instruments for each student to play, what are some ways we can make our arrangements work?

Procedures:

- Review the song, "Long Legged Sailor."
- Perform the movements to the song: the students sing and stand tall for long legged sailor; stand on their knees for short legged; join their knees together for knock-kneed; put one foot on their knee for bow-legged; and stand and cross their legs for crossed-legged.
- Sing again the first and second verses, but use these movements to show the bass line of the orffestration: G G D G—Stand on the Gs and bend down on the D.
- Sing the third through fifth verses again and transfer the bass line to their legs of G/Right G/Right D/Left G/Right.
- Open the Autoharp app and show the students the G and D chords. With this app, you can show how the virtual autoharp emulates characteristics of an acoustic autoharp:
  a. Touch-sensitive volume
  b. Play muted strings
  c. Stop strings with multiple fingers
  d. Show active strings
  e. Leave buttons pressed
  f. Use left-handed setup
  g. Reverse button layout
  h. Reverse chord sequence.
- Depending on the size of your class, give a few students a turn to play.
- Assign students to Orff instruments, boomwhackers, and the autoharp. All sing the first verse while playing the bass line and the autoharp playing the chords G G D G (see arrangement).
- Example the alto and soprano xylophone lines by patting ti-ti ti-ti ta rest | ti-ti ti-ti ta rest:|| on the R-R R-R R rest | L-L L-L R rest:||. Have them tap then play it. Use your preferred method of rhythm counting.

- Sing verse two with basses playing the bass line, autoharp playing the chords, and everyone else playing the alto and soprano xylophone line.
- Example the metallophone lines by snapping (or flicking) the whole note and whole rest rhythm: whole note hold it | whole rest hold it: | | or ta-a-a-a | rest rest rest rest: | |
- Sing verses three through five with all parts.

Higher Order Thinking Questions to Ask the Students:

- What were some ways that we could include certain instruments in our classroom when we do not have them, i.e., autoharp?
- What were some ways that we could include everyone in making music?

Extensions: Divide the class into two groups. Have them work together to create more verses and movements to the song. Address the topic of appropriate lyrics. Have each group perform their new verse for each other.

Sharing Your Music Classroom with Parents/Caregivers and Globally

Curriculum Note: *This has been addressed throughout the book in all of the approaches. I feel that it is important to share your classroom with parents/caregivers. By doing this, you give your students an authentic audience, your shyest students a voice, it answers the question, "What did you do in school today?", it assists you in documenting musical creations as they happen, and it empowers your students to reflect and answer higher order thinking questions. I will use Seesaw (web.seesaw.me) and Flipgrid (https://www.flipgrid.com), the digital learning portfolio, and/ or student engagement tools that empower students' voices, in this example. However, there are other portfolios out there, like ClassDojo (https://www.classdojo.com), ClassTag (https://www. classtag.com), Bloomz (https://www.bloomz.net), and FreshGrade (https://www.freshgrade. com/), that empower students' voices and can connect with an audience such as parents.*

Objective: To have your students "show what they know" to an authentic audience. This could occur with any lesson in your music classroom from singing songs to performing on instruments.

Grade Levels: PreK and up

Materials: We will use the free version of Seesaw (web.seesaw.me) and Flipgrid (https:// www.flipgrid.com) as two examples.

Standards: All performing, creating, responding, and connecting to music standards.

Essential Questions:

- How can my students "show what they know" to an authentic audience?
- How do I give my shyest students a voice?

Procedures:

- **Seesaw (web.seesaw.me)**—Check out Appendix, "Links Listed Throughout the Book and Descriptions of Programs," for a detailed description of Seesaw.
- **Ideas for your elementary music classroom that are based on the Orff Schulwerk approach:**
  - **One Device in the Classroom:**
    - **Video tool**: Use the video tool to video your students' orffestrations, performances, songs, dances, etc. Click accept and tag the student in the video. The parent or

caregiver has the Seesaw Family app and has signed up to receive posts from their children. They can only see their children's posts. The parents receive the post and can now see the video (Figure 5.3) that you posted.

- **Photo tool**: Use the camera tool (Figure 5.4) to take a picture of the students' music creations. An example is them using manipulatives to place the pitches mi, sol, and la on a staff. Use the record tool within the photo tool to record them performing their musical creation. Click the accept tool. Do this again for each student. The parent or caregiver of each student can now see and hear their child's musical creation.
- **Link tool**: Use the link tool (Figure 5.5) to share a link used in class. For example, my students love Staff Wars. This is a paid app for iOS and Google Play, but it can also be downloaded for free to your laptop at http://themusicinteractive.com/. When I have had the students review note names on the staff in a group activity using Staff Wars, they ask me how they can continue the activity at home. I place the link on their Seesaw journals with a caption or recording of how to download the program to their laptops and how to use the activity at home for family game

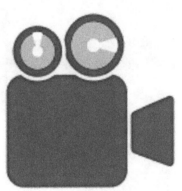

Figure 5.3.
Seesaw video tool.

Figure 5.4.
Seesaw photo tool.

night. In addition, I encourage the students to teach their parents how to name the notes on the staff.

- **Drawing tool**: Use the drawing tool (Figure 5.6) to write a rhythm pattern on the screen. Click the record button within the drawing tool and have the students perform the rhythm pattern together. Click accept and post the performance to the students' journals. The parents and caregivers can now see and listen to the rhythm pattern.
- **Upload tool**: Use the upload tool (Figure 5.7) to access anything you have taken photos or videos of from your classroom or performances, items in your Google Drive, or items on your device's hard drive. For example, if you add a photo of a new classroom instrument from your uploads tool, i.e., a glockenspiel, then use the record tool to have each student reflect on what that instrument can do, how to play it, what sound it can produce, what it is made of, and how it can play high and low. Ask them higher order thinking questions for them to answer as a group. Click accept and post the reflections along with the picture to the students' journals. Parents and caregivers can now see and listen to their reflections. Use the record tool within the camera tool to record the students' reflections.

Figure 5.5.
Seesaw link tool.

Figure 5.6.
Seesaw drawing tool.

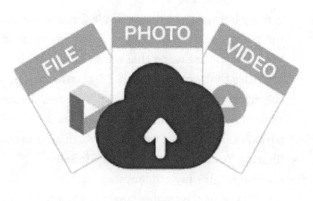

Figure 5.7.
Seesaw upload tool.

- **1:1 or a Few Devices in the Classroom**:
  - **Login**: The student logs in using a QR code (usually with students Grade 2 or younger) or a text code/email sign in (usually with students Grade 3 and up). They are now able to submit a post to you to post on their own journals. Nothing can be posted onto their journals until you approve it.
  - **Video tool**: Use the video tool for each child to video himself or herself performing the latest recorder melody (you can replace recorder with any instrument you choose to use in your classroom). Once they post it to their journals, you have the ability to approve it, discard it, tag a folder onto it to make it easier to filter the posts (for example, recorder folder), comment on it, or even assign skill sets to it and grade them (only paid versions can currently do this).
  - **Photo tool**: See the activity listed for the photo tool for one device in the classroom and have them record themselves performing and reflecting on their compositions. They click the check button to submit them. You have to approve it for it to appear in their journal and for their parents/caregivers to see and listen.
  - **Link tool**: If the students are using Chromebooks or the apps they are using will not "smash" to Seesaw (meaning that you can share from one app directly to Seesaw), then they copy the link and use the link tool to place it on their Seesaw journals. For example, if they created a Google site, then they can share their Google site link onto their Seesaw journals. You approve the post with the link and their parents can now easily access their child's Google site.
  - **Drawing tool**: Use the drawing tool to have the students write and perform a rhythm pattern. You can ask them to create a three-beat rhythm pattern using quarter and eighth notes and rests. They use the drawing tool to draw it and then click the microphone to record it. Once they click the check button to submit it, you can approve it, discard it, comment on it, tag a folder to it, etc. Once approved, their parents and caregivers can see their rhythm pattern and listen to their performances.
  - **Upload tools**: See the activity listed for the camera roll for one device in the classroom. Then click the check button to submit it. You have to approve it for it to appear in their journal and for their parents or caregivers to see and listen.
- **Activities**: Seesaw has activities included in their app (free and paid versions) that you can assign students to perform and submit. For example, you can go into the

activity library and browse Grade 1 music activities. You will find a plethora of activities to choose from written by Seesaw Ambassadors. Seesaw Ambassadors are mostly teachers who are using these activities in their classroom. Therefore, they have tested activities that work well. In a 1:1 classroom, you can assign activities to your students to perform and submit. You can approve, discard, comment, tag a folder, and assign skill sets to grade them on (skill sets are in the paid versions only). Once approved, the parents can see these activities, which are in some ways assessments.

- **Sharing Your Seesaw Journals Globally**:
  - I love to give my students an authentic audience. Their parents and caregivers, as well as their classmates, are only their first audience. I like to be able to connect their journals to other students' journals outside of our classroom.
  - **Seesaw blogs**: Seesaw has a blog feature to turn the posts that you choose into a blog to share with a larger audience. I choose posts that have no students' faces in them. Seesaw provides a Google doc that shows other classes' blog addresses so that you can easily contact them to connect to them. One year, my third graders shared their blog with a Grade 6 and 7 instrument class in Michigan. My students commented on their compositions. This was a great way for my young students to learn about compositions, instruments (they performed their compositions), to reinforce location (they were learning about the 50 states and could find the school's state on the map), and to learn about digital citizenship. My students had to use a design thinking tool of "I like," "I wonder," "What if." For example, "I like the melody and the way it moves high to low." "I wonder what it would sound like if it moved low to high." "What if you added a few measures with low to high notes?"
  - **Website example**: Go to www.oup.com/us/utema to see all of the preceding examples in action. If you are a member of NJMEA, you can earn PD hours for listening to and answering questions about the webinar.⊛
- **Flipgrid (flipgrid.com)**: Check out Appendix, "Links Listed Throughout the Book and Descriptions of Programs," for a detailed description of Flipgrid.
  - **Ideas for your elementary music classroom that are based on the Orff-Schulwerk approach using Flipgrid**:
  - **One Device in the Classroom**:
    - Create a free account.
    - Create a grid that represents your music classroom. Examples include one grid per classroom or one grid per grade.
  - Create topics for your grid that encourage performance and reflection.
    - There are options for sharing grids.
    - The students can log into your grid with their email addresses.
    - For students with no email addresses, you can create student logins so that they will have a QR code to scan to join the grid.
    - Or you can make the grid public with a password to enter the grid.
    - Suggestions for topics include orffestrations, simple melodies, recorder melodies, etc.
  - In the topic, click the + button and record the students performing orffestrations, singing simple melodies as a group, a trio, a duet, a solo, etc., performing recorder melodies in groups or as solos, and so much more.

- If they are shy, have them click the whiteboard button, where they can add emoji stickers and record their singing without having to appear in the video (Figure 3.8).
- **1:1 Devices**
  - Very similar to the preceding, but you can add the instructions.
  - Add a new topic within the class grid titled, "Recorder Songs."
    - The recording time for each video submitted will currently default to one minute and thirty seconds.
    - In the section marked "Prompt," type the instructions.
    - In the section marked "Focus (Optional)," you can video record yourself giving the instructions or an example of a Simple Song.
      - Have the students access your grid (via email addresses or QR code) and click the green + button.
      - Have them video record themselves performing a simple song.
        - If they are shy, have them click the whiteboard button, where they can add emoji stickers and record their singing without having to appear in the video (Figure 3.8).
        - Once they finish their video, they can add a selfie as their thumbnail (you can turn this off in the settings if needed).
        - In the settings, you can turn on the item that allows you to approve each video that is submitted.
    - In the Guest Mode, you can invite the parents/caregivers or other music classes in the school to view the videos. You can change the settings to allow the visitor to leave video comments.
    - Encourage students to use the Design Thinking process of "I like . . ." "I wish . . ." "What if . . ." For example, "I like your recorder song. I wish the notes did not pop. What if you cover the holes more so that the notes do not pop as much?"
    - Click on #Gridpals to find other music classes from around the world to share this grid.
  - **Website example**: Go to www.oup.com/us/utema to see all of the preceding examples in action. If you are a member of NJMEA, you can earn PD hours for listening to and answering questions about the webinar. ⊚

Higher Order Thinking Questions to Ask the Students:
As you use a digital student portfolio tool more in your classroom, the higher order thinking questions will come naturally. Examples:

- Since you knew that your post would be seen by others, did that affect the way you performed the music?
- If your science teacher viewed your post, how you would explain how your instrument makes sound using the knowledge you have learned from science and music classes?

Extensions: Where to Begin with a Student Digital Learning Portfolio
A student digital learning portfolio is a game-changer in your classroom. You can now bring your classroom to parents'/caregivers' mobile devices and connect globally. When you begin using them in your classroom, begin small. Start with one class and ask a teacher to join you in the class, for example, an art teacher or a classroom teacher. Begin with you posting and tagging the students. As you get comfortable, have the students

begin posting and reflecting. To bring parents on board, use the app's premade email/printouts to get the parents to sign up and connect to their child's portfolio. Or in the case of Flipgrid, share the link to the classroom's grid. Continuously approach them to get them connected through emails, going to PTA meetings, etc.

Using NYU Music Experience Design Musedlab's Groove Pizza to Create and Perform

Curriculum Note: *Using the free music creation tool of NYU Music Experience Design Musedlab's Groove Pizza* (https://apps.musedlab.org/groovepizza), *students can create drum grooves using mathematical angles. This is a great cross-curricular connection with math, but keeps music as the focus of the lesson.*

Objective: The students will create a drum groove to perform the melody of Queen's "We Will Rock You" on recorder (you can use other melodic instruments for this lesson besides recorder).

Grade Levels: Grades 3–6

Materials: A device that can access NYU Music Experience Design Musedlab's Groove Pizza, found at https://apps.musedlab.org/groovepizza, and Soundtrap, found at https://www.soundtrap.com (Soundtrap is easiest as Groove Pizza exports directly into it, but you can use other Digital Audio Workstations (DAW) like GarageBand or Audacity for this lesson), a projector to project this site onto a screen, and recorders. This is intended for one device in a classroom projecting onto a screen, but can easily be adapted to a 1:1 classroom..

Standards: Creating, Performing, Responding, and Connecting

Essential Questions:

- What is the relationship with mathematical angles and music?
- What is a groove?
- How are grooves and beats related?

Procedures:

- Before class, make sure that your device is connected to the internet and a projector and that you have created a free account in Soundtrap, found at https://www.soundtrap.com.
  - **Tech tip**: As long as you are using Soundtrap and not having each child use it on his or her own device, then the free version will work for this lesson. If you plan to use it with all children on their own devices, then I highly recommend the educational (EDU) version they offer, or you can acquire it through MusicFirst (https://www.musicfirst.com).
- Launch *NYU Music Experience Design Musedlab's Groove Pizza*, found at https://apps.musedlab.org/groovepizza.
- Click the play button and ask the students, "What is a groove?"
- Identify the shapes seen on the screen, which are a triangle and a line.
- Have you or the students come up to the device to change the shapes by clicking on the dots in each circle.
- Ask the students to reflect on how the groove changed when the shapes changed.
- Cross-curricular connection: Ask the students to name the shape.

- Click on "Specials" and scroll down to "Rock You." This will display the groove to the song, "We Will Rock You" by Queen.
- Since the first circle has a rectangle with the Rock You Groove, have the students use other shapes to create grooves for the other three circles. Or, copy the Rock You Groove into the other three circles by just clicking on each circle (it automatically copies the first groove into the other circles).
- Click the Share button and scroll over to "Continue in Soundtrap."
- If you are logged into Soundtrap, it will automatically open it in a new window and show the four circles as four separate drum tracks.
  - You can add another track by clicking on "Add New Track" and then the microphone icon.
  - Teach the students how to play the melody to "We Will Rock You": C B A G A A to the rhythm of ta ta ta ta ti-ta.
  - Click on the record button and answer the questions that come up on the screen.
  - Let the loop play the first two measures to set up the rhythm and tempo.
  - Have the students play the melody beginning on measure three.
  - Once finished, press the stop button.
- Play back the recording and have the students listen and respond to their performance.

Higher Order Thinking Questions to Ask the Students:

- What did you like about your performance?
- What do you wonder about what you could improve on?
- What if we record it again and see if we can improve on that aspect of the performance?

Extensions: This lesson is prepared with a guided groove and melody. In the next lesson, have the students create and compose their own groove with Groove Pizza and their own short melody using traditional staff paper or a web-based composition program like Noteflight (https://www.noteflight.com).

Using Odogy to Practice and Assess Recorder Songs

Curriculum Note: *Using the website* https://odogy.com/LearnToPlayRecorderSongs/, *you can have your students perform recorder melodies in a fun way. Currently, this website has a page titled "Recorder Karate." This site has traditional recorder melodies where the students can perform and be tested on their performances. No email addresses are required. Each student can add his or her name to the player's list. There are settings to turn off the recorder fingering chart, to turn off the note names or make them appear one to three times and then turn off, to change the tempo of the song, to turn off the game mode, and to turn off the accompaniment.*

Objective: Students will practice recorder melodies in a fun way using https://odogy.com/LearnToPlayRecorderSongs/.

Grade Levels: Grades 3–6

Materials: You can do this with one device in the classroom or 1:1 classroom. Your devices need to be connected to the internet, be able to access flash websites (Adobe Flash will be discontinued at the end of 2020), have working internal microphones, and it would be beneficial if they were either connected to a decent pair of speakers or, if a 1:1 classroom, that each student had headphones. A projector is beneficial so that you can demonstrate the website to the students and have the students perform all together if you are not a 1:1 classroom. You will need the website https://odogy.com/LearnToPlayRecorderSongs/ and their recorders.

Standards: Performing: MU:Pr4.1.3a, MU:Pr4.2.3a, MU:Pr4.2.3b, MU:Pr4.2.3c, MU:Pr4.3.3a, MU:Pr5.1.3a, MU:Pr5.1.3b, MU:Pr6.1.3a, MU:Pr6.1.3b, MU:Pr4.1.4a, MU:Pr4.2.4a, MU:Pr4.2.4b, MU:Pr4.2.4c, MU:Pr4.3.4a, MU:Pr5.1.4a, MU:Pr5.1.4b, MU:Pr6.1.4a, MU:Pr6.1.4b, MU:Pr4.1.5a, MU:Pr4.2.5a, MU:Pr4.2.5b, MU:Pr4.2.5c, MU:Pr4.3.5a, MU:Pr5.1.5a, MU:Pr5.1.5b, MU:Pr6.1.5a, MU:Pr6.1.5b, MU:Pr4.1.6a, MU:Pr4.2.6a, MU:Pr4.2.6b, MU:Pr4.2.6c, MU:Pr4.3.6a, MU:Pr5.1.6a, MU:Pr6.1.6a, MU:Pr6.1.6b

Essential Questions:

- How does the tempo of the song affect the way you perform it?
- Does performing a song with the motivational tool of it being a game, enhance or hinder the learning process?

Procedures:

- Before class, test the website https://odogy.com/LearnToPlayRecorderSongs/ (Recorder Karate) and your device's internal microphone by performing one of the Recorder Karate songs. In addition, add the player's name; if this is the whole class, add the name of the class, for example 3C. Project the website to a screen. If you have a decent pair of speakers, make sure your device is connected to them.
- Use the settings that best fit the needs of the class: note names on or off, fingering chart on or off, accompaniment on or off, game mode on or off, and set the tempo.
- When the class enters, sing "Hot Cross Buns."
- Pass out their recorders and review the notes to "Hot Cross Buns," which are B, A, and G.
- Launch https://odogy.com/LearnToPlayRecorderSongs/ and click on Recorder Karate.
- After answering the prompts of enabling the microphone and the player's name, click on "Hot Cross Buns."
- Demonstrate performing the song with the accompaniment. Have the students then perform with the accompaniment. Set the tempo accordingly. If the accompaniment distracts them, then turn it off and have them play without it.
- Demonstrate the game mode to show them how to achieve a score. The game mode assesses the student's performance of notes, not rhythms.
- With one device in the classroom, have the students play the game mode in small groups. As one group performs, the other group is "ghost fingering" the song.
- In a 1:1 classroom, have the students access the website, enable their microphone, put in their name as a player, put on their headphones, and individually perform and earn scores for their performances.
- **Tech tip**: In a 1:1 classroom, this can be challenging, as the devices can pick up other sounds being produced in the room. A solution is for the students to spread out, play into the device as close as they can, and to play the recorder quietly. If this does not work, use one device and divide into small groups, so that one group performs while the other groups "ghost finger."

Higher Order Thinking Questions to Ask the Students:

- How did the tempo affect the way that you performed?
- Which did you like better: performing with the accompaniment or not, and why?
- Which did you like better: performing in the game mode or not, and why?

Extensions: Record the scores by having you or the students write them down. Later in the school year, have them perform the lesson again to see if their scores improve.

Using DoReMi123 to Enhance Improvisation

Curriculum Note: *The free version of the app DoReMi 123 can be found at the iOS app store (https://itunes.apple.com/us/app/doremi-1-2-3-music-for-kids/id479692413?mt=8) and on Google Play (https://play.google.com/store/apps/details?id=com.creativity. doremi.lite&hl=en_US). There are also paid versions with in-app purchases that can be found for both systems.*
Objective: The students will improvise using boomwhackers and guided pitches.
Grade Levels: Grades 1–4

Materials: One device connected to a screen. I would suggest using an adapter so that when the students tap a pitch, the app responds quickly. You can mirror your device's screen through airplay/Chromecast/etc., but there might be a delay when the student taps a pitch and when the app plays the sound. You will need the free version of the app DoReMi 123 for iOS or Google Play. Google Play versions of the app can play on Android devices, as well as Chromebooks. You will also need boomwhackers, non-pitched classroom instruments, and Orff instruments. The song "Doggie Doggie," the notated melody of which can be found on the supplemental website for this book at www.oup.com/us/utema.⊛

Standards: Creating: MU:Cr1.1.1a, MU:Cr1.1.2a, MU:Cr1.1.3a, MU:Cr1.1.4a, **Performing:** MU:Pr4.2.1a, MU:Pr4.2.1b, MU:Pr4.2.2a, MU:Pr4.2.2b, MU:Pr4.2.3a, MU:Pr4.2.3b, MU:Pr4.2.4a, MU:Pr4.2.4b
Essential Questions:

- How does the understanding of musical concepts shape how a melody is improvised by a performer?
- How do musicians generate musical ideas?

Procedures:

- Before class, launch the app, DoReMi 123.
  - Press play.
    - **Tech tip:** If you are using the Google Play version on the Chromebook, it will tell you that the page is missing. Press the back arrow and click on guest user. It will then continue as listed in the following.
  - Press the rainbow button.
  - Press Rockin' River (the one with the dragon).
  - Press the panda bear to make music.
  - In the upper right-hand corner, change the pointer so it points at the eighth notes.
  - The pandas will now sing in their head voices using the solfege syllables.

- Greet the students and review the song "Doggie Doggie."
  - Sing the melody.
  - Tap the rhythm on their laps using the rhythmic syllables of your choice.
- Introduce improvisation.
  - Launch the app DoReMi123.
  - Assign a student to the device with DoReMi123.
    - Give the student a slow, steady beat by playing an alternating bordun on C and G on the bass or contrabass bars (or piano).
    - The student performs a pattern to the rhythm of the phrase, "Doggie Doggie" (ti-ti ti-ti), using the DoReMi123 app. The students sing back the improvisation by phrase, with the help of using hand signals.
    - Continue to have students come to the app to improvise a short melody using each phrase of "Doggie Doggie" that the class echoes with their singing voices.
  - Assign students to the boomwhackers and Orff instruments (remove the bars C, D, F, and B). Leave the E, G, and A bars on the instrument. If the students are young, I would only leave one set of E, G, and A bars on and take the other set off.
    - If there are not enough boomwhackers and Orff instruments per student, supplement with non-pitched classroom instruments or virtual instruments.
    - In the key of C, determine E to be mi, G to be sol, and A to be la.
    - Have a student improvise a melody using only the pitches mi, sol, and la and the rhythm of the words to each phrase of "Doggie Doggie" with the app, while the others echo on their instruments.
    - Continue until all students have had a turn improvising.
    - For some turns, play the alternating C and G bordun to create a steady beat.

Higher Order Thinking Questions to Ask the Students:

- How do the musical improvisations from the game turn into new melodies?
- Was it easier to echo the pattern back when a leader played the patterns with a steady beat? Why or why not?

Extensions: Use a staff on a felt board with music notes (or create a staff in a program like Google Slides, PowerPoint, Keynote, Notebook—see the beginning of the Kodály lesson section to learn how to do this) and have the students drag the same pitches to the staff to create a melody that they can sing and record themselves to share with others.

Practicing Reading Notes in a Fun Game-Like Way Using Staff Wars

Curriculum Note: *Staff Wars, a notation reading game in the style of Star Wars developed by Craig Gonci, is a paid app for iOS* (https://itunes.apple.com/us/app/staffwars/id810405576?ls=1&mt=8), *Google Play devices, and Chromebooks* (https://play.google.com/store/apps/details?id=air.com.themusicinteractive.staffwars), *and Amazon Kindle* (https://www.amazon.com/Craig-Gonci-Staffwars/dp/B00NN2TD8C/ref=sr_sp-atf_title_1_1?ie=UTF8&qid=1410992318&sr=8-1&keywords=staffwars), *as well as a free app that can be downloaded to a computer from the website* http://www.themusicinteractive.com.

Objective: The students will practice reading notes B, A, and G on the treble clef staff.

Grade Levels: Grades 3–5

Materials: A device that has Staff Wars on it, projected onto a screen or interactive white-board, with a decent pair of speakers. If you are going to perform this lesson in a 1:1 class-room, you will need to have the paid version of the app placed onto the individual devices. The school's administration would have to handle this and can purchase some of the apps through Apple's Volume Purchase Program or something similar.

Standards: Performing: MU:Pr4.1.3a, MU:Pr4.2.3a, MU:Pr4.2.3b, MU:Pr4.2.3c, MU:Pr4.3.3a, MU:Pr5.1.3a, MU:Pr5.1.3b, MU:Pr6.1.3a, MU:Pr6.1.3b, MU:Pr4.1.4a, MU:Pr4.2.4a, MU:Pr4.2.4b, MU:Pr4.2.4c, MU:Pr4.3.4a, MU:Pr5.1.4a, MU:Pr5.1.4b, MU:Pr6.1.4a, MU:Pr6.1.4b, MU:Pr4.1.5a, MU:Pr4.2.5a, MU:Pr4.2.5b, MU:Pr4.2.5c, MU:Pr4.3.5a, MU:Pr5.1.5a, MU:Pr5.1.5b, MU:Pr6.1.5a, MU:Pr6.1.5b

Essential Questions:

- How will the study of reading notes enable the student to better understand and appreciate music and become a more competent musician?

Procedures:

- Load Staff Wars onto a device and project it onto a screen. If you are using a device with the Staff Wars app that will airplay to the screen (this means it will project wirelessly), then I suggest using an adapter and hardwiring it into the projector so that the game will not have a delay in latency.
- Review the notes B, A, and G on the staff. I tend to do this with a large felt staff, asking students to place notes on the G or B lines or the A space.
- Launch Staff Wars and demonstrate the game.
  - Click on where you see the range.
  - If you click it several times, it will show you predetermined ranges, such as all lines or all spaces. The final click will be a customized range. Here is where I set the range to be the notes B, A, and G.
  - Click the treble clef and the game is ready to begin.
  - The game defaults to not showing the answer when an incorrect answer is given. You can click on "Show Answer" to show the correct answers when an incorrect answer is given.
  - It also defaults to C D E F G A B order on the screen. If you click on the arrows you can change the order.
  - Click start and demonstrate the game.
- This time, you play the game again, but the students will call out the letter name as it floats across the screen. You click the majority of the letter name called out. For example, if you hear most students call out a G, then you click on the G. Play until all lives run out.
- Play the game again, but this time, divide the class into two groups. Have the groups line up in front of the device or interactive whiteboard. Assign a group to go first. Click start and the child will tap the note name. Then, the student in the other group will come up and tap the note name. Continue until all lives run out. Play the game a few times until all students are getting at least two turns.
- Play the game again with small groups of no more than three students in a group. Each group takes turns answering the note name as it flies across the screen. For example, the first note is answered by group 1; the second note is answered by group 2; the third note is answered by group 3; etc.

- **Assessment**: Video record the lesson using a mobile device, such as your phone, to watch later. As you watch, you can take note of the students' responses.

Higher Order Thinking Questions to Ask the Students:

- You all are musicians in this classroom. Why is it important to learn to read notes?
- If you feel that it is not important, then why do you feel this way?

Extensions: Currently, there is the paid iOS app called Staff Wars Live that allows students to perform the notes being played on the screen in order to blow them up. This is a wonderful tool for learning to read notes while playing the recorder, an Orff instrument, or singing. It used to be a free downloadable app from the same site, but it is no longer being developed for computers. See the next lesson to learn more about Staff Wars Live.

Using Staff Wars Live to Assess Recorder Note Reading and Playing Skills

Curriculum Note: *Staff Wars Live is currently a paid iOS app found at* https://itunes.apple. com/us/app/staffwars-live/id1071622918?ls=1&mt=8, *developed by TMI Media LLC. The free version that you used to be able to download from* http://themusicinteractive.com *is no longer being developed.*

Objective: The students will read and perform notes on the recorder.

Grade Levels: Grades 3–6

Materials: This lesson requires Staff Wars Live, a paid iOS app found at https://itunes. apple.com/us/app/staffwars-live/id1071622918?ls=1&mt=8. This lesson is for one iOS device connected to a projector and speakers. To project the iOS device to the screen, use airplay (wirelessly, like Apple TV, around $149+, or the Reflector app, around $14.99) or an adapter (HDMI or VGA, depending on your setup). My advice is to use the adapter so that the device is hardwired into the projector and works more consistently.

Standards: Performing: MU:Pr4.1.3a, MU:Pr4.2.3a, MU:Pr4.2.3b, MU:Pr4.2.3c, MU:Pr4.3.3a, MU:Pr5.1.3a, MU:Pr5.1.3b, MU:Pr6.1.3a, MU:Pr6.1.3b, MU:Pr4.1.4a, MU:Pr4.2.4a, MU:Pr4.2.4b, MU:Pr4.2.4c, MU:Pr4.3.4a, MU:Pr5.1.4a, MU:Pr5.1.4b, MU:Pr6.1.4a, MU:Pr6.1.4b, MU:Pr4.1.5a, MU:Pr4.2.5a, MU:Pr4.2.5b, MU:Pr4.2.5c, MU:Pr4.3.5a, MU:Pr5.1.5a, MU:Pr5.1.5b, MU:Pr6.1.5a, MU:Pr6.1.5b, MU:Pr4.1.6a, MU:Pr4.2.6a, MU:Pr4.2.6b, MU:Pr4.2.6c, MU:Pr4.3.6a, MU:Pr5.1.6a, MU:Pr6.1.6a, MU:Pr6.1.6b

Essential Questions:

- How will the study of reading notes enable the student to better understand and appreciate music and become a more competent musician?

Procedures:

- Before class, hook the iOS device up to the projector and speakers.
- Launch Staff Wars Live.
- Click on the settings. Set them to the following:
  - Choose Key: G
  - Scale: Major
  - Instrument: Recorder
  - Range: Second line G to fourth line D

- Click Save.
- Click the treble clef.
- Greet the students and begin with your normal welcome routines.
- Pass out recorders and review the notes G, A, B, C, and D.
- Demonstrate Staff Wars Live
  - As the note flies across the screen, play the note to blow it up.
  - **Tech tip**: If the app is not hearing you, go to the settings on your iOS device, scroll all the way down to Staff Wars Live and tap it. In the right part of the screen, turn the microphone on so that the app can access the device's microphone.
- Have the students line up and have each one of them come up to the device to play the note that flies across the screen.
- Play the game a few times until everyone has had at least two turns.
- **Activity tip**: Divide the class into a few groups and have them take turns playing the game with one device. While one group takes its turn, the other groups are ghost fingerings.
- **Activity tip**: Set the device up as a station where students rotate through to perform and read notes on their recorders.

Higher Order Thinking Questions to Ask the Students:

- You all are musicians in this classroom. Why is it important to learn to read notes?
- If you feel that it is not important, then why do you feel this way?

Extensions: If your school is 1:1 devices, talk to your instructional technology about participating in Apple's Volume Purchase Program to place this app onto the students' devices. Besides recorder, the app has numerous instruments listed from treble clef (your voice singing into the app) to Orff instruments.

Using Book Creator and Orff Instruments to Make a Book Come to Life

Curriculum Note: *This lesson turns any book into an ebook into which you can add the students' music. Book Creator (https://bookcreator.com/) is an iOS app where you can make one ebook for free, or purchase the app (currently $4.99) to create numerous ebooks. You can also register for a subscription on the web-based app and create 40 ebooks for free.*

Objective: The students make a book come to life with sound by creating an ebook.

Grade Levels: Grades 1–4

Materials: For this lesson, we will use *Mortimer* by Robert Munsch, a device to take pictures, and the Book Creator app found at https://www.bookcreator.com. The device that has Book Creator is connected to a projector and displayed onto a screen or TV. Before this class, the students would have already experienced *Mortimer* by having it read to them, acted it out, and performed the song and melodic stair climbing on the Orff instruments and other pitched instruments. You will use those pitched instruments again for this lesson.

Standards: Creating: MU:Cr1.1.1a, MU:Cr1.1.2a, MU:Cr1.1.3a, MU:Cr1.1.4a, **Performing**: MU:Pr4.2.1a, MU:Pr4.2.1b, MU:Pr4.2.2a, MU:Pr4.2.2b, MU:Pr4.2.3a, MU:Pr4.2.3b, MU:Pr4.2.4a, MU:Pr4.2.4b

Essential Questions:

- When is a creative idea ready to share?
- When is a performance ready to share?

Procedures:

- Before class, launch Book Creator.
  - Click on a new book.
  - Click the + at the top of the screen and scroll down to the camera icon.
  - This will launch your device's camera.
  - Take a picture of the cover.
  - Add a new page (> or + on the side of the screen depending on your device).
  - Take a picture of the next page.
  - Do this for every page until you have a complete book in the Book Creator app.
  - **Tech tip**: In the web-based app, if you need to change around the order or delete a page, click on "Pages," move the page to the proper place, or click on the three dots to delete. When finished, click "Back" on the top left-hand side of the screen.
  - **Tech tip**: In the iOS app, if you need to change around the order or delete a page, click on "Pages," click "Edit," and the pages will begin to wiggle. You can now move a page to its proper place. To delete it, while it is wiggling, tap the page that you want to delete, and click delete. To return to the ebook, click "Done," and then click the page that you want. If you click "Cancel," it will discard the changes that you made.
- Greet the students and review the book *Mortimer* by Robert Munsch.
- Launch the ebook that you created before class in Book Creator.
- Have the students go to a pitched instrument or Orff instrument and review how to perform the low-to-high and the high-to-low stair climbing that occurs in the book (we used a C pentatonic scale for this).
- Have the students review the song that Mortimer sings. For my classroom, the students played an alternating C and G bordun while singing a melody that consisted of the pitches do, re, mi, and sol that I learned in a workshop. You can create your own melody to the words listed in the book.
- For the pages with words and no music, ask a student to read the page while you record their reading.
  - Click the + button at the top of the page.
  - Scroll down to the microphone.
  - Click "Start Recording" and let the student read the words on the page.
  - Click "Accept Recording" and the sound icon appears on the page.
- For the pages with the numerous "Thump" in the ascending and descending melodic lines, ask a student to read the page and the pitched instruments to play the "Thump."
  - Click the + button at the top of the page.
  - Scroll down to the microphone.
  - Click "Start Recording" and let the student read the words on the page and the students perform the "Thump."
  - Click "Accept Recording" and the sound icon appears on the page.
- For the pages with Mortimer singing the song, have the students perform the bordun while singing the song.
  - Click the + button at the top of the page.
  - Scroll down to the microphone.

- Click "Start Recording" and have the students perform the bordun while singing the song.
- Click "Accept Recording" and the sound icon appears on the page.
- Once finished, you and your students have made their own ebook version of the book.
- Since this book is the intellectual property of the author, you would need permission to share the book publicly. However, your class could share this ebook with another class in the school, or use it to be played for a younger class in the school, such as pre-kindergarten and kindergarten.
  - You can play the book within the Book Creator app.
  - You could also export the book as a video (if you are using the iOS app). If you are using the web-based app, you can download it as an ebook and open it in an app that can read ebooks, like iBooks or Kindle.

Higher Order Thinking Questions to Ask the Students:

- We finished our ebook. Do you feel that it is ready to share with another class at our school? Why or why not?
- Do you perform differently when you know that someone else besides the teacher and your classmates will listen to it?

Extensions: Since this ebook cannot be shared outside of school, use the version of this lesson in the Project-Based Learning section (Chapter 6) of the book to create their own ebook from scratch.

Enhancing Speech Rhythms with Incredibox

Curriculum Note: *This lesson focuses on creating an accompaniment to speech rhythms using the website or app Incredibox. If you can use the website, currently only four out of the seven versions are available. The paid Incredibox app (https://www.incredibox.com/mobile/) is available for iOS, Google Play, and Amazon Devices and has at least six versions.*

Objective: The students will create an accompaniment to their original speech rhythms that they will perform for the entire class.

Grade Levels: Grade 2 and up

Materials: Paper and pencils as well as the Incredibox app, either played through the website, https://www.incredibox.com, or through the iOS, Google Play, or Amazon mobile apps found at https://www.incredibox.com/mobile. This can be done with one device in a classroom projected to a screen, hooked to a decent pair of speakers, or a classroom with a few devices or 1:1 devices.

Standards: Performing and Creating for Grades 2 and up

Essential Questions:

- How does an accompaniment affect a performance?
- What is essential for a good accompaniment?

Procedures:

- **Create Speech Rhythms**
  - Ask the students to write a haiku. A haiku is a Japanese poem with 5 syllables in the first line, 7 syllables in the second line, and 5 syllables in the third line, with the lines not rhyming. It should leave the reader with a strong feeling.

- Give them ideas to write about, from animals to food.
- Group students together if you feel that they would not be able to write a haiku individually.
- Once finished, have them decode the rhythm of the words and perform them for the class.
- **Create an accompaniment using Incredibox (https://www.incredibox.com)**
  - On the teacher's device connected to a projector and screen (or airplay to a screen), launch Incredibox and one of the versions.
    - **Tech tip**: Version two has a good tempo for a rhythm composition.
    - **Tech tip**: Version one in the flash-based website has the cartoon beatboxers all wearing shirts, as opposed to the other versions where you add the shirts in the forms of melodies, beats, voices, and effects. However, you can only find this flash-based version through a Google search, and Flash will be discontinued at the end of 2020.
  - Create an accompaniment and have one student or group perform their haiku rhythm composition with the accompaniment.
  - Have the students create their own Incredibox accompaniments to their haiku rhythm compositions and perform them for the class.

Higher Order Thinking Questions to Ask the Students:

- Which did you like better: performing with the accompaniment, or without? Why?
- What did the accompaniment need to have in order for you to be able to perform your haiku rhythm composition well?

Extensions: Share their performances with a broader audience by using a mobile device to video their performances, or audio record their performances, and share via a school website, email, music classroom website, or a digital learning portfolio like Seesaw.

Statue in the Park

Curriculum Note: *Using the file titled Statues.pdf, found on the supplemental website*, www.oup.com/us/utema, *electronically display these stick figure statues for students to create when moving to music.*⊛

Objective: The students will move to music and create guided statues when the music is paused using the digital statue cards.

Grade Levels: PreK and up

Materials: The file titled Statues.pdf, found on the supplemental website at www.oup.com/us/utema, and a device to display the file that is connected to the internet, as well as a projector or airplay to a screen.⊛

Standards: **Creating**: MU:Cr1.1.PKa, MU:Cr1.1.Ka, MU:Cr1.1.Kb, **Performing**: MU:Pr4.2.PKa, MU:Pr4.2.Ka, MU:Pr4.2.1a, MU:Pr4.2.2a, **Connecting**: MU:Cn10.0.PKa, MU:Cn10.0.Ka, MU:Cn10.0.1a, MU:Cn10.0.2a

Essential Understanding:

- The movement lesson will assist the students in broadening their movement possibilities, especially focusing on the awareness of shapes, the awareness of levels, and the awareness of others.

Procedures:

- Project the Statues.pdf file onto a screen.
  - **Any Device**: Place the pdf file in a Google Drive and then you can project the figures onto a screen by opening the file within Google Drive from any device.
  - **Document Camera**: Print out the pdf version of Statues.pdf and place under the document camera to project onto the screen. The document camera must be hooked up to the projector in order to do this.
- **Activity tip: Why project the cards when I can just print them and hold them up?** You can always choose this option. However, the students can have a challenging time seeing the cards that you are holding up in the air. When they are projected, the students have an easier time seeing the card and creating the movement shape.
- Choose a piece of music for this movement lesson. You can choose a recorded piece, or have half of your students perform an orffestration while the other half perform the movement statues.
  - If your school district will accommodate the cost, I suggest having a subscription to Spotify, Google Play, or Apple Music so you have access to a plethora of musical selections when you have internet access.
- Have the students spread out in the room (if they cannot spread out because they are seated at desks, then feel free to adapt the movements).
- Tell the students that when the music pauses, they must create the movement shape that is displayed on the screen. Remind the students that when the music pauses and they are performing the movement shape, they can always breathe, blink, and swallow.
- Begin playing the music and have the students move independently to the music.
- Pause the music with one of the shapes projected onto the screen. The students are to pause and create the shape with their bodies.
- Ask the students if their movement shape is high, middle, or low (to reinforce the awareness of levels).
- Resume playing the music and showcase another shape onto the screen.
- Pause the music again and have the students create the shape that is projected onto the screen.
- Continue until you present all 22 shapes. Feel free to arrange them in a different order than presented. Encourage groupings by showing the slides that have 2+ stick figures in them.
- For the final shape, have the students create their own shape with their bodies; walk around the room to compliment the students on their shapes and statues.

Higher Order Thinking Questions to Ask the Students:

- What movement shape did you create?
- What level is your movement shape (high, middle, or low)?

Extensions: Guide the students to use stick figure drawings to create their own shapes. Take pictures of the drawings and add them to a PowerPoint, Google Slide, Keynote, or Notebook file, or project them directly from your device to the projector by using Airplay, Reflector App, Apple TV (MAC/iOS), Miracast (PC/Android), Chromecast, etc., (for wireless results), or attaching the adapter from the device to the projector (for hardwire results). Play another piece of music and have the students become these new shapes when the music pauses.

Using Edpuzzle to Assess Learning to Play the Recorder

Curriculum Note: *Edpuzzle* (edpuzzle.com) *is a website where you can take a video, one that is already available or one that you have created, and turn it into a student comprehension lesson or assessment.*

Objective: Students will be assessed on their knowledge of the recorder.

Grade Levels: Grades 3–6

Materials: You can do this with one device in the classroom or in a 1:1 classroom. You can do this activity during class, or assign it to be done at home. You will need to create a free account at edpuzzle.com.

Standards: Responding: MU:Re7.2.3a, MU:Re7.2.4a, MU:Re7.2.5a, MU:Re7.2.6a

Essential Questions:

- What did you learn about the recorder?
- Why is it important to know about hand position, covering holes, and other items of the recorder?

Procedures:

- Before class, login to edpuzzle.com and create a free account.
- In the search bar, type "recorder."
  - The search results give you videos that are included in Edpuzzle that teachers have made to quiz their own music students. You will also see YouTube videos in your findings that you can use to create your own assessment.
  - If you choose an Edpuzzle video, click on the link. You will see an edit tab on the side of the screen where you can edit, copy, assign, and share (Figure 5.8).
    - You can then edit the questions that are included. You can crop the video to make it shorter, add a voice-over, add more questions, and add audio notes to get your student's attention.
    - In one video on Edpuzzle, the questions about the recorder are about hand position, which hand is on top, covering the holes, and the degree of the angle to hold the recorder. You can edit these questions, take them out, or add more. The questions can be T/F, multiple choice, or open ended so that there is no correct answer assigned.
    - **Tech tip**: If you edit a question, click save at the bottom of the question you edited.
    - Once editing is finished, click the "Save" button at the top of the screen.
    - Click the "Finish" button and it will ask you how you want to share it.
    - You can add a new class in this window. The class can be a "Classic" class where your students login and sign up. The class can also be "Open," where your students just have to enter a class code to join—no account required (Figure 5.9). You will be able to see the students' progress with this type of class.
      - Click "Create." I then check the box that turns on the close captioning and click "Assign" (Figure 5.10)

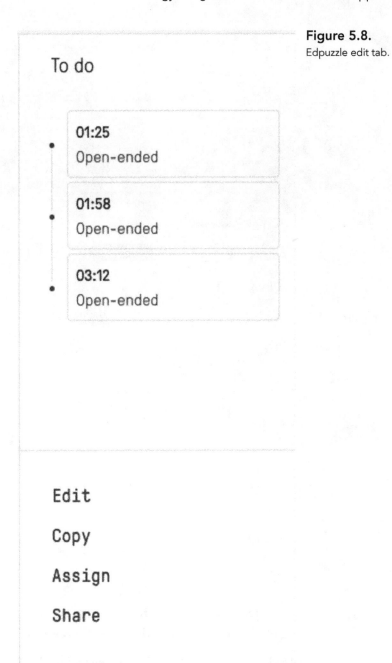

Figure 5.8.
Edpuzzle edit tab.

- I can share it to the class with a link or "Go Live." When I go live, the students follow a link to join my open class with the class code and the video now appears on their devices.
- Edpuzzle also shares directly to a Google Classroom, as well as imports the class roster from Google Classroom to Edpuzzle.
- You can see the students' progress at any time. You can set it up so that they cannot skip through the video, but must watch it, like we do with the safety videos at the beginning of the school year.
- Edpuzzle has numerous music education videos included. In addition, it will give you options from YouTube, or you could insert a YouTube link and edit the video with your questions. Finally, you can make your own video and upload it to Edpuzzle.

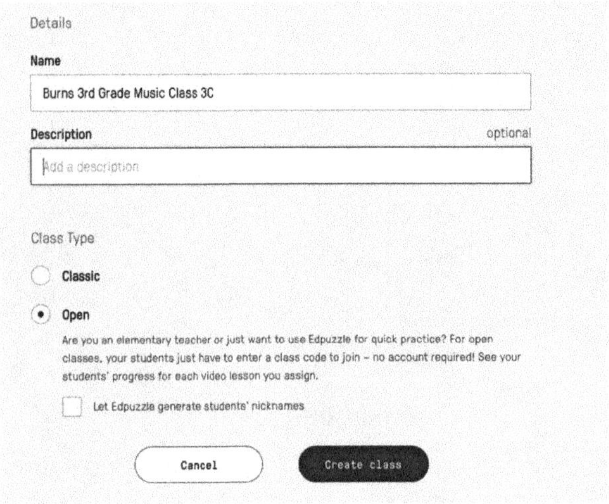

Figure 5.9.
Setting up a class in Edpuzzle.

Figure 5.10.
Creating an assignment in Edpuzzle.

- Edpuzzle is currently free for storing up to 20 videos. The pro paid versions have teacher and school editions and allow you to host more videos.

Higher Order Thinking Questions to Ask the Students:

- Why do we need to know about the basics of playing the recorder?
- Why are hand and finger positions important?

Extensions: Have the students create their own recorder tutorials to show the other classes about the basics of playing the recorder.

6

Project-Based Learning

Amy M. Burns and Cherie Herring

Project-Based Learning (PBL) is the teaching approach where, over a length of time, students learn the skills of research and problem-solving by answering essential questions. It enables students to master content knowledge and to develop real-world skills such as collaboration, problem-solving, and the use of technology. The essential questions involved in PBL encourage students to use higher order thinking skills, as well as working together to find potential answers for these questions. In the process of PBL, students develop their own meanings to the questions, they gain knowledge through research, and they continuously reflect and revise their work. They conclude by making their work into a presentation, publication, performance, exhibition, or some other type of exposition displaying the process beyond the classroom (HQPBL 2018; Buck Institute for Education, n.d.; Vander Ark & Liebtag, 2018; Teacher Thought Staff, 2019; Wolpert-Garwen, 2015).

In an elementary music classroom, PBL is a very natural process. Students in music class actively gain knowledge and skills through collaborating, performing, creating, responding, and connecting to music. This results in authentic music-making where the students make connections to the music that they are performing, creating, composing, moving to, recording, experiencing, and more.

Project-Based Learning also allows students to connect music across the curriculum. These types of connections help students see how music relates to math, reading, writing, world languages, science, physical education, art, library, social studies, history, STEAM (science, technology, engineering, arts, and mathematics), and so much more. However, when music educators utilize PBL, a fear that arises is that music becomes a "second fiddle" to the subject that music is connecting to throughout the PBL process. This is a legitimate concern, especially when some music educators might feel that they have to provide cross-curricular connections in order to advocate for keeping music in the schools.

I feel that the PBL process in the music classroom is meant to keep the music intact. When PBL is presented that way, it gives the students a deeper connection to music because it relates music to other subjects. It also empowers the students to take ownership of their learning. I have always felt that music is not a separate entity. The music taught to my elementary students does not only occur during a 40-minute music class that happens three times in a cycle. I want my students to feel that music is present in all subjects. The connections that they make in music class can be felt across the curriculum (Barry, 2018; Burns, Miller, Rubin, 2017; Miller, 2012).

Amy M. Burns and Cherie Herring, *Project-Based Learning* In: *Using Technology with Elementary Music Approaches.* Edited by: Amy M. Burns, Oxford University Press (2020). © Oxford University Press.
DOI: 10.1093/oso/9780190055653.003.0009

PBL Example

An example of this is when my students are researching their individual state for their Adventure America project in Grade 3 social studies. In music class, they are also using their musical skills to write an eight-measure song using Noteflight (https://www.noteflight.com—a web-based compositional software app) and Soundtrap (https://www.soundtrap.com—a web-based music making loop-based app) to create a state song for their individual states. They use their knowledge of their state to also write lyrics to their state songs (see Figure 6.1). The students are presented with a problem: their state needs a new state song. Currently, in New Jersey in 2020, this is an actual concern because we have never had an official state song. We have come close, but no New Jersey governor has ever made a song officially the state song. Therefore, students feel connected to this problem. When presented with writing a new state song for their individual states, they take their compositions and songwriting very seriously. The results are fantastic, with new state songs presented in a "Song ebook" made in Book Creator (www.bookcreator.com; see Figure 6.2). The ebook is shared in Seesaw (a digital student learning journal—web.seesaw.me), which is accessed by parents, as they have access to their child's digital Seesaw journal. The journals also contain reflections about the process and what they wanted their audience to know about their piece of music. These reflections can also be recorded in Seesaw or any type of exit ticket/assessment program like Socrative (www.socrative.com, see Figure 6.3).

This project eventually advanced into a science, technology, engineering, arts, and mathematics (STEAM) PBL, as the science teacher and I had the students dig deeper into the concepts of sound and how instruments produce sound. The students created instruments from recycled materials and performed their melody or percussion lines on their newly created instruments. For this STEAM PBL, the science teacher and I collaborated to teach the unit of sound together. Where we branched off was when she went on to use the unit of sound to have the students create blueprints of instruments that used the Design Thinking process of prototype and revisions, and I focused on the students working through the process of composing music and how they would perform their compositions on instruments that might only produce limited sounds (such as two pitches of high and low) (see Figures 6.4, 6.5, and 6.6).

Figure 6.1.
Third grader's state song about Maine.

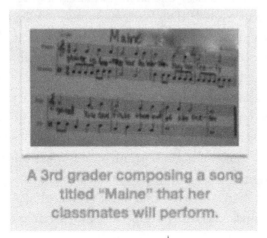

A 3rd grader composing a song titled "Maine" that her classmates will perform.

Figure 6.2.
Third Grade ebook of compositions.

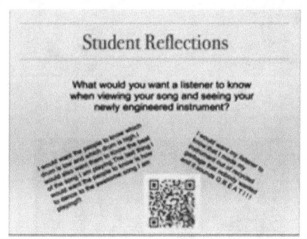

Figure 6.3.
Student reflections.

This is one of my favorite units because the students feel very connected to it. They are creating and performing music. They are understanding the relationship that music has with other subjects. The light bulbs go off when I begin focusing on sound in music class and they gasp, raise their hands, and state, "Mrs. Burns! Did you know that we are learning about sound in science class with Mrs. Wagar?" They are composing state songs for these newly created instruments that help them see the connections to science and to social studies (with their Adventure America unit). Through the creating, composing, performing, and the relationships, the students are experiencing PBL through an authentic musical experience. This unit is one that the students recall in later years because it was so meaningful to them.

Figure 6.4.
Student's guitar
made from recycled
materials.

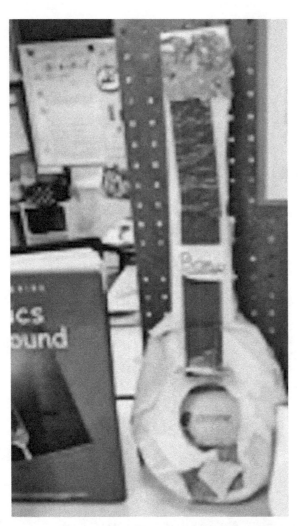

Figure 6.5.
Student's drum.

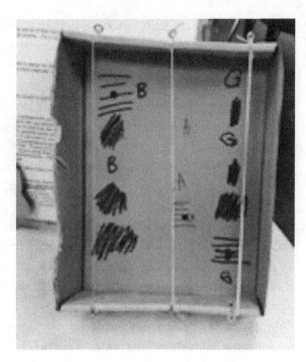

Figure 6.6.
Student's stringed
instrument.

Throughout this chapter, you will read examples of PBL in the elementary music class-room where technology enhanced the unit. Whether it was used as a tool for presentation or as a tool to enhance the process of learning music, the technology provides the teacher with a way to substitute or possibly redefine and extend the way the musical concepts were traditionally taught. All of these projects can be adapted. When you read through them, always think of them in a way that could possibly work in your teaching environment. Though the projects are broken into the cross-curricular connections, you can adapt these to perform all cross-curricular connections in your music room, as opposed to having all teachers included. Ideally, it would be wonderful to have all of the teachers working on the PBL together in their classrooms. However, realistically, you need to adapt the best way possible for your teaching environment. Finally, I am thrilled that Cherie Herring, from the Hammond School in South Carolina, contributed the final project included in this chapter.

Important Notes:

- *Before you use any tool with your students, please check with your school's administration regarding the technology policies of your school to make sure you can use students' information, including images, and that you have their support.*
- **Accompanying website for this book**: Type in any web browser, www.oup.com/us/utema or click on the link found here.[▶]

PBL Activities

Creating a Student Inquiry-Based Podcast: Part 1

For students in younger elementary, where the teacher will guide the making of the podcast.

PBL Concept: The students in Grades PreK/K/1 will learn a musical concept in class, such as melodic sequence, rhythm pattern, a composer, a SongTale, a song, a new instrument, etc., and create a podcast to "show what they know" to an audience.

Introduction:

In this example, the students are introduced to concepts of pitched instruments. In this case, we are using boomwhackers. The problem given to the students is that they are not allowed to be video recorded, but they have to tell their parents about what they learned in music class. In addition, since they cannot bring the boomwhackers home, they have to brainstorm a way to create something in music class that would "show what they know." Depending on whether or not their parents have access to mobile phones, many young children will tell you that you can use your phone to record them talking about boomwhackers. This is where I introduce podcasting and play a couple of podcasts as examples, such as *Elementary Tech Time* found at https://anchor.fm/elementary-tech-time, which are short podcasts produced by the elementary students at Leeds Elementary.

Materials:

One device in a classroom: In this example, we are using Soundtrap (https://www.soundtrap.com) to record the podcast, though GarageBand, Soundation (educational version), Anchor, or other music production apps or software can be used. We are using a USB Blue Spark microphone (https://www.bluedesigns.com) to record so that the sound quality is better. However, you can use the internal mic found in the device. For our audience, we are using Seesaw (web.seesaw.me), the digital student learning portfolio, but any platform for presentation can be used.

Website example: There is an example of this project on the supplemental website to this book, found at www.oup.com/us/utema. [▶]

Essential Questions:

- What is the same about two red boomwhackers? (Show a low C and a high C)
- What is different about the two red boomwhackers?
- Why do they play two different sounds, even though they have the same pitch/syllable and they are the same color?
- How does the boomwhacker produce sound?

Music:

This PBL portion comes after you have introduced the boomwhacker and have played it in a song. With younger students, we play ostinato patterns or repetitive rhythm patterns found in a song. An example would be the "oh yes" found in the song "John the Rabbit."

Launch Soundtrap (https://www.sountrap.com). Soundtrap is a free digital audio workstation (DAW) where you can make music online by recording, using loops, editing audio files, inviting others to collaborate, and more. You can create a free account for you to use as a teacher to do all of the preceding. If you have students using Soundtrap, look at the pricing for the educational (EDU) version, which you can use through Soundtrap or a music education platform like MusicFirst (https://www.musicfirst.com).

You can create a free account to perform this since you would be using it and not the younger elementary students. Click "Enter Studio" and click on a blank project (the podcast demo is a great way to learn about how to begin a podcast with Soundtrap). For this podcast, I used a USB Blue Spark USB microphone (https://www.bluedesigns.com) and attached it to the laptop.

Each student is seated in a circle and has a boomwhacker. Place the laptop near you with the microphone. Click the red record button and begin recording. Begin the podcast by introducing yourself and your class (you can have the students brainstorm a name for the podcast through a circle thinking map). Ask the essential questions to the students and have them answer. Then ask them to demonstrate the boomwhacker and to explain the process. Finish by asking them to reflect on one thing they love about the boomwhacker or one thing that challenges them.

When finished, click stop and save the recording. Together, give the students two choices of loops: one to add at the beginning and one to add at the end of the podcast. These loops could be a bass line, a drum track, a strings track, etc. Guide them with choices as it will help you corral numerous young children to give a solid answer. To add a loop, click and drag the loop to the screen. Once finished, title the file and click save.

Writing/Language Arts:
Writing is incorporated by asking the students to create a circle thinking map or a bubble thinking map (descriptive) to answer the essential questions. In addition, use a thinking map to brainstorm names for the podcast. You will be doing the writing for this age group.

Science:
In music class or science class, talk about how sound is produced. In addition, address how the shape and size of the boomwhacker affect the pitch. Finally, when the students observe the soundwaves created when they recorded in Soundtrap, talk about the shape of the waves.

Art:
You can extend this PBL to include art. Have them draw a logo or picture for your podcast. Use traditional art materials and take a picture of the artwork to include in the podcast. Though Soundtrap currently does not include pictures or videos, that could change. In addition, you could use WeVideo (https://www.wevideo.com) (cloud-based) or iMovie (https://www.apple.com/imovie/) (iOS/MAC only) to include artwork with audio.

World Languages:
In younger elementary grade levels, the students are learning how to say colors. Therefore, add a question about how to say their boomwhacker's color in another language.

Sharing the Project:
I feel that PBL is most effective when the students can share it with an audience. For these young children, our audience is the parents. Therefore, we shared it through the digital student learning portfolio Seesaw (web.seesaw.me). Alternatives are ClassDojo (https://www.classdojo.com), Bloomz (https://www.bloomz.net), Flipgrid (https://www.flipgrid.com), FreshGrade (freshgrade.com), or ClassTag (https://www.classtag.com/), to name a few.

Activity **tip when using** Flipgrid: Since Flipgrid is based in video, the teacher could use the whiteboard tool for the students to create the artwork for the podcast, and then press record. This will produce a recorded podcast with no video, just the whiteboard artwork. To read more details about Flipgrid, please visit Appendix, "Links Listed Throughout the Book and Descriptions of Programs."

Website example: There is an example of how to do this with Flipgrid on the supplemental website to this book, found at www.oup.com/us/utema. [▶]

Activity **tip when using** Seesaw and Soundtrap: Seesaw is a free digital student learning portfolio. You can set up a free account and add up to 10 classes with two teachers.

To read more details about Seesaw, please visit Appendix, "Links Listed Throughout the Book and Descriptions of Programs."

Create a class and invite the parents to join (Seesaw includes the parent/caregiver email invite and QR code so you can easily send it out to invite the parents/caregivers). If you used Soundtrap on the laptop, download the file from the main screen (tap on the file, click download, and it downloads as an MP3). Since Seesaw will not upload an MP3 file, I place the MP3 in my Google Drive. From there, I can create a link and copy the link. In your teacher Seesaw account, tap the + button, post student work, click "Link," and drag paste the link's address. From there, you can add a caption. Once finished, click the green check to approve, then click the students you want to post on their journals (if a student was absent, you could leave him or her out, but I would include all of the students), then click the green check to submit. If you make a mistake, click the back arrow until you get to the "delete and start over" option.

Activity **tip if you do not have access** to Seesaw or Flipgrid: If you do not have access to a digital student learning portfolio, you can download the file and email it to the parents/caregivers. In addition, you could ask for it to be posted to a school website or social media account, a music classroom website or social media account, etc.

Reflection:

An easy way to promote student reflection is to ask the students the following and record their answers with any recording app or software (like Soundtrap, Seesaw, Flipgrid, or your mobile device's recording app like Voice Memos).

- What did you like about the podcast?
- What do you wish you did better, or what do you wonder about the podcast?
- What if we did that next time?

If you are using digital student learning portfolios, ask the students to reflect as an exit ticket. Have them log into their Seesaw journal or their Flipgrid Grid and leave an activity, or ask them to video record themselves answering the question. This works best for a 1:1 classroom. My kindergartners and first graders have done this successfully.
Podcasting with younger elementary was authentic and impressive.

After I completed this once, the reading specialist jumped on board and had her students begin creating numerous podcasts about their reading games and goals. When I placed the podcasts on the Seesaw journals, the students were thrilled to see the parents liking and commenting on them (this is a feature can be turned off in Seesaw, but it is an effective way to teach digital citizenship).

When the students have learned a new song or concept, they now ask if they can podcast and Seesaw it. It makes me smile because they want to reflect and share. These two concepts are the foundations to higher order thinking skills and ownership of their learning.

Creating a Student Inquiry-Based Podcast: Part 2

For students in older elementary, where the teacher will begin by guiding, but will let the students direct and lead.

PBL Concept: The students in Grades 2–5 will learn a musical concept in class such as a composer, musical style, music history, melodic sequence, rhythm pattern, a SongTale, a song, a new instrument, etc., and create a podcast to "show what they know" to an audience.

Introduction:

In this example, the students have studied the music of Johann Sebastian Bach through moving to music, listening to and learning about the organ and the recorder (this correlates with our curriculum), studying his music and chord structures, and learning about him through books and movies (we use *Bach's Fight for Freedom*).

Materials:

This can be done with one device in a classroom. In this example, we will use a 1:1 classroom, with every student having a device that he or she brings to class. If you have one device per classroom and want to do something similar to this, use the steps in Part 1 of this PBL.

We are using Soundtrap EDU (https://www.soundtrap.com) to record the podcast, though GarageBand, Soundation (educational version), Anchor, or other music production apps or software can be used. We are using a USB Blue Spark microphone (https://www.bluedesigns.com) to record so that the sound quality is better. However, you can use the internal mic found in the device.

We are using headphones for each student, but you can ask students to bring in their own or not use headphones. You will have a better-quality recording with headphones. I would also suggest finding places in the room to record so that the background noise does not impede each recording. In addition, use a recording box (a large box where the students place their device and they record) to dampen the background noise.

For our audience, we are using Seesaw (web.seesaw.me), the digital student learning portfolio, but any platform for presentation can be used.

Essential Questions:

- What is an organ (show picture of an organ) and how is sound produced?
- What is a recorder and how is sound produced?
- How do you think Bach felt when he angered Duke Wilhelm for wanting to leave his position to work for Prince Leopold and then was jailed?
- Why was composing his own music important to Bach?
- Why would it be important to you if you were in Bach's shoes?
- Why would another famous composer, Johannes Brahms, state, "Study Bach: there you will find everything"?

Music:

This PBL portion comes after the students have studied the music and life of Johann Sebastian Bach.

Launch Soundtrap EDU (https://www.sountrap.com). Soundtrap is a free digital audio workstation (DAW) where you can make music online by recording, using loops, editing audio files, inviting others to collaborate, and more. You can create a free account for you to use as a teacher. If you have students using Soundtrap, look at the pricing for the educational (EDU) version, which you can use through Soundtrap or a music education platform like MusicFirst (https://www.musicfirst.com). You want to use the EDU versions from Soundtrap or MusicFirst because they have safewalls. MusicFirst also has the learning management system built in so you can easily create and receive assignments.

Have one student in the pair log in to the Soundtrap account. For this project, it is ideal to group the students so that they can create the podcast together. Since a podcast is usually a broadcasting interview, having the students paired to create questions and answers is ideal. Since Soundtrap is like GarageBand and Google Docs merged together, when they enter through one student's account, they can invite the other student on and share their project.

Click "Enter Studio" and click on a blank project (the podcast demo is a great way to learn about how to begin a podcast with Soundtrap). For this podcast, I used a USB Blue Spark USB microphone (https://www.bluedesigns.com) and attached it to the laptop.

For the written material that they will use, look at the Writing/Language Arts portion that follows. For music, I will give the students 30-second selections of Bach's music. They have the choice of what they would like to use. Before class, I would upload the Bach selections to my Soundtrap account. I would then edit them to 30 seconds and download them to my laptop. I can then add them to the students' accounts by creating a new studio, dragging each loop to a track, and then saving them into the "my loops" tab. This helps me control how the loops get into their Soundtrap account. You could also share it with them, either via Google Drive, or Google Classroom, or whatever learning management system you are using in your school. They would add the musical selections after they record their written material.

When finished recording the written material, click stop and save the recording. Then add the music to the podcast. Remind the students of the podcasting examples so they know to "duck"—turning down the music when the voices are talking. Once finished, title the file and click save.

Writing/Language Arts:

Writing is incorporated by asking the students to create a circle thinking map or a bubble thinking map (descriptive) to answer the essential questions. In addition, use a thinking map to brainstorm names for the podcast.

Science:

In music class or science class, talk about how sound is produced on the organ and the recorder. There are several videos and sites that reinforce this. One of my favorites is on YouTube and is called The House of Sound. The woodwind video about making a carrot clarinet fascinates my older elementary students. Finally, when the students observe the soundwaves created when they recorded in Soundtrap, talk about the shape of the waves.

Art:

You can extend this PBL to include art. Have them draw a logo or picture for your podcast. Use traditional art materials and take a picture of the artwork to include in the podcast. Though Soundtrap currently does not include pictures or videos, that could change. In addition, you could use WeVideo (https://www.wevideo.com) (cloud-based) or iMovie (https://www.apple.com/imovie/) (iOS/MAC only) to include artwork with audio.

World Languages:

Many times, the students' audiences are bilingual. Have the students podcast in more than one language. If you are uncomfortable publishing a podcast in a language that is not native to you, ask your world languages colleagues to listen to them before you publish them.

Sharing the Project:

I feel that PBL is most effective when the students can share it with an audience. For these young children, our audience is the parents. Therefore, we shared it through the digital student learning portfolio, Seesaw (web.seesaw.me). Alternatives are ClassDojo (https://www.classdojo.com), Bloomz (https://www.bloomz.net), Flipgrid (https://www.flipgrid.com), FreshGrade (freshgrade.com), or ClassTag (https://www.classtag.com/), to name a few.

Activity **tip when using** Flipgrid: Since Flipgrid is based in video, the teacher could use the whiteboard tool for the students to create the artwork for the podcast, and then press record. This will produce a recorded podcast with no video, just the whiteboard artwork. To read more details about Flipgrid, please visit Chapter 8, "Links Listed Throughout the Book and Descriptions of Programs."

Website example: There is an example of how to do this with Flipgrid on the supplemental website to this book, found at www.oup.com/us/utema. [⊙]

Activity **tip when using** Seesaw and Soundtrap: Seesaw is a free digital student learning portfolio. You can set up a free account and add up to 10 classes with two teachers. To read more details about Seesaw, please visit Chapter 8, "Links Listed Throughout the Book and Descriptions of Programs."

Create a class and invite the parents to join (Seesaw includes the parent/caregiver email invite and QR code, so you can easily send it out to invite the parents/caregivers). If you used Soundtrap on the laptop, download the file from the main screen (tap on the file, click download, and it downloads as an MP3). Since Seesaw will not upload an MP3 file, I place the MP3 in my Google Drive. From there, I can create a link and copy the link. In your teacher Seesaw account, tap the + button, post student work, click "Link," and drag paste the link's address. From there, you can add a caption. Once finished, click the green check to approve, then click the students you want to post on their journals (if a student was absent, you could leave him or her out, but I would include all of the students), then click the green check to submit. If you make a mistake, click the back arrow until you get to the "delete and start over" option.

Activity **tip if you do not have access** to Seesaw or Flipgrid: If you do not have access to a digital student learning portfolio, you can download the file and email it to the parents/caregivers. In addition, you could ask for it to be posted to a school website or social media account, a music classroom website or social media account, etc.

Sharing as a School Broadcast: One great example was a school that used a podcast about classical music to broadcast throughout the halls as the students traveled from one class to another. Think outside the box for your audience, as it makes it so meaningful to the students.

Reflection:

An easy way to promote student reflection is to ask the students the following and record their answers with any recording app or software (like Soundtrap or Seesaw or your mobile device's recording app like Voice Memos).

- What did you like about the podcast?
- What do you wish you did better, or what do you wonder about the podcast?
- What if we did that next time?

If you are using digital student learning portfolios, ask the students to reflect as an exit ticket. Have them log into their Seesaw journal or Flipgrid Grid and leave an activity or ask them to video record themselves answering the question. This works well for a 1:1 classroom.

Podcasting with older elementary was authentic and impressive. The students love to lead and take control. It empowers their learning. When giving them guidelines, but with the room to let them lead and take charge, the students' creativity and knowledge explode. They become passionate about their learning and about sharing it to all who will listen. Older elementary students have a lot to share. By using this type of PBL, you give them a great outlet for them to "show what they know."

Green Screen + Younger Elementary = Assessment!

A green screen PBL activity that involves younger elementary students.
PBL Concept: The students in kindergarten and Grade 1 will utilize a green screen to showcase what they know about musical instruments.

Introduction:

The students have been studying specific instruments of the orchestra. They can show what they know by creating a video of themselves with a life-size instrument.

Materials:

A green screen, as well as a green screen program will be needed. A green screen can be purchased from vendors such as Amazon. However, if you use the iOS app, Green Screen by Do Ink (https://itunes.apple.com/us/app/green-screen-by-do-ink/id730091131?mt=8), you can use the Chroma Key within the app to match the color of the background. Therefore, if your background is one solid color, you can avoid purchasing the green screen. However, I do feel that using a green screen is ideal. One that is the color of "Sprite bottle" green works best.

Another green screen app is WeVideo (https://www.wevideo.com). WeVideo is web-based, so you can access it from almost any device with internet access. You can create a five-minute video for up to 1 GB with the free version. To create more, you will have to purchase a subscription. WeVideo also has the Chroma Key so that you can match the background as long as the background is one solid color. Finally, you must make the floor match the background or the floor will stick out in the video. To accomplish this, lay a cloth on the floor that matches the green screen, or if you are using a green screen cloth, order it long enough to cover the floor and wall. You could also paint the floor to match the green screen, but you would need permission to do that to a classroom.

Another green screen resource is iMovie. iMovie can superimpose one clip over another using a green- or blue-screen effect. Perform a Google search to learn more about how to do this.

You will also need a picture of the instrument your students will be showcasing. You can perform a Google search for a transparent trumpet so that the trumpet has a transparent background and you do not have to make it transparent in the app.

Essential Questions:

- How does the instrument produce sound?
- If the instrument is one size, how does it make high and low sounds?
- Does what the instrument is made out of make a difference in how the instrument sounds?

Music:

After you have taught and reviewed certain instruments of the orchestra, take out the green screen. Launch the Do Ink App. Click the + sign and then "Create a New Project." Click the middle track, the + sign, then "Image," and then choose the transparent instrument picture from the camera roll. Tap the + sign on the top track and then click the video camera. Place the iOS device on a music stand facing the green screen. You might need to adjust the Chroma key a bit to see yourself in front of the picture you placed on the middle track or flip the camera if necessary. If you need to make the background transparent, you can use the "Mask" tool to erase items in the picture. The crop tool will also help you crop the picture. Once your background is set, you are ready to record the video.

Website example: Go to www.oup.com/us/utema to watch a video with steps on how to do this. [◉]

Writing/Language Arts:

Create a descriptive/bubble thinking map about the instrument. For example, place trumpet in the middle circle and ask the children to use words to describe the trumpet. Those adjectives would go in the surrounding bubbles.

Science:

In music or science class, the students can review the basics of sound with how it is produced.

Art:

The students could draw their own picture of the instrument and that could be used for the background image in the green screen app. The mask tool in Do Ink would be needed to make the background transparent.

World Languages:

Since the audience for this project will be the children's caregivers, many of them speak multiple languages. Check with your world languages teachers on how to say the instrument name and color in another language. Add them to the descriptive/bubble thinking map.

Green Screen:

With the green screen and Do Ink app ready to go, click record and have the students show what they know about the instrument. When finished, click stop and save it to the camera roll or export it to a shared drive, like Google Drive. If you need to record the video again, discard the video and record it again. Since they record, show what they know, and save it, you will not need to edit the video. If you did, you can with WeVideo (https://www.wevideo.com) or iMovie (MAC or iOS only).

Sharing the Project:

I feel that PBL is most effective when the students can share it with an audience. For this particular activity, you can share it on their digital student learning portfolios, like Seesaw (web.seesaw.me), Class Dojo (https://www.classdojo.com), Bloomz (https://www.bloomz.net), Flipgrid (https://www.flipgrid.com), FreshGrade (https://wwww.freshgrade.com), or ClassTag (https://www.classtag.com/), to name a few. You can see how to use Seesaw and Flipgrid in the podcasts projects listed earlier.

Reflection:

The parents and students loved this project. The students loved seeing themselves next to a large instrument. They adored being able to point at it when describing it. The parents were fascinated to watch their children interact with a large instrument, as well as hearing them describe it so well.

STEAM + Green Screen + Musical School Message = Magic!

A more involved green screen PBL activity that involves students from younger to older elementary.

PBL Concept: The students in PreK-4 will utilize the science, technology, engineering, arts, and mathematics (STEAM) philosophy to create a musical school message. This message can range from school spirit to a weather-related school closing message. For this project, the students were creating a snow day video for the school.

Introduction:

The school needs a snow day video to announce a school closing due to inclement weather. In the past, the teachers and/or administration had created a music video to announce the closings. However, this year, they were very busy and have asked the students to create one that will be used to announce school closings.

Materials:

This can be done with one device in a classroom or in a multiple devices/1:1 classroom. In this example, since we are using a variety of grade levels, we will use one device. However, more can be done with the video if you give older students some of the video editing and audio mixing privileges on their own devices.

To record the song, we are using Soundtrap (https://www.soundtrap.com), the web-based digital audio workstation (DAW) that can be accessed from almost any device. If you are the only one using Soundtrap, the free version will suffice. If you have students using Soundtrap, look at the pricing for the educational (EDU) version, which you can use through Soundtrap or a music education platform like MusicFirst (https://www. musicfirst.com). You want to use the EDU versions from Soundtrap or MusicFirst because they have safewalls. MusicFirst also has the learning management system built in, so you can easily create and receive assignments. I also use a USB microphone for this project from Blue (https://www.bluedesigns.com) so that Soundtrap can access it. GarageBand (iOS and MAC only) is also an alternative.

A green screen, as well as a green screen program, will be needed. A green screen can be purchased from vendors such as Amazon. However, if you use the iOS app, Green Screen by Do Ink (https://itunes.apple.com/us/app/green-screen-by-do-ink/ id730091131?mt=8), you can use the Chroma Key within the app to match the color of the background. Therefore, if your background is one solid color, you can avoid purchasing the green screen. However, I do feel that using a green screen is ideal. One that is the color of "Sprite bottle" green works best.

Another green screen app is WeVideo (https://www.wevideo.com). WeVideo is web-based, so you can access it from almost any device with internet access. You can create a five-minute video for up to 1GB with the free version. To create more, you will have to purchase a subscription. WeVideo also has the Chroma Key so that you can match the background as long as the background is one solid color. Finally, you must make the floor match the background or the floor will stick out in the video. To accomplish this, lay a cloth on the floor that matches the green screen, or if you are using a green screen cloth, order it long enough to cover the floor and wall. You could also paint the floor to match the green screen, but you would need permission to do that to a classroom.

Another green screen resource is iMovie. iMovie can superimpose one clip over another using a green- or blue-screen effect. Perform a Google search to learn more about how to do this.

For this project, we acquired costumes that the students brought in from home. If your school has a theater department, there might be costumes that you can borrow.

Scenes of snow will be needed to upload to the green screen program. To do this, perform a Google search for the scenes that you will need. We used pictures of the school as well as still pictures and animated, transparent videos of snow.

Students will be writing. Therefore, writing utensils, paper, and thinking maps will be beneficial.

Since the PBL activity involved numerous grade levels and classes, I used iMovie (iOS and MAC) to mix together the video clips and the audio track. WeVideo would work well and can be used on most devices with internet access. Since this video would probably go over the limit of the free account, a subscription would be necessary.

Essential Questions:

- What are the qualities of a well-produced video?
- What do you need to know about the topic to be able to write and produce a video?
- What do you need to know about your audience?
- How do lyrics affect the music?
- What do you need to know about recording sound?

Music:

This PBL STEAM project begins by stating the problem: when our school has snow days, the caregivers are expecting one of those viral "snow day" videos. It is our job to be able to write, record, and produce one with all of our students. Then, view some snow day videos to ask the students questions to help them begin. The questions can vary from, "What did you like about the videos?" "What did you wonder about the videos?" "What if we tried some of those ideas?" "What do we need to be able to make a video?"

Song Choice: When we did this, we began with the song choice. You can ask the students what song we should use to rewrite the lyrics, or if you have students that are capable, you could have them create their own original song. Due to our timing, we took a song and rewrote the lyrics.

Writing/Language Arts:

The older elementary students decided to use the idea of snow day superstitions. They used a circle thinking map to list their ideas of what they do to help bring on a snow day. This ranged from putting on their pajamas inside out to throwing ice cubes out the window. Share this thinking map with other classes so that they can add their ideas (Figure 6.7).

Once the ideas are there, begin the songwriting process. Review how you must count syllables as opposed to words to create the lyrics. In addition, review the form of the song and look at how many verses, choruses, and bridges there are so that they can recreate them.

Science:

In music class or science class, talk about the weather and how snow formed. In addition, when the students record their voices singing the song, talk about how sound is produced. Finally, when the students observe the soundwaves created when they recorded in Soundtrap, talk about the shape of the waves.

Figure 6.7.

An example of the "Snow Day" thinking content circle map.

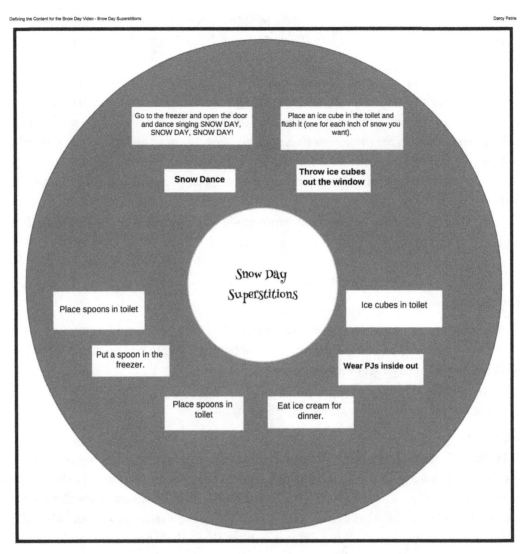

Defining the Content for the Snow Day Video - Snow Day Superstitions   Darcy Petrie

Snow Dance

Go to the freezer and open the door and dance singing SNOW DAY, SNOW DAY, SNOW DAY!

Throw ice cubes out the window

Place an ice cube in the toilet and flush it (one for each inch of snow you want).

Snow Day Superstitions

Place spoons in toilet

Put a spoon in the freezer.

Ice cubes in toilet

Wear PJs inside out

Place spoons in toilet

Eat ice cream for dinner.

Art:

Since the older elementary classes created the thinking map and rewrote the lyrics, the younger elementary students can choose the backgrounds for the video. Remind them of the lyrics to help them find pictures that will enhance the video. This can be done by projecting one device onto a screen. Then, perform a Google search for their ideas, such as a snowy mountain. Give them three choices so that you can guide them into one choice. Also, find pictures of the school and use those as well. Once you find pictures that you like, save them to your device's laptop or Google drive. If you use the Do Ink app for your green screen recording, place those saved images in your iOS device.

World Languages:

In order for the students to reach all audiences, ask the students to add bilingual words to describe a snow day.

Recording:

Once the lyrics are written, practice the song over two or three classes. As they practice the song, they can also be helping with the background for the green screen or deciding on clothing and costumes for the video. In addition, since we wanted to level it up, the students wrote rhythm patterns to perform during the bridge on classroom percussion instruments and tone chimes.

Each class will record the song. For the younger elementary, I either taught them the chorus or the repetitious words in the bridge section. The older elementary students sang and recorded the entire song.

Launch Soundtrap and enter the studio. Find a karaoke track of the song on your streaming service, or such. Place the karaoke track in the Soundtrap file by clicking and dragging it into the project screen. Add another track by clicking "Add New Track" and clicking on the microphone icon. Make sure that the device you are using with Soundtrap is connected to a decent pair of speakers. Add a USB microphone (we use https://www.bluedesigns.com) to get a more focused-sounding recording where there will be less white noise. In the Soundtrap screen, change the "Default—Internal Microphone (Built-in)" to the name of your USB microphone.

Note: *Ideally, you would want to record this with all students wearing headphones. And if they have a 1:1 classroom and all have Soundtrap EDU accounts, that might be the best way to go. However, since timing and devices come into play, this can be done with recording each class onto their own track. The only problem with this is the karaoke track is recorded into every class's track.*

Click record on the new track and answer the questions about not having headphones. Once the karaoke track plays, have the students sing along. You will know that it is recording as you and the students will see the recording appear on the track. Once finished, click the save button at the top of the screen.

When recording the next class, mute the other class's track, but keep the karaoke track active. If your younger elementary students are only recording a certain part of the song, place the header right before their part begins. Soundtrap gives you seven seconds and plays a few measures before the recording begins.

Once all of the classes have been recorded, use headphones to help you mix the recording together. Use the volume sliders to help balance the classes' recording tracks with the karaoke track. I also pan certain tracks left or right to create more balance.

When it is to your liking, click save and exit the studio. Once the song is mixed (this could take a few minutes), click on the track and find the download button. Download the track, and you now have your soundtrack for your video.

Green Screen:

I use the iOS Green Screen app by Do Ink. Launch the app. Click the + sign and then "Create a New Project." We chose the background picture depending on which part of the song that class was featured. For example, for verse one, we used a school background. For the chorus, we used a picture of a mountain of snow with a snowboarder in the picture. We placed that specific background photo by clicking the middle track, the + sign, then "Image," and then chose the picture from the camera roll. Tap the + sign on the top track and then click the video camera. Place the iOS device on a music stand facing the green screen. You might need to adjust the Chroma key a bit to see yourself in front of the picture you placed on the middle track or flip the camera if necessary. Or you can use the "Mask" tool to erase items in the picture so that they become transparent. The crop tool will also help you crop the picture. Once your background is set, you are ready to record the video.

This was a great way for students to learn that most artists lip-sync their music when creating a video. We played our Soundtrap mixed recording throughout the room. The students clicked on the red record button when they were ready. When their part came up, they acted out the lyrics. If the lyrics included "wear your PJs inside out," there were students jumping up and down in the video with their PJs inside out (they brought them, changed in the restroom before class, and then went back to the restroom to change back to school clothes). If the lyrics included, "throw the ice cubes out," the students imitated throwing something out, and we added the ice cubes with the animated add-on in the Do Ink app. In addition, all of the students brought their winter coats and gear to class to create the effect of cold temperatures.

Once recorded, I would click to save it in the camera roll so I could edit it all together later. If you wanted to export the clips into Google Drive, then click "Show the export options" and click on Google Drive. Then, the next group would come up. We had the device airplay to a large screen so that the students waiting could watch the current recording. If they needed to delete a recording, they clicked on the track, and the "Trim Cut Copy Paste Delete" menu appeared at the bottom of the screen.

Editing It All Together:

I imported all of the video clips into iMovie (MAC or iOS). You can do this by using the iMovie app on the same device you used to video the students and access the videos from iPhoto. If you are editing on a different device, you can access them by airdropping them from the iOS device to the editing device, or placing the videos in Google Drive and accessing them from there.

Once the videos are imported and placed in the correct order, I trim the videos so that we cut out the time right before their part and right after. Once that is complete, I add the soundtrack we recorded in Soundtrap. I then match up the videos with the soundtrack. If there are not enough videos, copy and paste some of them to other parts of the track. You will notice in iMovie that if you import the music and the video track is shorter than the music track, you will need to extend or add more videos in order to make them match up.

Website example: For a quick tutorial on how to edit in iMovie, go to the supplemental website that correlates with this book, found at www.oup.com/us/utema. [▶]

Design Thinking:

This project uses the Design Thinking process: empathize, define, ideate, prototype, test, and share. The final step of sharing is not always included, but it is important for the PBL activity. The students empathized with the problem that their school was lacking a snow day video that many schools have and that had gone viral. The students defined the problem and came up with a solution of rewriting a new song based on the superstitions of trying to get a snow day called. They used thinking maps to organize their knowledge on the topic and mapped out a plan to create the song and video. Throughout creating and testing their prototype, they made necessary changes to improve the song recording, the props in the video, etc. Finally, they shared their video.

Sharing the Project:

I feel that PBL is most effective when the students can share it with an audience. For this particular activity, you can share it on their digital student learning portfolios, like Seesaw (web.seesaw.me), ClassDojo (https://www.classdojo.com), Bloomz (https://www.bloomz.net), Flipgrid (https://www.flipgrid.com), FreshGrade (https://wwww.freshgrade.com), or ClassTag (https://www.classtag.com/), to name a few. You can see how to use Seesaw and Flipgrid in the podcasts projects listed earlier.

Since the school needed a video, this could also be shared on the school website (with permission from the parents), when there is a snow day.

Reflection:

The students loved this project and recalled it a year later in hopes that they would be able to make another snow day video. The STEAM philosophy in this PBL integrates in the following ways: Science: the students incorporated how snow is formed in the original phase of creating lyrics for the song. Technology: technology was used throughout the project to create and share it. Engineering: the recording process of sound and video, along with editing, incorporated their engineering, musical, and technical skills. Arts: the project keeps the music curriculum intact as the students were songwriting, writing rhythm patterns, performing, and playing instruments. In addition, their artistic vision came into play when worked with the green screen. Mathematics: the rhythm patterns created did extend to learning about beats and rhythms in a certain meter.

Students felt connected to each other. This aspect surprised me, as I forget that many students have siblings. This project became a topic discussed at home because all of the students had an investment in it. The siblings would compare notes about what their part was in creating and making the song and video.

Creating an ebook to Share with an Audience

PBL Concept: The elementary students will create an ebook that will involve creating the concept, electronically writing the ebook, recording music for the ebook, publishing the ebook to share with an audience, and learning about copyright.

Introduction:

The students have experienced and enjoyed numerous books in music class during their elementary years. They are now to create their own ebook that will involve a story, characters, improvised music, drawings, and publishing to share with an audience.

Materials:

This project should be a collaboration among grade levels and subjects. For example, Grade 4 can write the book. Grade 3 can illustrate the book. Grade 2 can improvise the music. You can vary this, but distributing the responsibilities makes this a cross-grade level project, which is something special that we can do in music classes. If you can have other specialists work on the visual art in Art class and the writing in Language Arts class, then it becomes a wonderful collaboration across subjects and grade levels. However, if not, you can do this all in music class.

To write the ebook, have the students base it on a book that they loved to read when they were children. For example, if they loved the Elephant and Piggie series, written by Mo Willems, then they can create a story about two characters and their friendship. Another suggestion is *Going on a Bear Hunt* by Michael Rosen.

To create an ebook, we can use the Book Creator app found at https://www. bookcreator.com. This is an iOS and web-based app, which means that it can be used on iOS devices as well as Chromebooks, computers, and Android devices. The iOS app lets you create one ebook for free. If you want to create numerous ebooks, the paid iOS version is currently $4.99. The web-based version allows you to currently create a subscription and 40 ebooks in one library for free. After that, there are paid subscriptions that allow much more.

To create the music, utilize pitched instruments set to a pentatonic scale (do, re, mi, sol, and la) and non-pitched instruments. Therefore, it will sound pleasant no matter how the students create and improvise the music.

Essential Questions:

- What qualifies as a good children's book?
- What will we need to write an ebook?
- What will we need to record and produce music?
- What music would enhance a children's ebook?
- What is copyright and why is it important?
- Whom should we share this ebook with?

Writing/Language Arts:

This project begins with the grade that will be writing the ebook. The ebook is presented as a PBL in which we will share this with younger elementary and parents/caregivers. In addition, describe the publishing process so the students know that the ebook will be published for a wider audience to view and read.

Begin with a concept. Ask the students what books they enjoyed when they were younger. If ideas are too vague, begin with the Elephant and Piggie Series by Mo Willems. These books focused on two friends always trying to solve a problem that occurs daily in a young child's life (for example, not wanting to try a new food or making new friends, etc.). Or use the book *Going on a Bear Hunt* by Michael Rosen, where the characters are searching for the bear and move through various scenes that have built-in sound effects.

Once the concept is formed, draw a circle ideas thinking map for all of the students to brainstorm ideas for the book. From the circle map, create a flow map to show a timeline progression of the ideas. For example, if you base the book on *Going on a Bear Hunt*, the students might create an idea where it is an ebook about students going on a school hunt trying to find the principal to bring back to the music room to create music. Figure 6.8 gives an example of a flow map where my kindergartners mapped out a timeline of a few events from Mozart's childhood.

Once the flow map is complete, have the students create a simple text for each page of the ebook. You can divide the class into small groups so that each group creates a page based on each box of the flow map. Once finished, launch Book Creator and have them type the text into the ebook.

World Languages:

In order for the students to reach all audiences, ask the students to add bilingual words to the text.

Book Creator:

If you are using the free versions or collaborating on one device, then when it is time to create the ebook, launch the app on a device that is projected onto a screen. Ask one student from each group to type the text onto each page. To do this, launch the app, create a new ebook in square mode, click the button on the right-hand side to progress to the page after the first cover page, tap the + button at the top of the screen, and scroll down to the text tool. Add the text to the page. To change the font and size of the text, click on the text box and click the "i" button at the top of the page. This will give you a menu that allows you to change the font and text size and more. Continue to add the text to each page.

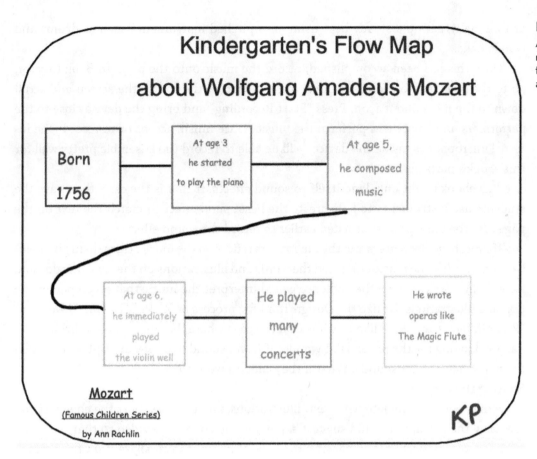

Figure 6.8.
An example of a flow map by kindergartners from what they learned about Mozart's life.

If you are using the paid versions of Book Creator in a 1:1 classroom, then you can collaborate in real-time so that each group can work together on their own devices and update their pages.

Art:

Once the pages are written in Book Creator, assign a class to illustrate the book. Have the class read the book and then brainstorm ideas to what the characters look like. These illustrations can be very simple or complex. Have the students work in groups to create one for each page on paper using writing and drawing utensils.

To add the illustrations to Book Creator, click on the page, click the + button at the top of the screen, and scroll down to the camera app. Take a picture of the illustration. Accept the picture. The picture now blocks the text. To correct this, click on the picture, click the "i" button at the top of the screen, and scroll down to "Move to Back/Front." This will order the illustration to go behind the text box.

If there is time, have the students who wrote the ebook reflect on the illustrations. If possible, have them give feedback in ways that help the illustrators either improve on their vision of the illustrations or on how an audience would interpret their illustrations.

Music:

Once the text and illustrations are complete, assign a class to create music for the ebook using pitched and non-pitched instruments. Depending on the text, guide the students in creating and improvising some of the text to a pentatonic scale. For example, if there is text that is used consistently throughout the ebook, like a chorus, then decode a rhythm pattern to the text. Once decoded, use that rhythm pattern to improvise a melody using pitched instruments set to a pentatonic scale (I would suggest the key of F). Finally, set up a steady beat using non-pitched instruments such as drums and woodblocks.

Once this has been accomplished, record the music onto the page. In Book Creator, go to the page in the ebook. Click on the + button at the top of the screen and scroll down to the microphone icon. Press "Start Recording" and bring the device close to the performers and have them perform the music. Once finish, accept or re-record. The internal microphones inside the devices will be able to record the ensemble pretty well for this ebook's purpose.

This ebook might only lend itself to sound effects. If that is the case, then have the students use instruments to help create the best sound effect to match the text on the page. Use the same process as listed earlier to record the sound effects.

If time, have the writers and the illustrators reflect on the music. Have them give feedback on whether the music enhanced the words and illustrations on the page. In addition, have them reflect on how the audience would interpret the music that accompanies the text and illustrations. Utilize the Design Thinking process of "I like," "I wish," "I wonder," "What if." For example, "I like the music on the page where the children walk through the hallway looking for the principal. I wonder if it can sound like they are tiptoeing. I wish the music had shorter sounds. What if they added a woodblock?"

Sharing the Project:

Once the ebook is complete with text, illustrations, and music, export the ebook. If you are using the iOS app, I would suggest exporting the ebook as a video so that the audio is played automatically when viewing the ebook. Then, you can share it on the school's website, or the music website, or a student digital portfolio like Seesaw (web.seesaw.me), ClassDojo (https://www.classdojo.com), Flipgrid (https://www.flipgrid.com), FreshGrade (https://www.freshgrade.com), Bloomz (https://www.bloomz.net), or ClassTag (https://www.classtag.com/), to name a few. You can see how to use Seesaw and Flipgrid in the podcasts projects listed earlier.

If you used the web-based version, then share the ebook by publishing it online and copying the link to send to others. Book Creator has this as an option for both the iOS and web-based app. The ebook would be published to Book Creator's website and a link would be provided for you to share with others. The link can be private or public. When sending the link, you can include it in an email, adding the link to a school newsletter, add it to the students' digital learning portfolios, or placing it on the school's website or music website.

To share the ebook with other schools, I would suggest publishing it publicly as a library that is allowed to be published and read by Book Creator users. This still allows you to share a link as well. Here is an example of a music library that my students created: https://read.bookcreator.com/library/-LZWcCSmHVhcAyd08Ckw

Copyright:

This PBL lends itself to a great discussion over copyright and ownership. It helps the students to realize what it means to create and own something, and how they would feel if someone copied and sold it without their permission.

Reflection:

When finished, have the students reflect on the essential questions.

Students felt connected to each other. Since this a cross grade-level project, many students created this ebook with their siblings. This brought on conversations at home about the process of writing, creating, producing music for, and publishing an ebook.

Coding Percussion

For younger elementary students.

PBL Concept: The elementary students will create a drum set using https://scratch.mit.edu.

Introduction: Why address coding in music class?

Coding has been an edtech buzz word for over the past few years because many current jobs require coding skills. According to research conducted by code.org, 58% of all new jobs in STEM are based in computing, 10% of STEM graduates are in computer science, and computing jobs are the number one source of new wages in the United States (code.org, 2019). More schools are offering coding classes and addressing events like the Hour of Code, which occurs at the beginning of December. Some of the benefits of teaching coding range from problem-solving to team-building skills.

One would then say that music does the same, and I would agree. However, as music educators, we are trying to reach every child in our classroom. If our traditional methods are not reaching all of them because only some like to sing, dance, perform, and move to music, how do we reach the ones that do not? What if we use coding, with music being the focus, to reach those students who are not being reached?

Materials:

For this PBL, we will use the website https://scratch.mit.edu/. This will be done in a classroom with one device connected to a projector that projects onto a screen/TV/IWB and connected the internet. It is beneficial if the device is connected to a decent pair of speakers. This PBL will require that the students have prior knowledge of percussion instruments.

Website example: Go to www.oup.com/us/utema to see a video of step-by-step motions on how to code with Scratch. [⊙]

Essential Questions:

- How do coding and music work together?
- Are there musical skills that correspond with coding?
- How would coding a drum set assist you in music class or at home?

Coding: (These are the step-by-step instructions. I also have a video tutorial on the supplemental website to the book, found at www.oup.com/us/utema.)

Coding is basically the computer language used to create apps, websites, and more; https://scratch.mit.edu is one of many sites where you can learn to code. When you code, you are creating step-by-step instructions to tell the computer how to complete a task.

Give the students a real problem to solve: they have to code a drum set so that there are enough instruments for all students to perform.

To do this, go to https://scratch.mit.edu and click "Create." If this is the first time you have done this, there will be a tutorial that will show up on the screen, which you can click off. There is a cat on the screen that is called a sprite. We will delete this, so click the "x" in the trashcan of the cat's sprite box to delete it.

Add a backdrop: Click the "Backdrop" tab and in the backdrop menu that appears, click the add button (see Figure 6.9). A new menu of backdrops will appear. Look for "Concert" as your backdrop. It is a big stage that is perfect for a drum set.

Code Sprites to create a drum set: When you deleted the cat, you deleted a sprite. A sprite is a bitmap image that is a part of a larger screen and can be static or animated. To find the sprite that we need, there is a cat-menu at the bottom of the screen. Click the cat-menu, which will bring up a menu of sprites (Figure 6.10). Click on the instrument tab. Find the "Drum Kit" and click on it. It will now appear on the stage.

Coding: Remember that coding is telling the computer to do something. Therefore, you will want to start with the event of clicking on the drum set so it makes a sound. Ask the students which color is for events (yellow). Click on the yellow "Events" circle and drag the "When this sprite is clicked" onto the screen. Ask the children what the drum set should do. They should answer that it will make a sound. Click the pink "Sound" circle. Look at the codes and read them to the students. Ask them which code would make the

Figure 6.9.
Adding a backdrop in scratch.mit.edu.

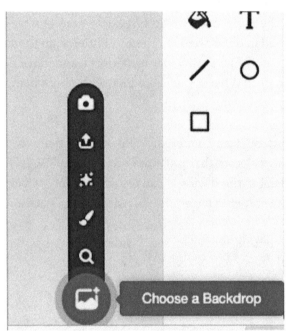

Figure 6.10.
Sprite menu in scratch. mit.edu.

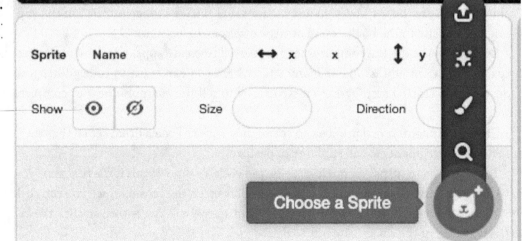

drum play: "Start sound. . . ." Click and drag that to the screen and test the bass drum sounds. Choose a "Drum Bass" sound (I like #3). Then click and drag "Play sound . . . until done" and scroll down to the same bass drum. Finally, drag the code "stop all sounds" to the screen. Go to the orange "Control" circle and place the "repeat 10" code box around the bottom two codes so that the bass drum plays 10 times in a row (see Figure 6.11).

Do the same steps for adding a low or high tom sound to the same drum set. In addition, add more percussion sprites, such as a snare drum, high hat, and cymbal. You are essentially having the children help you build and code a drum set.

Sharing the drum set: Use your mobile device to video the students' reflections on the process and results of coding a drum set. Finally, talk about how the results created a steady beat. If it did not, what could they do to the code to change that so that they could perform a simple melody with this drum set?

Problem solving: There will be hiccups when trying to teach your students to code this project. Coding teaches your children how to problem solve and the importance of failing, starting over, and trying again.

Coding a Soprano Recorder

For older elementary students.

PBL Concept: The elementary students will create a soprano recorder using https://scratch.mit.edu.

Introduction: Why address coding in music class?

Coding has been an edtech buzz word for over the past few years because many current jobs require coding skills. According to research conducted by code.org, 58% of all new jobs in STEM are based in computing, 10% of STEM graduates are in computer science, and computing jobs are the number one source of new wages in the United States (code.org, 2019). More schools are offering coding classes and addressing events like the Hour of Code, which occurs at the beginning of December. Some of the benefits of teaching coding range from problem-solving to team-building skills.

One would then say that music does the same, and I would agree. However, as music educators, we are trying to reach every child in our classroom. If our traditional methods are not reaching all of them because only some like to sing, dance, perform, and move to music, how do we reach the ones that do not? What if we use coding, with music being the focus, to reach those students who are not begin reached?

Materials:

For this PBL, we will use the website https://scratch.mit.edu/. This can be done in a classroom with one device connected to a projector that projects onto a screen/TV/IWB and connected the internet. It is beneficial if the device is connected to a decent pair of speakers. This PBL will require that the students have prior knowledge of how to play the recorder. This also can be done in a 1:1 classroom. Finally, you will need the file "recorder for coding.png" found at the supplemental website, www.oup.com/us/utema.

Website example: Go to www.oup.com/us/utema to also see a video of step-by-step motions on how to code with Scratch. [⊚]

Essential Questions:

- How do coding and music work together?
- Are there musical skills that correspond with coding?

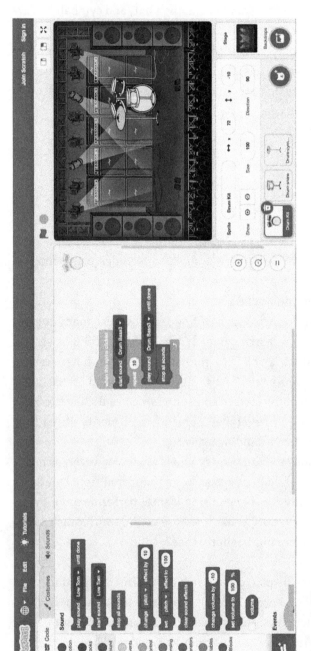

Figure 6.11.
Coding a drum set with scratch.mit.edu.

- How would coding a recorder assist you in music class or at home?
- How can coding a recorder assist a person who could not play it traditionally?

Coding: (These are the step-by-step instructions. I also have a video tutorial on the supplemental website to the book, found at www.oup.com/us/utema.)

Coding is basically the computer language used to create apps, websites, and more; https://scratch.mit.edu is one of many sites where you can learn to code. When you code, you are creating step-by-step instructions to tell the computer how to complete a task.

Whether you do this in a 1:1 classroom, or do this together as a class project, this is a PBL that has the students coding a recorder fingering chart. Give the students a real problem to solve: they have to create an interactive recorder fingering chart for them to use in class so that they can just tap the note name and the interactive recorder on the screen fingers and plays the note.

To do this, go to https://scratch.mit.edu and click "Create." If this is the first time you have done this, there will be a tutorial that will show up on the screen, which you can click off. There is a cat on the screen that is called a sprite. We will delete this, so click the "x" in the trashcan in the cat's sprite box to delete it.

Add a backdrop: Click the "Backdrop" tab and in the backdrop menu that appears, click the upload button and upload the "recorder for coding.png" file found at the supplemental website, www.oup.com/us/utema. [◉] Once you upload it, it will now appear on the scratch screen.

We need to move the recorder picture to the left side of the screen. To do this, click the button "Convert to Vector," click the pointer tool, and move the recorder to the left side of the screen. Finally, click on the left side of the screen where you see "Backdrop 1" and click the trashcan to delete "Backdrop 1" because we will not need it.

Duplicate the backdrop to show fingerings: The students will now duplicate the backdrop. Right-click (PC) or control-click (MAC) on the square that shows the current backdrop that is most likely to the left side of the screen. A menu will appear. Click on "duplicate" and duplicate it three times so that you will end up with four empty recorder charts. The first one is to stay empty. The second one will be used for the B fingering. The third one will be used for the A fingering. And the fourth one will be used for the G fingering.

With the duplicated backdrop on the screen, go to the second one for the note B. Click "Convert to Bitmap," click on the paint can, change the fill color to blue, and fill in the circles that represent a B fingering. Follow the same steps for duplicating and filling in the circles for the fingerings (you must be in Bitmap to fill in the fingering circles) to show the fingerings for the notes A (red—in the third one) and G (green—in the fourth one). Be careful here as once you fill in the circles, it is challenging to undo it. Use the "undo" button near the filler button to undo an action. If the students fill in the circles with the incorrect color and undoing the task will not suffice, then delete the backdrop and start again by duplicating the original empty recorder chart.

Create a sprite: When you deleted the cat, you deleted a sprite. A sprite is a bitmap image that is a part of a larger screen and can be static or animated. To find the sprite that we need for the B fingering, click on the empty backdrop that is #1 and shows a recorder with no filled in holes. Then, click the cat-sprite menu at the bottom of the screen and scroll up to the magnifying glass so that you can choose a sprite. Click on letters and click on the letter B. There are block, glow, and story letters. Once the B appears, do the same steps to add the letters A and G to the screen.

Since they are on top of each other, click on the sprite box you want to move (i.e., click on the sprite B box) and then move the letter B on the screen.

Coding: Start with the backdrop that has the empty recorder fingerings. Click the "Code" tab. Click "Events," which is color-coded in yellow. Click on the B sprite box. Now drag the code that reads, "When this sprite is clicked" to the empty screen. If you dragged the incorrect code, just drag it off the screen and it will go away. Click the purple "Looks" and drag "Switch backdrop to" onto the screen so that it lays under the yellow code box. In the purple code, use the pull-down menu so that it reads "Switch backdrop to recorder for coding 2." This is the B fingering chart.

200

Click at the bottom of the left-hand side where you can add more code. (Figure 6.12) When you click on this, you will see more items to code with, such as music, Makey Makey, etc. Click on "Music." Drag "set instrument to . . ." and scroll down to "(13) Wooden Flute." Then drag over "play note 60 for .25 beats." Click on 60 and use the keyboard that appears on the screen to change it to what a recorder sounds like when one plays a middle line B on a treble clef staff (83). Change the beats to 2. Go back to the "Looks" code and drag "switch backdrop to . . ." and scroll down to recorder for coding to switch the background back to an empty recorder chart.

Click the "B" and see if your coding worked. It should show the fingering chart, play the note B, and then go back to an empty fingering chart. Perform the same process for A and G. You now have an interactive recorder fingering chart. (Figure 6.13)

Figure 6.12

Scratch's coding menu.

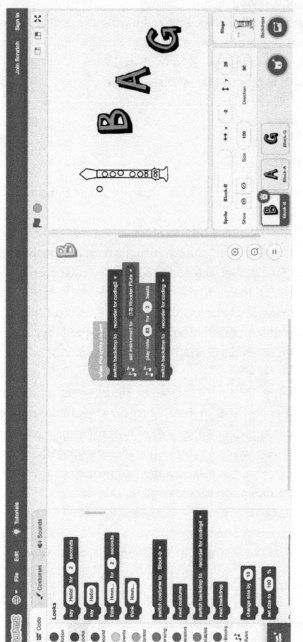

Figure 6.13

Interactive recorder fingering chart coded in Scratch.

Sharing the interactive recorder chart: For students to save this, they must create an account with their email addresses. If that is not possible, have them use a tool like Screencastify (Chromebook extension) or QuickTime (MAC) to screen record themselves showing how to code this project and reflecting on the process.

Problem solving: There will be hiccups when trying to teach your students to code this project. Coding teaches your children how to problem solve and the importance of failing, starting over, and trying again. When I coded this interactive recorder chart, I failed many times before finally succeeding and having the code work well. I relate this type of challenge to learning a new song. There are times when I have to start over and work diligently on a new passage to get it to work well.

Level up: If you have access to Makey Makeys, use them to also code instruments. Scratch has the Makey Makey addition where you can code certain items to perform as instruments. To learn more about this, please visit https://www.makeymakey.com.

Commercial Jingle Project

By Cherie Herring, Elementary General Music Teacher at the Hammond School in South Carolina

Fourth grade students in South Carolina study the states and regions of the United States. The Commercial Jingle project is a cross-curricular unit involving core teachers as well as the Science, Art, Music, Digital Media, and Library teachers.

Introduction:
Divided into regional groups, students brainstormed problems common in their assigned region. The problems could be caused by climate, landscape, population growth, transportation, natural resources, modernization, clash of cultures, etc.

Materials:
Do Ink iOS Green Screen App ((https://itunes.apple.com/us/app/green-screen-by-do-ink/id730091131?mt=8), Keynote (iOS or MAC, https://www.apple.com/keynote/), Pages (iOS or MAC, https://www.apple.com/pages/), Soundtrap (https://www.soundtrap.com), GarageBand (iOS, https://www.apple.com/ios/garageband/ or MAC, https://www.apple.com/mac/garageband/), Seesaw (web.seesaw.me), a green screen, which can be a green sheet found at a store or one pricier found online, iMovie (iOS or MAC, https://www.apple.com/imovie/), Thinglink (https://www.thinglink.com/), and HP Reveal (https://www.hpreveal.com/, formerly Aurasma).

Website example: Go to www.oup.com/us/utema to find all of the links listed here.[⊚]

Essential Questions:

- What makes places unique and different in this region?
- How do a region's geography, climate, and natural resources affect the way people live and work?
- What challenges do people face because they live in this region?
- How does where I live influence how I live?
- What would improve the quality of life in this region?
- What would improve tourism in this state/region?
- Next, students were given the assignment to think of a product, real or invented, that could solve a problem in their region.

Create/Design:

Students had to write a commercial to sell the product, design a logo, create a musical jingle, create background music for the commercial, gather costumes, design props, and find appropriate images to use in the filming of the commercial using green screen technology.

The beauty of this project is how it naturally embedded the arts in the PBL process.

Language Arts:

Students learned about persuasive writing, commercial style. They brainstormed product features, identified the most marketable uses, and wrote the TV commercial to persuade consumers to buy their product. After watching brief examples, they asked, "What aspect of each commercial, such as words, images, creative dialogue, or spokesperson, is most effective in persuading consumers?"

These are some of the strategies teachers highlighted with our students:

- **Bandwagon**: suggesting that everyone else is buying it, so you should, too.
- **Testimonial**: having an expert or famous person persuading the audience.
- **Repetition**: repeating an idea over and over again.
- **Bargain or free**: suggesting the consumer can get something for nothing or almost nothing.
- **Reasoning**: explaining why the product is a good idea/beneficial to them.
- **Criticizing the opposition**: explaining why one product is better than another.
- **Slogan**: creating a catchy phrase to help the consumer remember the product.
- **Personal pronouns**: talking directly to the audience/consumer (*we, us, you*).

Science:

The teacher guided students in the Design Thinking process for inventing a product to fix the problem found in their state/region.

Library:

Students researched their region, found public domain images for use in their commercial scenes, analyzed commercial examples, and rehearsed their commercial before filming.

Art:

Students studied the graphic design of an advertisement doing research into graphic forms, colors and their meanings, and even brand recognition. Students learned about headline, copy, visual, tagline, signature, and layout as they designed their own logos for their product. Logos were drawn, colored, or painted on large art paper. Students took pictures of their logo and used Keynote or Pages to include it in their magazine layout design.

Music:

Students compared commercial jingles and researched how to make an effective earworm, a jingle that stays in your mind long after it is heard on TV. We discussed the importance of choosing a musical style or genre that matches the product and targets the audience. Students also learned that creating a tune that is snappy or melodic, and as entertaining and short as possible, helps create a core message that is easy to remember. When creating their musical jingle, they also created a "bed" to set the tone for the commercial. In the past, GarageBand was our only tool on the iPad, but starting this year, students used Soundtrap, making the creation process much more collaborative.

Students signed up for extra help "studio" time before school, during recess, and after school. I was available to help with composing their jingle, melody, or commercial "bed." Along the way, we used Seesaw, the learning journal, to share our jingles in progress; taking pictures of the first brain-storming ideas, recording a bit of the melody, sharing the "pad" for approval, etc. In fact, Seesaw was such a wonderful way to record the collaboration as students journaled their "next steps" each week.

Digital Media:

Students learned how to film and edit using the Do Ink Green Screen app. We purchased the app for every fourth grader so that they could completely own the process and the project.

Building and Filming the "Green Screen" Commercial:

Because it was a team approach, we were able to set aside a few afternoons for filming the commercial and the green screen editing process. There were three teachers trained in filming and editing using a green screen, the Do Ink app, and iMovie. This took the burden of filming and editing off the teachers and we were able to just assist the students with their own editing. If needed, students were able to rotate through stations for extra help:

- Art—put final touches on their logo or magazine layout, made props or costumes;
- Library—practiced acting out the commercial right before filming;
- Music—filmed the commercial using a green screen or worked on their jingle;
- Science—edited their movie in Do Ink and iMovie;
- Digital Media—filmed the commercial or received help editing the commercial, worked on their magazine layout for their product (Keynote or Pages);
- Homeroom—filmed, edited with their teacher's guidance, etc.

Sharing the Commercial Project:

This project was completed during the final quarter of the school year and shared first with all of the elementary students during a special assembly and then with their parents at the "Step-up" ceremony during the last week of school. They received a standing ovation each time. Additionally, I created and embedded a Thinglink, with the commercials linked to individual students, on our school website for all to see. I also made HP Reveal (formerly Aurasma) triggers out of the logos and hung a few of them along our "Bragging" hall for parents and guests to view when visiting our school.

Reflection:

When filming, some teams had students who wanted to be behind the camera, while others wanted to create the music or only act. Since students were responsible for every step of the process, they would review, delete, and film again until all were satisfied. It was amazing how engaged *all* of the students were during this project.

The Commercial Jingle Project was easy and inexpensive. Green screen technology is not hard and doesn't have to be expensive. I made my 8' x 16' green screen with four $10 foam insulation boards and green paint. The Do Ink app was very intuitive to use and no more complicated than editing using iMovie. Fourth graders have no problem figuring out the editing process.

The Commercial Jingle Project was authentic. To me, this was such an authentic way for students and teachers to pool their talents, resources, time, and effort to maximize connection across the curriculum. Students were completely engaged in deeper learning as technology allowed us to do what was previously inconceivable. We all were so inspired by the process and the results that we've made plans to purposefully collaborate on even more projects next year.

Resources

Barry, T. (2018, June 4). PBL in Music: Driving Questions Invoke Deeper Musical Learning. Retrieved August 5, 2019, from https://www.pblworks.org/blog/pbl-music-driving-questions-invoke-deeper-musical-learning

Buck Institute for Education. (n.d.). What is PBL? Retrieved August 5, 2019, from https://www.pblworks.org/what-is-pbl

Burns, A., Miller, S., & Rubin, K. (2017). Project-Based Learning across the Curriculum. Retrieved August 5, 2019, from https://www.nais.org/magazine/independent-teacher/fall-2017/project-based-learning-across-the-curriculum/

Diana, K. (2012). "Logos and Design." *Art for Kids!*, art-educ4kids.weebly.com/logos-and-design.html

Framework for High Quality Project Based Learning (HQPBL)(Publication). (2018). Retrieved August 5, 2019, from Project Management Institute Educational Foundation and the William and Flora Hewlett Foundation. The Buck Institute for Education facilitated the development of the Framework for HQPBL. https://hqpbl.org/wp-content/uploads/2018/03/FrameworkforHQPBL.pdf

Furstein, Brianne. "Graphic Arts Lesson Plan: Parts and Design of an Advertisement." *BrainPOP Educators*, BrainPOP, educators.brainpop.com/lesson-plan/graphic-arts-lesson-plan-parts-and-design-of-an-advertisement/.

Lynch, Erin. (2017, January 17). "Super Bowl Advertising Activity; A Persuasive Writing Lesson Students Love." *William H. Sadlier, Inc.*, www.sadlier.com/school/core-literacy/persuasive-writing-lesson-super-bowl-advertising-grades-5

Miller, A. (2012, March 5). Use PBL to Innovate the Music Classroom. Retrieved August 5, 2019, from https://www.edutopia.org/blog/project-based-learning-music-andrew-miller

Teacher Thought Staff. (2019, June 7). 5 Examples of Project-Based Learning Protocols. Retrieved August 5, 2019, from https://www.teachthought.com/project-based-learning/5-examples-of-project-based-learning-protocols/

Vander Ark, T., & Liebtag, E. (2018, March 7). Introducing a Framework for High Quality Project Based Learning. Retrieved August 5, 2019, from https://www.gettingsmart.com/2018/03/introducing-a-framework-for-high-quality-project-based-learning/

Wolpert-Gawron, H. (2015, August 13). What the Heck Is Project-Based Learning? Retrieved August 5, 2019, from https://www.edutopia.org/blog/what-heck-project-based-learning-heather-wolpert-gawron

7

Conclusion

Amy M. Burns

Using technology with elementary music approaches means keeping the approach as the focus and utilizing technology when it can enhance the curriculum. Technology is a tool that can help students achieve success in music-making where traditional methods could not.

As you use this book, please keep in mind the dessert buffet: If you try everything in this book, you will become very full, very quickly, and inevitably become ill. Take small bites so that you do not feel overwhelmed. Start simple and find those who can help you when you get stuck. These forms of help could be the tech department in your school, or a colleague who loves technology, or social media networking groups for elementary music educators. As with anything you try that is new, ease up on yourself if you fail. Review what went wrong and problem solve. We continuously tell our students to have a growth mindset. We have to live that example that as well.

Finally, think of technology as a way to reach students who are not being reached with current methods. Utilize technology to enhance and excite learning. And use it when it is the best tool to accomplish the goals and to help the students achieve success.

Acknowledgments

I am passionate about teaching. Like many of you, I strive to be the best teacher I can possibly be. I also strive to be a good mother to my daughters, a supportive partner to my husband, and a good friend. When I took on writing this book, I knew that it would be a labor of love. I am thrilled with the way it turned out. It only turned out well because I had a lot of help.

I thank and am in awe of Missy Strong, Glennis Patterson, Ardith Collins, and Cherie Herring. When I brought the concept of this book to these amazing elementary music educators, they jumped right in and contributed their expertise with the Feierabend approach (Missy), Kodály approach (Glennis), Orff Schulwerk approach (Ardith), and project-based learning (Cherie). They helped me make this book come to life. I am so grateful to and thankful for these truly phenomenal educators!

Many thanks to Norm Hirschy, who believed in this book and supported me in writing it. In addition, many thanks to the Technology In Music Education Organization (TI:ME: www.ti-me.org) and all of its fine leaders who started the organization for the purpose of assisting music educators in integrating technology into their classrooms.

Amy M. Burns, *Conclusion* In: *Using Technology with Elementary Music Approaches*. Edited by: Amy M. Burns, Oxford University Press (2020).
© Oxford University Press.
DOI: 10.1093/oso/9780190055653.003.0010

I sincerely thank my family for supporting me as I worked many late nights to complete this book. My husband gave me time to work in silence, which is not an easy task at our house. I thank him profusely for this and for the many cups of coffee he made me as I sat on the couch and wrote. I thank my daughters, who would literally cheer me on and reminded me to never give up and to always go for my dreams.

I thank my colleagues and administrators at Far Hills Country Day School. They supported this project and encouraged me to write it. I have worked at Far Hills for over 20 years. They have mentored me and shaped me into a teacher who loves what I do every day. I am extremely grateful and thankful for them.

APPENDIX   Links Listed Throughout the Book and Descriptions of Programs

Amy M. Burns

Supplemental Website to This Book

- www.oup.com/us/utema: This site will list all of the links noted in the following, as well as supplemental downloadable manipulatives in multiple formats.◉

Links Listed in the Feierabend Approach

- **Feierabend Association for Music Education** (FAME) (https://www.feierabendmusic. org/): Organization for music educators who utilize Dr. Feierabend's First Steps in Music and Conversational Solfege approaches.
- **Feierabend Fundamentals Facebook Group** (https://www.facebook.com/groups/ feierabendfundamentals/): A Facebook group where you join and ask questions about the materials and receive answers from experts.
- **FAME Podcast** (https://www.feierabendmusic.org/the-tuneful-beatful-artful-music-teacher-podcast/): A series of podcasts that interview various educators successfully using the approach, as well as interviews with Dr. Feierabend himself.
- **Classroom Screen** (https://classroomscreen.com/): A website that holds tools that educators can quickly access and use daily.
- **Draw Island** (https://drawisland.com/): An online drawing tool.
- **ShowMe App** (https://www.showme.com/create): ShowMe is an interactive whiteboard that allows you to easily create and share videos.
- **Visualize Pitch Explorations** (https://creatability.withgoogle.com/seeing-music/): An online tool that lets you visualize music.
- **Skype in the Classroom** (https://education.microsoft.com/skype-in-the-classroom/ overview): A free online community where you can connect with other educators, other classrooms, guest speakers, virtual field trips, and more.
- **Emoji Creator for Ariosos** (http://byrdseed.com/emoji): An online tool to assist students with creating Ariosos.
- **Story Dice Free App to create Ariosos** (https://itunes.apple.com/us/app/story-dice-story-telling/id1105668334?mt=8 for iOS and https://play.google.com/store/apps/ details?id=com.zuidsoft.storystones&hl=en_US&pageId=none for Google Play): An app to assist students with creating Ariosos.

- **GIA Music** (https://www.giamusic.com): Publishing company of sacred choral music, hymnals, sacred music recordings, music education materials, and more.
- https://www.youtube.com/user/GIAPublications (the GIA publications YouTube channel) or the Kindle app (which can be installed on most mobile devices and laptops).
- **Free Kindle app on your device found at amazon.com** (https://www.amazon.com/kindle-dbs/fd/kcp) to display the SongTale Kindle versions.
- **Blue Designs USB Mics** (https://www.bluedesigns.com): Blue offers a ling of USB and XLR microphones, as well as headphones, and more.
- **Groovy Music** (https://www.musicfirst.com/applications/groovy-music/): Developed by Michael Avery and sold by MusicFirst, Groovy Music is a music-making tool for young students.
- **Online Guitar** (https://www.apronus.com/music/onlineguitar.htm): A virtual online guitar.
- **Autoharp iOS app** (http://www.autoharpapp.com/): A virtual autoharp app.
- **Beats Per Minute** (http://www.beatsperminuteonline.com): An online tool to calculate beats per minute through tapping on the keyboard or screen.

Links Listed in the Kodály Approach

- **International Kodály Society (IKS)** (https://www.iks.hu): The International Kodály Society is active in 34 countries and has Affiliated National Organizations in 16 countries.
- **Organization of American Kodály Educators** (https://www.oake.org): Organization inspired by the vision of Zoltán Kodály to support music education, music-making, and music literacy.
- **Organization of American Kodály Educators Facebook Group** (https://www.facebook.com/oakeorg/): The Facebook group you can join and ask questions about the approach.
- **Holy Names University's Kodály Center American Folk Song Collection** (http://kodaly.hnu.edu/collection.cfm): An online free resource created by HNU faculty members, Anne Laskey and Gail Needleman, from HNU's collection of American Folk Songs for Teaching, developed over 35 years by faculty and students at HNU's Kodály Center.
  - http://kodaly.hnu.edu/song.cfm?id=694—Doggie Doggie—Song found in Chapter 4.
- **Kodály Song Analysis Directory** (https://ksadirectory.blogspot.com): A blog with a searchable database of folk songs for teaching with the Kodály approach.
- **Kodály Song Website** (http://kodalysongweb.net/): An online free resource for music educators inspired by the Kodály concept of teaching music.
- **My Song File—Music Resources for the Classroom** (https://mysongfile.com): An online free and paid resource of a database of songs that are thoroughly cross-referenced, created by Miriam and Graham McLatchey.
- **The Global Jukebox** (https://theglobaljukebox.org): An online global resource of music, dancing, and conversing from around the world.

- **Beth's Notes** (https://www.bethsnotesplus.com): An online subscription-based music education community created by Beth that contains numerous lessons, resources, manipulatives, games, Orff arrangements, and so much more.
- **Kodály Collaboration Board** (https://www.pinterest.com/linzyjo7/kodaly-collaboration-board/?fbclid=IwAR14oD1DfRGj6fPVOJitQF6MSeqPWgJBsef_ZBkIxrnO6syllLIXGT4d4eY): A Pinterest board of Kodály websites.
- **Kodály Corner** (http://kodalycorner.blogspot.com): An online resource of music education bloggers who are inspired by Kodály.
- **Kodály Crafts** (https://www.kodalycrafts.com/): Jenny Ferris, a music educator based in Melbourne, Australia, created this blog to share ideas and crafts inspired by the Kodály approach.
- **Kodály Inspired Classroom** (http://www.kodalyinspiredclassroom.com/): Lindsay Jervis's blog about all things Kodály, with numerous ideas, resources, links to her store, and more.
- **Katie Wardrobe Midnight Music** (http://www.kodaly.org.au/creating-rhythm-flashcards-in-sibelius/): Blog post by Katie Wardrobe about how to make stick notation using Sibelius.
- **Mrs. King's Music Class** (http://mrskingrocks.blogspot.com): Tracy King's (The Bulletin Board Lady) website that includes ideas, links, resources, and more.
- **Music a la Abbott—A Kodály-Inspired Blog** (http://www.musicalaabbott.com/): Amy Abbott's blog with numerous resources, articles, lessons, ideas, and more.
- **Yellow Brick Road** (https://yellowbrickroadblog.com/): Jennifer Hibbard's blog about music literacy including ideas, articles, lessons, and more.
  - https://yellowbrickroadblog.com/2018/11/doggie-doggie.html—Doggie Doggie—One of the songs used in Chapter 4.
- **"Placing Mi and Sol on the Staff"** (https://docs.google.com/presentation/d/1XnWitQl34lr7c7D-4Q_RKrQixHSO7RwSxMrTqNuyRJo/copy)
- **Peardeck Extension** (https://chrome.google.com/webstore/detail/pear-deck/dnloadmamaeibnaadmfdfelflmmnbajd?hl=en)
- **"Creating a Rhythm Composition with Seesaw"** (https://docs.google.com/presentation/d/17E14sMrfdyWJgondEPg9gvbrGYBZzWLNj2M3ZhOruAU/copy)
- **Herbie Hancock's Chameleon's backtrack** (https://www.youtube.com/watch?v=8IdBAmJmlK0)
- **Bounce High Bounce Low** (https://docs.google.com/presentation/d/1lqTJnfbIE-rmDlwCetZHMeoXGDppV0EkTqjj0C0iK-k/copy)
- **Reflector app** (https://www.airsquirrels.com/reflector): This paid app downloads to your laptop and when you connect your laptop to a projector, Reflector allows you to mirror other devices wirelessly onto the screen.
- **Sol-Mi Poison Game** (https://docs.google.com/presentation/d/13SyeQ-hjWq9lBkz1oe18kNqxhrBrFNqEeNylPAXi8Ts/copy)
- **DoReMi123** (iOS—https://itunes.apple.com/us/app/doremi-1-2-3-music-for-kids/id479692413?mt=8) and on Google Play (https://play.google.com/store/apps/details?id=com.creativity.doremi.lite&hl=en_US)
- **Kahoot! Assessment** (https://create.kahoot.it/share/low-la-and-low-sol-review/b048121a-084d-4L0a1-90fd-eb2fd738856a)

Links Listed with Orff Schulwerk Approach

- **International Orff Schulwerk Forum Salzburg (IOSFS)** (http://www.orff-schulwerk-forum-salzburg.org/): The center of the international Orff Schulwerk associations.
- **American Orff Schulwerk Organization (AOSA)** (https://aosa.org/): A professional organization of music educators dedicated to the creative music and movement approach developed by Carl Orff and Gunild Keetman.
- **American Orff Schulwerk Organization (AOSA) Facebook Group** (https://www.facebook.com/americanorffschulwerkassociation/): A Facebook group that anyone can join to discuss and ask questions about the Orff Schulwerk approach.
- **The American Center for Elemental Music and Movement** (https://acemm.us/): This organization promotes the artistic and educational opportunities of music and movement.
- **AOSA Resource Page** (https://aosa.org/resources/useful-links/): A list of resources and links from assessments to teaching resources.
- **O For Tuna Orff** (https://ofortunaorff.blogspot.com/): Aimée's blog with numerous ideas, lessons, articles, links, and so much more.
- **Mama Lisa's World** (https://www.mamalisa.com/): An online tool to help music educators find cultural songs and dances from around the world.
- **David Row's Make Moments Matter** (https://makemomentsmatter.org/): David blogs, podcasts, vlogs, has a great YouTube channel, and more, all about music education with fantastic examples from his own classroom.
  - https://makemomentsmatter.org/links/music-education-blogs/: David has a list of blogs for Kodály, Orff Schulwerk, and General Music Education.
- **Musication Boomwhacker Play-Along YouTube Video Channel** (https://www.youtube.com/channel/UCuNYP6sYWgjAddNo534PEKQ): Grab a Boomwhacker and play along to these videos.
- **Professor Pedro Morales Rhythm Videos**: Search YouTube to find rhythm play-along videos with minions, Mario Brothers, Angry Birds, and more.
- **Tim Purdum's iOS Xylophone App (Figure 2.3)** (https://itunes.apple.com/us/app/xylophone-orff/id1092959126?mt=8): Excellent Orff instrument app where a student can prepare the instrument in missing bars, add flats and sharps, and more [INSERT FIG 2.3]
- **Virtual Recorder App** (by AtPlayMusic (PlayAlong Recorder—https://itunes.apple.com/us/app/playalong-recorder/id600713930?mt=8 and AtPlayMusic Recorder—https://itunes.apple.com/us/app/atplaymusic-recorder-free/id580567733): An app that a student can use to perform songs on a virtual recorder.
- **Interactive Recorder Fingering Chart** (https://www.musick8.com/rkdojo/rkchart.php): A great online tool for students to check fingerings or learn new ones.
- **Virtual Boomwhackers** (https://www.musick8.com/boomwhackers/playboomwhackers.php?bwswitch=TRUE): This online tool can assist when you do not have enough Boomwhackers or need a chromatic set.
- **Autoharp App** (http://www.autoharpapp.com): A virtual autoharp app.
- **NYU Music Experience Design Musedlab's Groove Pizza** (https://apps.musedlab.org/groovepizza): An online tool to create groove's and beats using math concepts.

- **Odogy** (https://odogy.com/LearnToPlayRecorderSongs): An online tool for students to learn and play along with on recorder.
- **DoReMi123** (iOS—https://itunes.apple.com/us/app/doremi-1-2-3-music-for-kids/id479692413?mt=8 and on Google Play— https://play.google.com/store/apps/details?id=com.creativity.doremi.lite&hl=en_US): An app that has solfege and numbers where students can improvise singing patterns.
- **Staff Wars** (themusicinteractive.com): A great student-favorite note reading game that can be downloaded to a laptop or purchased as an app.
- **Staff Wars Live** (iOS only—https://itunes.apple.com/us/app/staffwars-live/id1071622918?ls=1&mt=8): An app that students can use to test their knowledge of reading and performing notes in a fun, game-like atmosphere.
- **Incredibox** (https://www.incredibox.com): A student favorite where they can create music with cartoon beatboxers.
- **Edpuzzle** (https://www.edpuzzle.com): Turn YouTube videos or your own videos into assessments to use in class or in a flipped classroom. Also look over the video library included in Edpuzzle.

Links Listed with PBL Approach

- **Soundtrap** (https://www.soundtrap.com): See discussion later in the chapter.
  - **GarageBand** (iOS, https://www.apple.com/ios/garageband/or MAC, https://www.apple.com/mac/garageband/): A digital audio workstation (DAW) for iOS and macOS devices. This comes free with the device.
  - **Soundation** (https://www.soundation.com): An online digital audio workstation (DAW) where you can collaborate with others online to make music. Educational version available.
  - **Anchor** (anchor.fm): An online podcast tool where you can create and host episodes, as well as distribute them.
- **USB Blue Spark microphone** (https://www.bluedesigns.com): Blue offers a line of USB and XLR microphones and audiophile headphones for recording, podcasting, and more.
- **Seesaw** (web.seesaw.me), **Bloomz** (https://www.bloomz.net), **ClassDojo** (https://www.classdojo.com), **FreshGrade** (freshgrade.com), **ClassTag** (https://www.classtag.com/): Seesaw, Bloomz, ClassDojo, FreshGrade, and ClassTag are student-driven digital portfolios. Each program has their own specialty. Seesaw has free and paid versions, both with numerous tools and activities included. Students can easily connect with parents, and no email addresses are required. The activities are written by teachers and can be used as lessons, assessments, and more. Bloomz has tools that make it easy to import classes, create groups, schedule posts, place office hours on the app so you are not disturbed at home, and also includes behavior management. ClassDojo has the classroom management and mindfulness tools included, as well as students connected to their parents and contributing to their portfolios. FreshGrade specializes in its grade book and parent communication for blended learning. ClassTag has good calendaring tools that allow you to schedule events and posts in advance and gives you the ability to see the week ahead. It gives students the ability to showcase their work and is connected to parents. It is free, so there are advertisements in the app. It will also allow you to earn coins that can be used in places like Teachers Pay

Teachers. *Note: Since this book focused on Seesaw, a more in-depth description of it is listed later in the chapter.*

- **Flipgrid** (https://www.flipgrid.com): A social learning platform that allows teachers to create grids for students to be invited and leave video messages, assignments, etc. It is a tool to empower students' voices through videos. It also includes a whiteboard features for students to show their work. *Note: Since this book focused on Flipgrid, a more in-depth description of it is listed later in the chapter.*
- **MusicFirst** (https://www.musicfirst.com): A learning management system where you can customize the music tools needed for a class to make and create music, along with creating assignments and monitoring classes.
- **WeVideo** (https://www.wevideo.com): An online video editing tool.
- **iMovie** (https://www.apple.com/imovie/): An iOS and macOS video editing tool.
- **Do Ink** (https://itunes.apple.com/us/app/green-screen-by-do-ink/id730091131?mt =8 or http://www.doink.com/: An iOS app to create and make animations and videos with green screens.
- **Book Creator** (https://www.bookcreator.com): An online and iOS tool to create ebooks.
  - **Exampleofalibrary:**https://read.bookcreator.com/library/-LZWcCSmHVhcAyd08Ckw
- **Scratch** (https://scratch.mit.edu): An online block coding tool for younger students.
- **Keynote** (iOS or MAC, https://www.apple.com/keynote/): An iOS and macOS tool for presentations.
- **Pages** (iOS or MAC, https://www.apple.com/pages/): An iOS and macOS tool for writing.
- **Thinglink** (https://www.thinglink.com/): An online tool that can turn images into interactive graphics.
- **HP Reveal** (https://www.hpreveal.com/, formerly Aurasma):An online tool to create and see augmented reality.

Online Music Curriculum or Music Learning Management Systems Mentioned in This Book

- **Denise Gagne's Musicplay Online** (musicplayonline.com): A PreK–6 music curriculum that assists music educators with online tools, manipulatives, recordings, videos, songs, and more.
- **MusicFirst Junior** (https://www.musicfirst.com/musicfirst-junior/): The junior version of MusicFirst, featuring learning management systems and tools for musical creations for younger students.
- **MusicFirst** (https://www.musicfirst.com): A learning management system where you can customize the music tools needed for a class to make and create music, along with creating assignments and monitoring classes.

Website Creation Tools

- **Google Classroom** (https://classroom.google.com): A blended learning management system that allows students and teachers to share work and assignments.
- **Google Sites** (https://sites.google.com/): A website tool that allows creation and collaboration among various editors.

- **Weebly** (https://education.weebly.com/): A free website building tool.
- **Adobe Pages** (https://spark.adobe.com/make/website-builder): An online and app to create web pages.
- **Wordpress** (https://wordpress.com/): An online tool to build websites and blogs.

Orchestral Websites

- **San Francisco Kids** (http://www.sfskids.org)
- **Dallas Symphony Orchestra Kids** (http://www.dsokids.com)
- **New York Phil Kidzone** (http://www.nyphilkids.org)
- **Carnegie Hall Listening Adventures** (http://listeningadventures.carnegiehall.org/ypgto/index.aspx)
- **Toronto Symphony Orchestra Teacher Resources** (https://www.tso.ca/education/teacher-resources)
- **Classics for Kids** (http://www.classicsforkids.com/)

Interactive Websites

- **Music Tech Teacher** (http://www.musictechteacher.com): Karen Garrett's website that was an extension of her music classroom. It holds lessons, games, activities, and more.
- **The Music Interactive** (http://www.themusicinteractive.com): A website that holds games and activities that can be downloaded or purchased as apps and used in the music classroom, developed by Craig Gonci and Marc Jacoby.
- **The Rhythm Trainer** (http://www.therhythmtrainer.com): A free rhythms trainer website developed by John Blank.
- **Phil Tulga** (http://www.philtulga.com): A website developed by Phil Tulga that hosts cross-curricular activities revolving around music.

Chrome Music Lab (Musiclab.chromeexperiments.com)

- **Rhythm**: Built by George Michael Brower. This consists of animated characters playing rhythms in meters of 3, 4, 5, and 6
  - o **Uses**: Use this tool to show meters as well as having students move to the meters. In addition, have a student create a rhythm pattern within in the meter. For older elementary, students can decode the rhythm pattern that was created on screen.
- **Sound Waves**: Built by Mark Lundin. This consists of an exploration and visualization of a sound wave moving through air molecules.
  - o **Uses**: I use this activity to introduce a STEAM unit. I collaborate with the science teacher as we work together on teaching about sound and music. With Sound Waves, I have a student play the keyboard provided in the app and they watch the blue dots move. The blue dots represent air moving through molecules. The higher the pitch, the faster the air moves. When the magnifying class is clicked, a red line will appear that draws the shape of one molecule moving through the air.
- **Kandinsky**: Built by Active Theory and inspired by Russian abstract artist Wassily Kandinsky. This app turns anything you draw into sound.
  - o **Uses**: Have the students draw a pattern on paper. This pattern can include shapes and lines. Set a guideline such as two shapes and three lines so that they can

perform all of their drawings. Have the students draw their pictures into the app and listen to the results. Ask them if they thought if it would sound the way the Kandinsky app played it. In addition, make the cross-curricular connections with learning about the artist in art class.

- **Song Maker**: Built by Google Creative Lab, Use All Five, and Yotam Mann. This app can make simple songs with melody, harmony and rhythm. The songs can be shared via a link or social media, where others can collaborate and add to or change the song. Click the "Settings" button to determine the song's length, beats per bar, subdivisions, scale (major, minor, pentatonic), tonic, and range.
  - o **Uses**: You can create a melody in the app, like "Snail Snail", and have the students try to identify the melody. Then hand out boomwhackers and have them perform the melody. Song Maker uses the colors that are closely related to boomwhacker colors.
  - o You can show a visualization of beat subdivisions by creating a song in a simple, triple meter and having the "Settings" show "Beats per bar 3/Split beats into 1". Have the students or the teacher create a melody when the notes will appear as dotted half notes. Then go back into the "Settings" and change "Split beats into 3". The melody now changes and shows the subdivision within each measure.
- **Sharing the Song**: When finished, click the "Save" button and the app will generate a link. The students can share this link on your music classroom's Facebook or Twitter page. You can also copy the embed code to embed in a music classroom webpage. Finally, the students can copy the link and email you the link (if you do not share your email address with your students, consider setting up a gmail account just for students to send you work, ie examplemusicteacherschoolexample@gmail.com), place the link on their Seesaw journal, or place the link on their Google classroom. Finally, share the link with another elementary music classroom and have the students collaborate and comment on each other's musical work.

Tech Tools That Enhance the Classroom

- **Audacity** (https://www.audacityteam.org/): A free downloadable digital audio workstation (DAW) that allows you to edit audio.
- **Soundtrap** (https://www.soundtrap.com): As Mic Wright stated at thenextweb.com, Soundtrap is a lovechild of Google Docs and GarageBand. This app works on web-based devices as well as iOS and Android devices. The educational (EDU) version is Children's Online Privacy Protection Rule (COPPA) compliant and has a walled garden to keep your students safe. The EDU version allows students to create and share music with other students online. Teachers have access to an admin panel and can create assignments, as well as integrate with Google Classroom.
- **Class Tools** (https://www.classtools.net/): A free website that hosts a plethora of classroom tools, from random name chooser to a timer that can be used in the classroom, created by Russel Tarr.
- **Noteflight** (https://www.noteflight.com): An online app that allows users to compose, view, and share music notation, developed by Joe Berkovitz and published by Hal Leonard.
- **GarageBand** (MAC—https://www.apple.com/mac/garageband/?cid=oas-us-domains-garageband.com, or iOS app—https://itunes.apple.com/us/app/garageband/id408709785?mt=8)

- **123Apps** (https://123apps.com/): An online tool that hosts audio and video editing apps.
  - 123 Apps online video recorder (https://webcamera.io/)
- **Online Voice Recorder** (online-voice-recorder.com/beta): An online voice recorder that allows you to record, crop the recording, and save as an MP3 file.
- **Vocaroo** (vocaroo.com): An online tool that allows you to record, send, and download recorded messages.
- **WeVideo** (https://www.wevideo.com): An online video editing tool.
- **Flashnote Derby** (https://flashnotederby.com/): An app for iOS, Android, and Amazon devices that tests your students' note-naming knowledge.
- **iDoceo** (idoceo.net): An iOS app that holds assessments, video recordings, audio recordings, seating charts, grades, and so much more, to assist with a teacher's organization.
- **Classroom Screen** (https://classroomscreen.com/): An online tool developed by Laurens Koppers. Project the website onto a screen and you now have numerous tools, from a traffic light to an interactive whiteboard screen, to use in the classroom.
- **Teacherkit** (http://teacherkit.net/): Similar to iDoceo but can be hosted on numerous platforms from iOS to Android.
- **iMovie** (https://www.apple.com/imovie/): An iOS and macOS video editing tool.
- **Book Creator** (bookcreator.com): An online and iOS tool to create ebooks.
- **YouTube** (youtube.com): You can find almost any video to enhance your classroom.
  - Can't show YouTube in the classroom? Try safeshare.tv or viewpure.com and insert the YouTube URL into their site. This will create a clean version of the YouTube video without comments and advertisements.

217

Assessment Tools

- **Edpuzzle** (https://www.edpuzzle.com): Turn YouTube videos or your own videos into assessments to use in class or in a flipped classroom. Also look over the video library included in Edpuzzle.
- **Google Forms** (https://www.google.com/forms/about/): Choose from a variety of question options, from multiple choice to dropdowns to a linear scale. Add images and YouTube videos, or get fancy with page branching and question skip logic. Place your assessment created in Google Form on your students' Google Classroom (or create a form directly into Google Classroom). Create assessments with pictures, YouTube videos for sound examples, multiple choice questions, short answers, long answers, linear scales, dropdown boxes, and check boxes.
- **iDoceo** (https://idoceo.net): An iOS app that holds assessments, video recordings, audio recordings, seating charts, grades, and so much more, to assist with a teacher's organization.
- **Kahoot!** (https://kahoot.com/): A gameshow type of assessment that can be done in a 1:1 classroom or a classroom with a few devices and students grouped in teams. You create a free account, search pre-made music assessments/quizzes/games, or create original ones to use in the classroom. I use this before a concert to assess the students on memorization of their lyrics. My students love Kahoot!
- **National Core Arts Standards for PreK-8 General Music** (https://nafme.org/wp-content/files/2014/11/2014-Music-Standards-PK-8-Strand.pdf): These standards

were developed in 2014 and include creating, performing, responding, and connecting to music, as well as essential questions and enduring understandings.

- **Nearpod** (https://www.nearpod.com): An interactive tool to bring your lesson to the students' devices and have them follow along. There are ready-to-teach interactive lessons to use immediately in the classroom. You can also easily create lessons in minutes for your next class. Import files (pdf, ppt, jpg) or Google Slides and add interactive activities, websites, and videos to keep your students engaged in their learning. Finally, you can synchronize your lessons across all student devices in the classroom and receive real-time feedback and post-session reports on student comprehension.
- **Pear Deck** (https:// https://www.peardeck.com/googleslides): Much like Nearpod; however, you can add it to your Google Slide presentations and turn your lessons into assessments.
- **Plickers** (https://www.plickers.com/): Plickers is an assessment tool that is perfect for exit tickets or multiple choice questions. This is also perfect for a classroom that has one device. The teacher creates the account on a computer, creates the questions, uploads the students' names so that Plickers can assign the students their number, download the free Plicker cards (you can also buy the matte laminated version on Amazon), download the free app (iOS, Android), and use your mobile device to assess the students. It records their answers and allows you to evaluate them at a later time.
- **Socrative** (https://socrative.com/): A formative assessment website where you can create T/F, multiple choice, and short answer assessments, along with a gaming assessment, and students can utilize without email addresses. The data is collects are accessible in the teacher account.

Student Digital Learning Portfolio, Blended Learning, or Video-Platform Student Empowerment Tools

- **Flipgrid** (flipgrid.com)
  - Flipgrid is compatible with web browsers such as Safari, Google Chrome, Firefox, and Edge. It works best on Google Chrome. It also works on iOS devices with iOS10 and above and Android devices with Android 5 and up. Flipgrid is COPPA and Family Educational Rights and Privacy Act (FERPA) compliant.
  - Flipgrid is a free video social learning platform that students can use to showcase and reflect on their progress, especially musical progress. It is a tool that can empower students' voices.
  - Create a free account and then begin a grid. Flipgrid gives you the opportunity to create a grid, which is like a classroom community, where you can add videos and invite students and parents to view and contribute. In order for parents to contribute, they would have to have or create a Google or Microsoft email account. Within each grid, you can add topics for students to reflect, perform, comment, and more.
  - You can make a grid private by letting students join with an email address or student ID (you create the student IDs and they log in with a specific QR code), or you can make the grid public. Once created, you can share the grid through a link or app-smashing with Google Classroom, Remind, and more.

- From there, you can add CoPilots. This is great if you are just beginning to use Flipgrid. When you start small with another teacher, then you have a support system.
- I like that Flipgrid gives you the first grid, which is a "Welcome" grid that has students introducing themselves through video. Flipgird gives you the ability to view as a student. You can click the "View" button and either enter a student's ID code or log in from another email address, depending on how you set the class up.
- Students log in and tap the topic and then the green + button. They are now ready to record with their device. You can set the timing of the recording so that they can record from 30 seconds to five minutes.
- Students can also access Flipgrid from home and share their musical progress at any time of the day.
- In the topic's "Actions" tools, you can do a variety of things. One is that you can edit the grid. When you click on edit, you are able to turn on and off notifications so you approve the videos, turn on and off downloading the videos, turn on and off the video captions, edit the languages you would like for the captions, turn on and off students receiving notifications about the grid, and turn on and off the grid.
- Another is to add the topic to the "Disco Library." The Disco Library is where many educators share their topics so other educators can find new ideas. You can filter the topics so you can find music topics for elementary grade levels.
- Another thing you can do in the edit mode is "Add Topic Guests." When you click on this, you can set the parameters for adding guests, such as parents and caregivers. These parameters are allowing guests to access the topic through a link and allowing them to video a response.
- Flipgrid also has "#GridPals" and "MixTapes." "#GridPals" shows a list of educators using Flipgrid in their classrooms so you can connect with them. "MixTapes" allows you to create a grid with your favorite videos from numerous topics.
- You can create "Shorts," which are videos three minutes or less of you speaking, singing, performing, etc., and share with your students' Google Classroom.
- Finally, if you have students who do not feel comfortable being video recorded, Flipgrid has a whiteboard tool that turns the screen into a whiteboard. The students can then sing without being seen. Or they could compose and perform rhythm patterns.
- Flipgrid is a great tool to help students feel empowered and to allow them to be heard.
- **Seesaw** (web.seesaw.me)
  - Seesaw is a free student-learning digital portfolio and engagement platform where students can showcase their musical creations, compositions, pitch explorations, orffestrations, etc., by using video, audio, drawings, pictures, links, and more.
  - Seesaw is free for up to 10 classes with two teachers. There is a paid app as well that hosts a few more items, but the free version can do plenty.
  - Seesaw works on multiple platforms from Android, to iOS, to Kindle Fire, to web-based devices such as Chromebooks. Seesaw is compliant with FERPA, COPPA, General Data Protection Regulation (GDPR), and the Australian Privacy Act.
  - You can utilize the free version to set up a class by inputting their names manually or uploading from Google Classroom when you set up the class, or having them join via QR or text code.

- The students join your class through a QR code (if your students are using tablets and iOS devices and have no email addresses) or through their school email address using a text code.
- Students can showcase their musical creations, compositions, pitch explorations, orffestrations, etc., by using video, audio, drawings, pictures, links, and more.
- I always suggest that if you are piloting Seesaw in your classroom, to pair up with a classroom teacher. Have the classroom teacher use it in his or her classroom as well as your music classroom. This way, there will be more posts and more parent communication. Through Seesaw, you can add parents to the student's portfolios. Only parents can see their own children's posts. The teacher can approve or deny any posts before they are submitted to the journal. The free account can do many things. As you use it more, the paid version will allow you to add skill sets, add a private teaching journal with notes and posts, and schedule and include activities in a schoolwide library.
- Once the students log in, either through email, text, or QR code, they can post on their journal using many tools. You can empower them by giving them a choice on how they will post themselves singing a solo, or recording themselves playing an excerpt, or writing and performing an ostinato or rhythm pattern, and so much more.
- You can set it up so the parents can comment on the posts, as well as other students, so that you can reinforce digital citizenship skills.
- Through Seesaw Blogs, you can connect your classroom with others from around the world that use Seesaw.
- Seesaw has activities within the app that you can use to assess students. Other activities serve as great manipulatives to reinforce a lesson or concept that you have taught. These activities are free to use and are written and tested by Seesaw Ambassadors, who are teachers. You can filter activities to music for Grade 1, and the result will be over hundreds of activities at your disposal.
- You can also create activities. An example would be creating an activity within Seesaw where you would add a picture of the simple song and ask the students to tap the record button to record themselves singing the song. Once they submit their recordings by pressing the check button, you can now assess them and have the recording in their journals. You can approve the recordings to be placed on their journal pages, where parents can listen to their child sing.
- Seesaw gives that advantage of connecting with your students on another level. The students have the ability to access Seesaw from home and can submit their musical progress to you at any time.
- Seesaw is an excellent tool to engage student learning and giving the students the ability to find their voices and express themselves.
- **Bloomz** (bloomz.net): see earlier description.
- **ClassDojo** (classdojo.com): see earlier description.
- **ClassTag** (classtag.com): see earlier description.
- **FreshGrade** (freshgrade.com): see earlier description.
- **Google Classroom** (https://classroom.google.com): see earlier description.

Important note: Websites that require Adobe Flash might be blocked by your school. In addition, Adobe Flash will be discontinued in late 2020.

220

GLOSSARY

1:1   One device per student in the classroom.

123Apps   Various free apps from online voice recorders to online video recorders.

21st Century Learners/Skills   Skills that schools are focused on teaching, such as problem-solving, collaboration, critical thinking, digital literacy, and more.

Airplay   Allows you to stream music to speakers, documents to a printer, videos to a TV, and more.

Anchor.fm   An online podcast tool where you can create and host episodes, as well as distribute them.

Android devices   This device has an operating system developed by Google and plays apps found at Google Play. Mobile phones and tablets are examples of Android Devices.

App smashing   Utilizing multiple apps together to create projects.

Audacity   Developed by Dominic Mazzoni and Roger Dannenberg at Carnegie Mellon University in 1999, Audacity is a free digital audio editor and recording application software, available for Windows, macOS/OS X, and Unix-like operating systems. You will need to download it onto your computer. It is not currently a cloud-based software, so it cannot be used on a mobile device, tablet, or Chromebook.

Audio file formats   Some include WAV, AIFF, MP3, MP4/M4A, and more.

Blended learning   Students learn through face-to-face traditional methods as well as methods enhanced with online technology.

Blue Designs   A line of Blue Line USB and XLR microphones and headphones.

Bloomz   An online digital portfolio that gives students the opportunity to showcase their work and to connect with an audience.

Book Creator   An iOS or web-based app that gives your students the opportunity to create ebooks using tools such as recording audio, drawing, taking pictures and video, using a text tool, adding photos, app smashing with Google Maps, and so much more. It is intuitive for young students to learn and create musical ebooks. Book Creator is free for one ebook (iOS version) and for 40 ebooks (web-based version). The paid versions give you more ebooks, libraries, and real-time collaboration.

Boomwhacker   A hollow, lightweight, color-coded, plastic tube, tuned to diatonic and chromatic pitches.

Chrome Music Lab   A website filled with interactive music exploration and creation tools.

Chromebooks   A machine that runs Google Chrome where all work is saved in the cloud and usually requires internet access.

ClassDojo   an online digital student portfolio that allows students to showcase their work and provides the teacher with positive reinforcement tools for behavior management and mindfulness.

ClassTag   An online digital student portfolio where students can showcase their work; also provides teachers with good calendaring tools to communicate with parents and schedule events.

Coding   The computer language used to create apps, websites, and more.

Common-Core Standards   A set of educational standards for teaching and testing math and English to students in grades K–12.

Conversational Solfege A developmental program written by Dr. John Feierabend to teach musical literacy with older elementary students.

COPPA Children's Online Privacy Protection Rule

Design Thinking This is a learning process that promotes problem-solving, empathy, and looking at situations differently to provide alternative strategies and solutions. It is based around five steps: empathize, define, ideate, prototype, and test.

Digital storytelling The practice of using technological tools to tell a story.

Do Ink An iOS app to create and make animations and videos with green screens.

Document camera A device that allows users to project objects onto a screen.

Educational technology (edtech) Digital technology used to enhance and assist in learning.

FERPA Family Educational Rights and Privacy Act

Flipgrid Flipgrid gives you the opportunity to create a grid where you can add videos and invite students and parents to view and contribute.

First Steps Approach by Dr. Feierabend An approach developed by Dr. John Feierabend involving eight steps in teaching music to preschool and beyond to help students become "tuneful, beatful, and artful." See Chapter 3 for more details.

Flashnote Derby A paid iOS and Google Play app to reinforce note reading skills.

Flipped classroom Through blended learning, instruction is "flipped" so that tools such as online formats and videos are used outside the classroom to assist in learning the content.

FreshGrade An online digital student portfolio tool that allows students to showcase their learning and work with an audience such as their parents and caregivers, as well as providing a gradebook.

Gamification The elements of game-playing applied to other areas, such as learning in the classroom.

GarageBand A digital audio workstation that is Mac-based, with iOS and macOS versions, where you can create, jam, edit, and record music.

GDPR General Data Protection Regulation

Google Drive A web-based storage system that is currently free for 15 GB of storage of any type or sized files.

Google Play An online store that offers Android apps, movie rentals and purchases, music, games, ebooks, and more. Formerly Android Market.

Google Sites A web-based website creation app

Google Slides A web-based presentation app that saves to the cloud.

Groovy Music Offered by MusicFirst, Groovy Music is like GarageBand for younger students. It allows them to create music in various styles.

Groove Pizza A web-based drum creation tool created by MusEd Lab.

iDoceo iDoceo is an iOS app that acts as a teacher's assistant. It serves as a gradebook, planner, diary, timetable, seating chart, resource manager to keep track of pdfs, audio, video, links, images, and more, that can export as pdfs, Excel files, and more. iDoceo is stored locally on your iPad. Therefore, no internet is needed. You can back it up to a Google Drive, Dropbox, etc. Alternative: Teacherkit (http://teacherkit.net/).

iMovie Mac-based iOS app or macOS program that allows you to create and edit movies.

iOS Devices These are devices that run the operating system developed by Apple, Inc. An iPad and an iPhone are examples of iOS devices.

Interactive whiteboard (IWB) This is a board that has a touch screen the user(s) can interact with. A SMART Board or a Promethean Board is an example of an IWB.

Keynote   A multi-platform presentation app in iOS and macOS for Mac devices.

Kindle app   Dr. Feierabend's SongTales are available as digitized Kindle versions. Download the free app to be able to display those Kindle versions you have purchased so that the students can see the tale projected onto a screen.

Kindle devices   Amazon's versions of e-readers and tablets.

Kodály Approach   The approach developed by Zoltán Kodály that focuses on melodic and rhythmic sequences involving introducing concepts through preparation, presentation, and practice using folk songs. See Chapter 4 for more details.

Learning management system (LMS)   A program that tracks, documents, reports, and delivers online learning.

Multiple intelligences   Dr. Howard Gardner's theory from cognitive research that "documents the extent to which students possess different kinds of minds and therefore learn, remember, perform, and understand in different ways" (Lane, 2015, p. 2).

MusicFirst   A music education digital platform and learning management system (LMS) that offers Noteflight, Soundtrap, Groovy Music, and other tools to assist in learning in the elementary music classroom. This also includes MusicFirst Junior.

Musicplay Online   Denise Gagne's award-winning comprehensive music teaching curriculum with the accompanying website for grades PreK through 6.

National Core Arts Music   Standards Developed in 2014, the music standards include the context and assessment for creating, performing, responding, and connecting to music at various grade levels. It also gives essential questions and enduring understandings.

Notebook Software   The multi-platform software application that works with the SMARTBoard.

Noteflight   An online, web-based music composition program.

Online voice recorder   A free online voice recorder that saves audio files as MP3 files and downloads them to the computer's hard drive or to a Chromebook's Google Drive. Use the beta version as it is currently much faster with saving the files and is not flash-based.

Orff instruments   Barred instruments such as xylophones, metallophones, and glockenspiels.

Orff Schulwerk   An approach developed by Carl Orff involving playing, singing, speaking, moving, exploring, imitating, improvising, and creating. See Chapter 5 for more details.

Pages   A multi-platform presentation app and program for iOS and macOS devices.

Personalized learning   The pace and the approach of the learning style is based around the need of the student.

Podcast   A digital audio file that is accessed on the internet and downloaded onto a device or streamed through a service. It is typically a series with new shows that are listened to by those who subscribe.

PowerPoint   A multi-platform presentation app for Mac or PC.

Project-Based Learning (PBL) and Problem-Based Learning   The teaching approach where, over a length of time, students learn the skills of research and problem-solving by answering essential questions. The research will evolve around solving a problem and is based in creating a project.

QR Code   A quick response (QR) code that contains information about the item that it is attached to and can be read by a device.

Reflector App   Allows you to mirror your device to a screen for a lower price than some other devices that do this. Similar apps are Miracast, Chromecast, and Apple TV.

Safeshare.tv, safeyoutube.net, and Viewpure   Websites that allow you to input the YouTube url and they will create a link that cleans up the YouTube video so that there are no comments, advertisements, and pop up videos present when you show them to students.

223

SAMR An acronym for substitution, augmentation, modification, and redefinition, developed by Dr. Ruben Puentedura, to assist with integrating technology into the classroom.

Seesaw Seesaw is a free student-learning digital portfolio and engagement platform where students can showcase their musical creations, compositions, pitch explorations, orffestrations, etc., by using video, audio, drawings, pictures, links, and more. Seesaw is currently free for up to 10 classes, with two teachers per class.

Skype in the Classroom You can find another classroom to skype or invite an expert into your classroom.

Staff Wars and Staff Wars Live Apps created by TMI Media that encourage note reading through fun games and performing on instruments.

Solfege A system for teaching how to sing pitches, music literacy, aural skills, and sight-singing. Also called sol-fa, solfa, and solfeo, among other names.

Soundation An online digital audio workstation (DAW) where you can collaborate with others online to make music. Educational version available.

Soundtrap This is a web-based digital audio workstation that is online and involves music creation, collaboration, and recording tools. There is a free version that can be set up for the teacher to use to record students. Soundtrap is like the love child of Google Docs and GarageBand. It is a cloud-based online digital audio work station (DAW), where it saves your music-making so you can access it from multiple devices, invite people to collaborate, and revert back to previous revisions.

STEAM An acronym for science, technology, engineering, arts, and mathematics.

STEM An acronym for science, technology, engineering, and mathematics

Stick notation Taking traditional notation and removing the note-head.

Student digital learning portfolios An engagement tool where students can share their works through various formats such as videos, links, pictures, reflections, writing, and more, with others in their family or across the globe. Seesaw, ClassDojo, ClassTag, FreshGrade, and Bloomz are a few examples of these.

Thinking map Thinking maps are eight visual and spoken learning tools, each based on a thinking process and used together for showing relationships.

Triple E Framework Developed by Liz Kolb, this framework focuses on integrating technology into the classroom through engagement, enhancement, and extension of technology tools to enhance authentic learning in the classroom.

Virtual classroom An online classroom where students participate and collaborate virtually.

Virtual instrument An online instrument that can be performed on a device such as an iPad or Chromebook.

Vocaroo This is a free online recorder that saves audio files that can be shared via social media, or downloaded onto the computer's hard drive or Google Drive (if you are using a Chromebook).

WeVideo WeVideo is very similar to iMovie, but it is web-based and therefore can be used on most devices with internet access and a web browser. Currently, a free account on WeVideo allows you to create 5 minutes of video per month with 1GB of cloud storage.

YouTube A video-sharing service where users can post and upload videos that can be shared on other sites.

INDEX